IMAGES
of America

GEORGETOWN AND SCOTT COUNTY

Cover Image: The cover photograph depicts the American Legion Post 29 Drum and Bugle Corps. The unit disbanded in 1938. Pictured from left to right are: (first row) Mrs. James R. Lewis (sponsor), and Roy Mulberry (color guard member); (second row) L.S. Odell, J.D. Kirkpatrick, W.P. "Pack" Humphrey, Harvey Towles, Brack Offutt, Elmer Shelton, and unidentified; (third row) Charles Smith, Estill Glass, James Baird, Charles McDaniels, J.O. Oldham, and Buddy Perkins. At the top are Hugo Hassloch Sr., William G. Blackburn, Griff Baird, and Frank Canan.

IMAGES
of America

GEORGETOWN AND SCOTT COUNTY

Ann Bolton Bevins, Frederick A. Johnston, and Lindsey Apple

ARCADIA
PUBLISHING

ISBN 978-0-7385-6898-0

Published by Arcadia Publishing
Charleston, South Carolina

Printed in the United States of America

Library of Congress Catalog Card Number: 98-86672

For all general information contact Arcadia Publishing at:
Telephone 843-853-2070
Fax 843-853-0044
E-Mail sales@arcadiapublishing.com
For customer service and orders:
Toll-Free 1-888-313-2665

Visit us on the Internet at www.arcadiapublishing.com

Contents

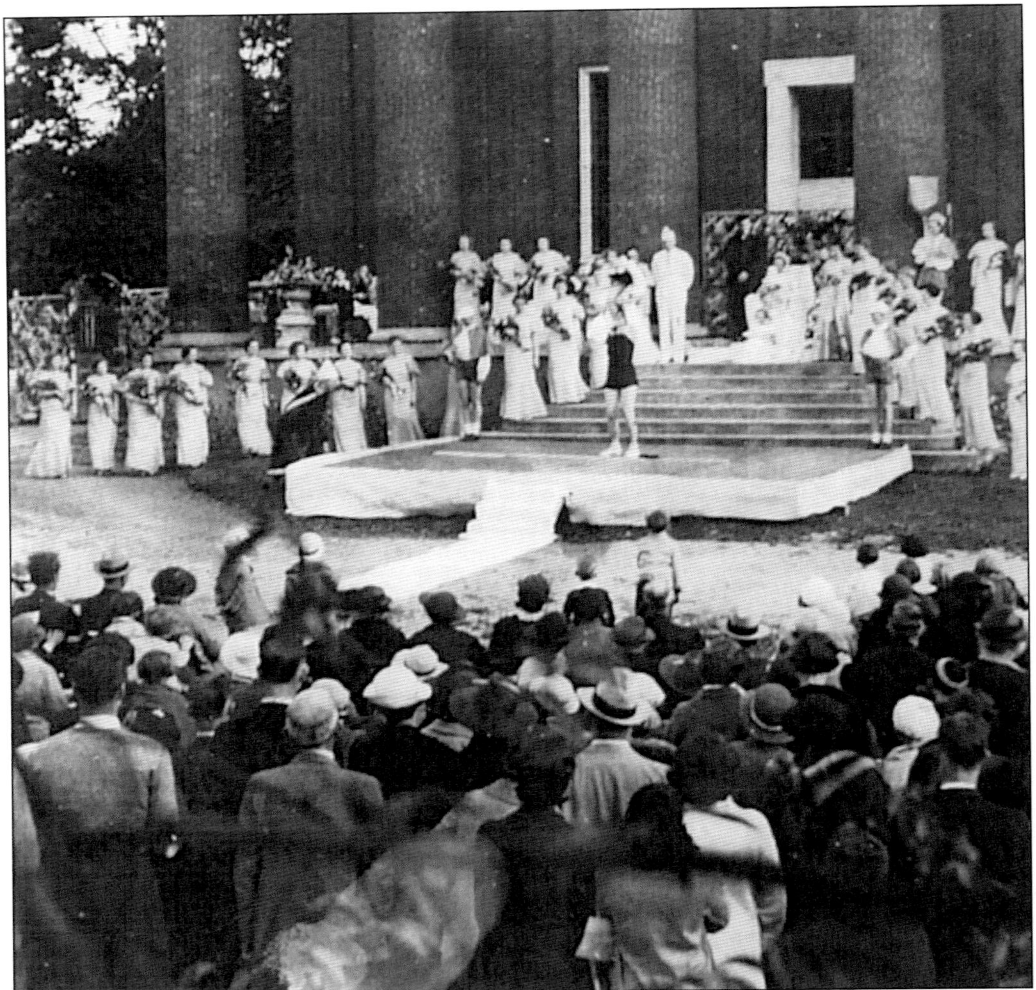

Days of Yore! This 1930s photograph of a May Day celebration at Georgetown College recalls the past. It also speaks for change and for the absence of change. Giddings Hall is much the same as it always was, but access to the building is not. The gravel circle was paved shortly after this photograph was taken, and Dr. Robert L. Mills added concrete retainers and a plaza in the late 1960s. The celebration suggests change as well. Giddings may be Greek Revival but the theme of this ceremony seems to be Roman, with the emperor on his throne. May Day was a popular celebration involving community and campus until about 1970. Activities of elaborate proportion heralded the crowning of a May Queen and the presentation of her court. We assume there was no dancing around the May Pole at the Baptist college, but who knows? The young woman at center stage appears to be wearing a bathing suit, but Georgetown College did not allow women to wear shorts in public until the 1960s. Photographs tell us much about ourselves, our institutions, and perhaps our tendency to bend history to present values. Admittedly, the editors were somewhat astonished when we first looked at this photograph. It seems out of character for the college and the community of that era. We think, however, the photograph reflects the effort of a community to celebrate itself. In the days before television, communities exhibited far more creativity in efforts to entertain themselves.

Another important element in defining a community is the myths that develop as a part of it. Did you know there is a keg of Elijah Craig's whiskey in the fourth column from the left?

INTRODUCTION

In a sermon, the Reverend Lewis Craig described heaven as "a mere Kentucky of a place." Since he had close ties, Scott County must have been his frame of reference for the state as a whole. Others felt similarly because European-American settlers flocked to the region, replacing Native Americans who fought to preserve their own control over it. The land supported large quantities of game, including huge herds of buffalo, which gave names to places like Great Crossings and Stamping Ground. European-American settlers were most interested in the fertility of the soil, and pioneers like Elijah Craig, Robert Johnson, and Robert Saunders carved out large farms where they grew corn, hemp, and raised horses, among other things. The county, though named for General Charles Scott, was created because of the influence in state politics of Robert Johnson. It officially came into existence on June 22, 1792.

As the years passed, the county and its major city, Georgetown, grew. The coming of the railroad created towns like Sadieville, and the interstate system in the 20th century assured the continued growth of the region. Electricity, the telephone, and television linked isolated areas, and a consolidated school system created greater unity in the 20th century than had been known before. Scott County residents have always been interested in education. Schools defined communities, and sports teams rallied people of all races and classes. Georgetown College provided a cultural forum that few small communities enjoy. Scott County residents toiled long hours to make a better life for their families, attended church, voted, and, when called, left the county to fight the nation's wars. Local citizens, through service clubs, churches, and government consistently sought to improve the quality of life in the county. Sometimes we thought small, and sometimes our ideas and ideals were grand.

In the last years of the 20th century, Scott County began to change with lightning speed. Perhaps the image of the county as a quiet, agrarian community has always been something of a myth, but the coming of Toyota Motor Manufacturing and the industries that support it has made Scott County like few other small counties. That change, real and perceived, is in large part the impetus for this book. In 1990, we gathered a large group of community residents to write a new county history. *Scott County Kentucky: A History* was published in 1993. The response to the book was one of excitement and renewed interest in the county's past. Longtime residents shared stories from their communities and families with us, and a number of people mentioned collections of photographs that illustrated aspects of the history we had attempted to describe in words. As a result, we decided to create a pictorial history to complement the earlier effort.

We have three basic goals for this book. First, we want to preserve the photographic record of this county. Photographs collect in boxes in attics or basements. A generation later, the people and events portrayed are often forgotten. It is a tragic loss to families and, in many instances, to the community. We hope this is a partial remedy. Second, we want to create a pictorial history of the county to welcome new residents. It is said that a picture is worth a thousand words. Perhaps that is true, but it has to be the right picture if the story is to be told. From thousands of pictures we have chosen ones we feel reflect not only the physical development of the county, but the feelings of other times and places. We hope this record will help new citizens understand their home, Scott County, Kentucky. Finally, the times are changing. The community motto says "Where Tradition and Progress Meet!" We seek to compile more than a history. This book seeks to provide for longtime residents an avenue of nostalgia. As we have looked at these photographs, images of the past have returned from deep in our memories. In some instances, we might long to go back. Others are best left in the past. Buildings that no longer stand, people who used to be, bluegrass vistas that are now subdivisions—each hopefully will speak to the viewers of this book in a special way. It is important to remember our past as we chart the future.

Scott County is more than a place—it has been a way of life. Tobacco setting, pony rides, a splash in the Elkhorn or in the pool at Suffoletta Park, Oxford High and SCHS, political rallies and children playing, a Christmas parade and people gathered in prayer—these are the scenes that make a community. We hope this book, like fine wine, gets better with age. We could not use all the photographs we would have liked. There are enough for two more books this length. We ask for your understanding. We did not try to use only photographs of pristine quality. Sometimes the age of the photograph itself stimulates the memory. And we did not identify every person in the photographs. One of the joys of a book like this is remembering those long forgotten. Join us in the process of remembering.

Our earnest desire is that the citizens of Scott County, longtime or newly arrived, will enjoy the pages within.

One
Scott County's Changing Landscape

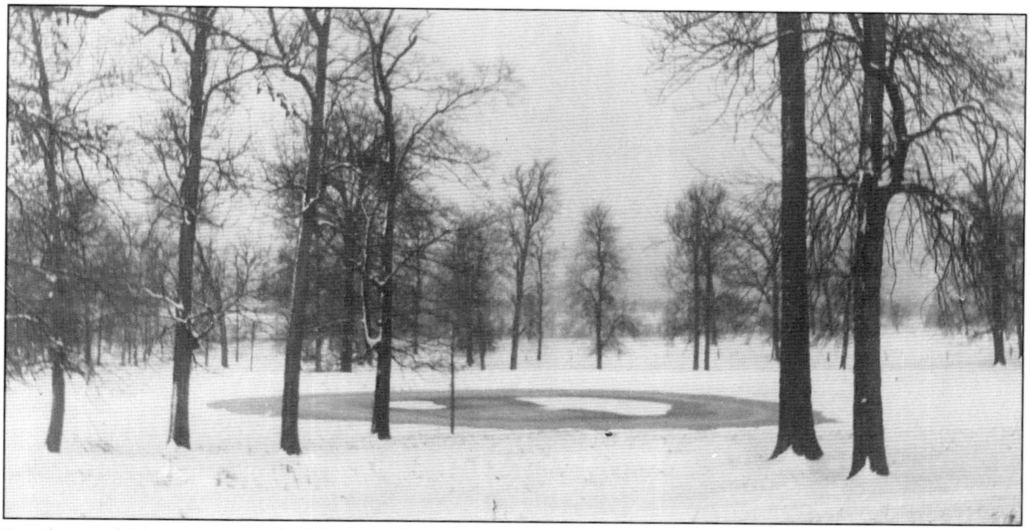

Settlers of European and African descent arriving in the 1770s in what became Central Kentucky's Inner Bluegrass Region found majestic grasslands with trees spaced widely enough apart to allow the sunshine to inspire growth of rich weeds, grasses, and clovers. Between the woodlands and grasslands were vast fields of cane. Woodland pastures such as the one pictured above are rare survivors of the early landscape pattern. This pasture, located on the Cincinnati Road on the Milton Graves Price farm, was photographed in the early 20th century. The Price woodland's trees include white and blue ash, bur oak, chinquapin and Shumard oak, and shagbark hickory.

Roadways made firm by huge herds of buffalo, elk, deer, and other migratory game cut through these fertile lands of limestone-based soils, which are rich in magnesium and phosphorous. The new settlers brought with them domesticated cattle, horses and mules, and hogs and sheep, beginning a trend that resulted in Kentucky's role as a major national livestock producer. The new settlers limited commercial cultivation to grains, flax, and hemp, and they produced vegetables, dairy and poultry products, and tobacco for home consumption. Mills and other manufacturers processed agricultural products into flour and meal, distilled beverages, cloth, paper, leather, and harnesses. The economy's focus was agriculture, an industry in which 94.9% of Scott County's working people found employment in the 1820s. Towns, villages, and crossroads hamlets served as rural service and social centers. The choicest areas became cities.

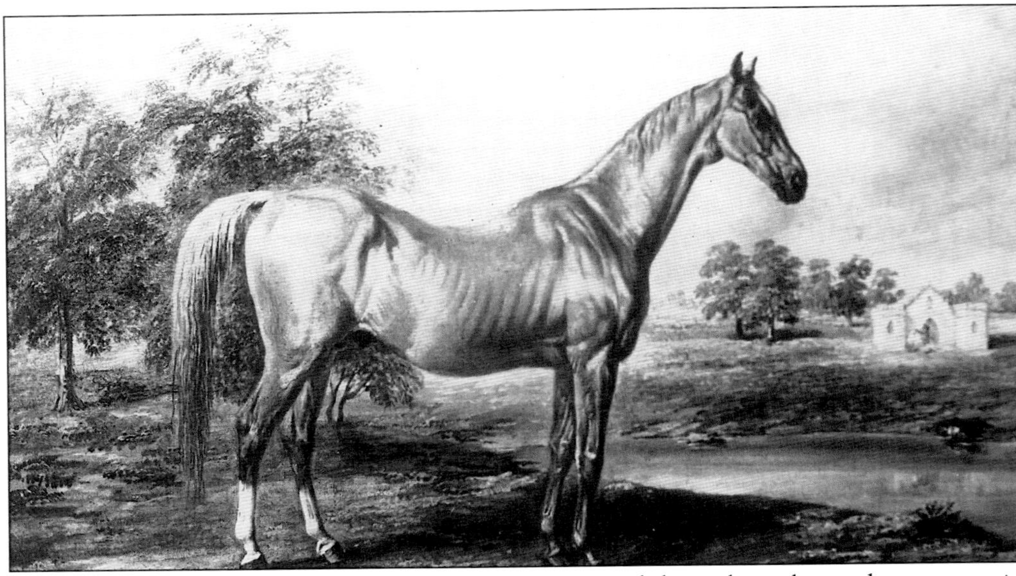

Horses for work, transport, pleasure, and sport accompanied the early settlers and were a crucial part of everyday as well as sporting life. In 1857, artist Edward Troye painted the aged Glencoe, the nineteenth century's greatest Thoroughbred sire, near a Gothic barn on Keene Richards's Blue Grass Park. Among the county's champions of more recent times were Kingman, Venetian Way, and Winning Colors—respective winners of the 1891, 1960, and 1988 Kentucky Derbies.

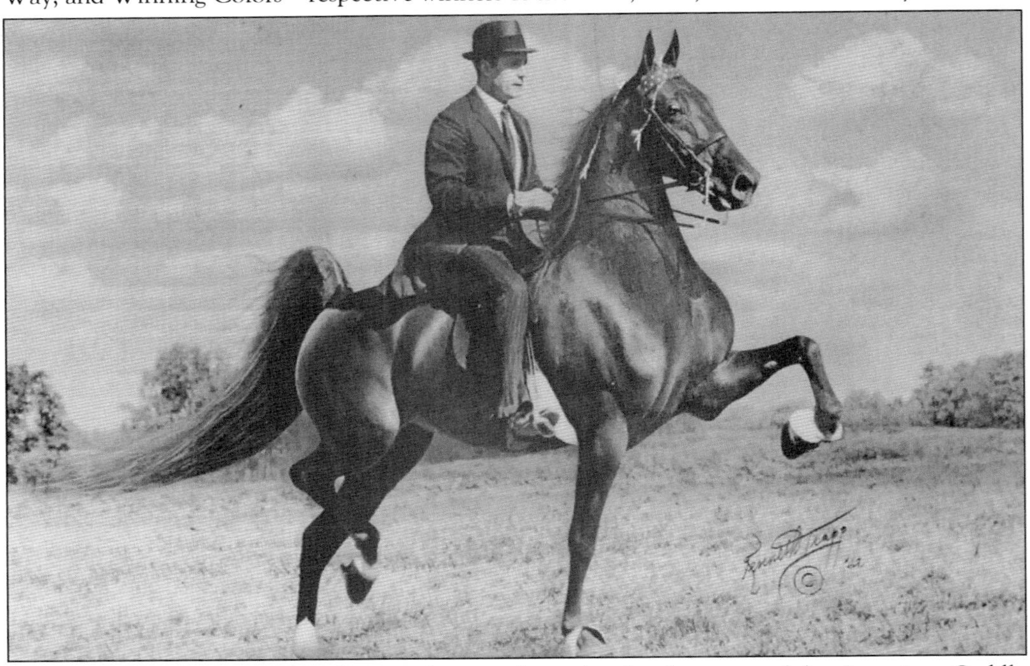

Scott County horsemen played a significant role in the development of the American Saddle Horse breed. Edward P. Gaines's Gaines Denmark, foaled in 1851, is the ancestor of most of today's Saddlebreds. Trainer Frank Bradshaw (above) is shown atop Jolie Richardson's Standardbred, My My, the world's five-gaited grand champion in 1963, 1964, 1965, 1966, 1967, and 1968. Fred and Bonnie Neuville's Morgan Shaker Supreme took breed honors in 1990.

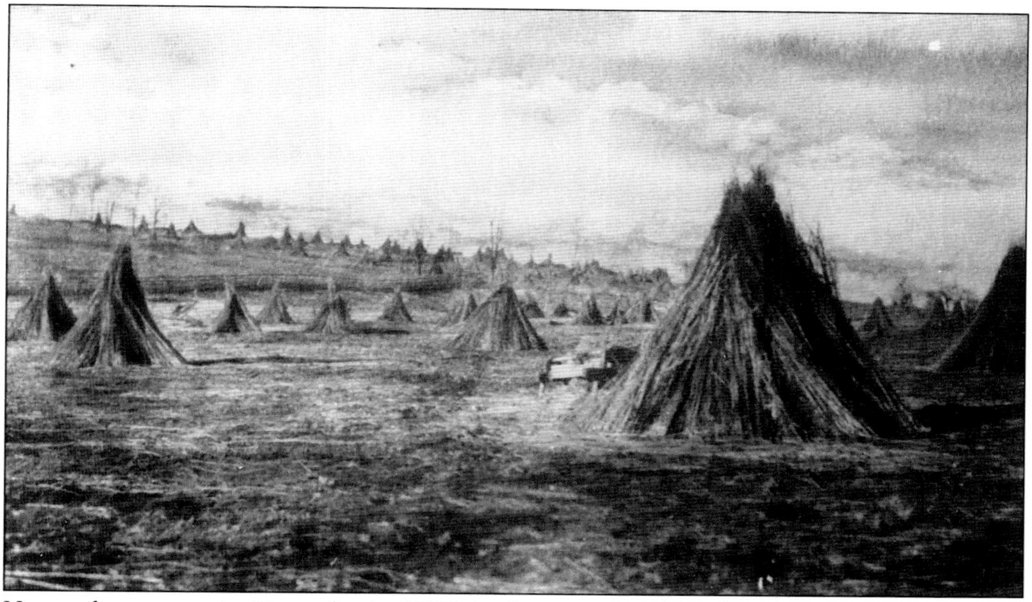

Hemp, first grown in Kentucky in 1775, is the crop that brought great wealth to Central Kentucky and ensured the proliferation of the unfortunate institution of slavery. Workers and machines in local mills and factories converted hempen fiber into rope, sailcloth, coarse clothing, and paper. Southern planters packed cotton in Kentucky-produced hempen bagging. Gradually, imported jute replaced hemp in American markets. In this view are hemp fields, photographed by Eugene Bradley.

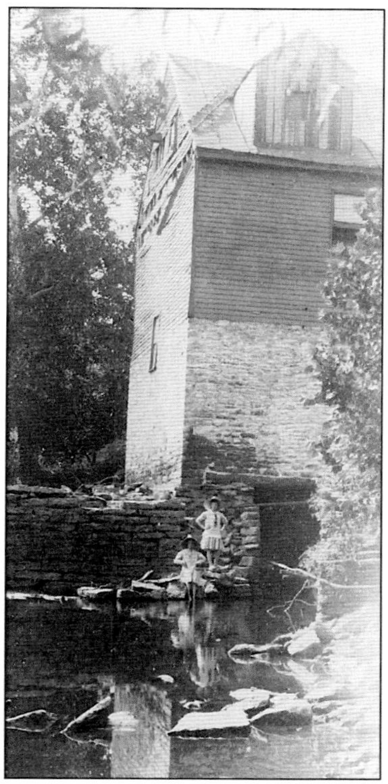

In 1783, on North Elkhorn Creek at a large buffalo crossing, Robert and Jemima Suggett Johnson established Johnson's Station, then Big Crossings, and subsequently Great Crossings. In the village were paper and gristmills, blacksmith shops, stores, taverns and inns, a post office, a bank, a school, and a church. Milton Viley Offutt's daughters, Archie and Willie Herndon, pose at the gristmill. In 1934, the WPA supervised the construction of a new dam at the old mill site.

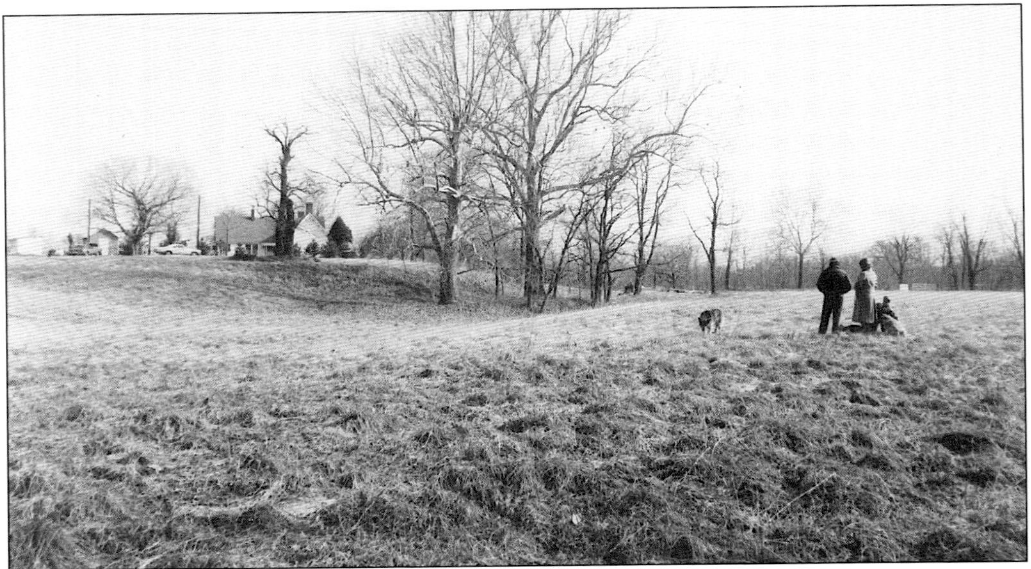

Water-powered mills were crucial to the rural Kentucky economy through the early 20th century. An 1819 scheme to refine South Elkhorn Creek for navigation resulted in the cutting of a canal that allowed river craft to circumvent the dam and mills of a creek-crossing village incredibly named Sodom. The village receded into archaeology after the antebellum period, but if one looks closely, remnants of the old canal can be discerned on the topography.

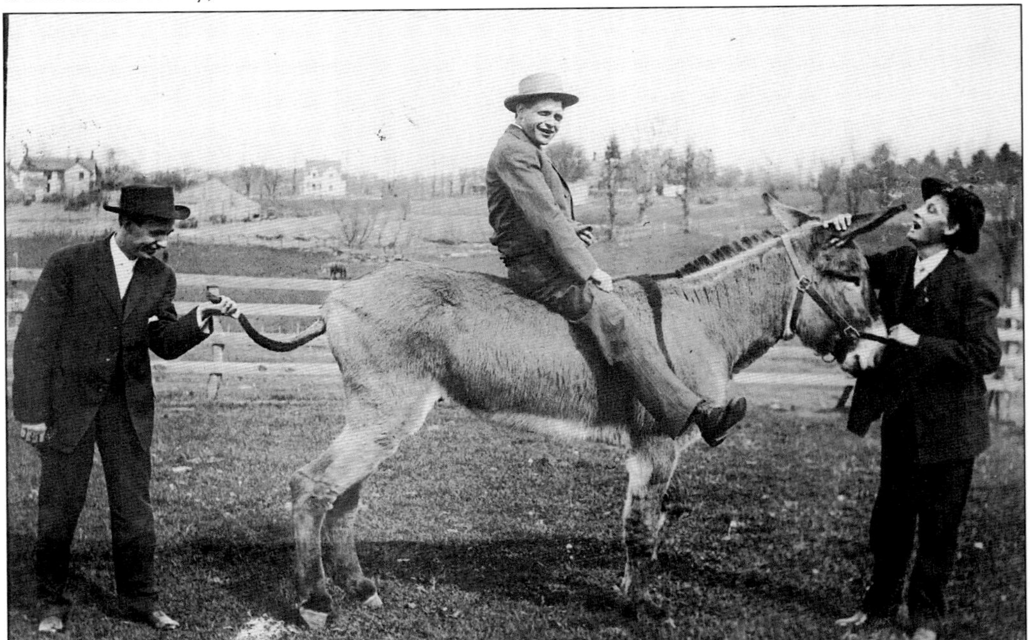

North Georgetown's landscape has changed vastly since a group of young men found merriment with a mule in a field near North Hamilton Street. To the west, one can see early residential development on the former Elijah Craig paper mill tract. On the left is the back of the Cary Clark house, and just left of center are Lee Jenkins's 1890 house (minus the tower), the W.D. Long house, a portion of the Craig-Stedman house, and properties associated with the mill.

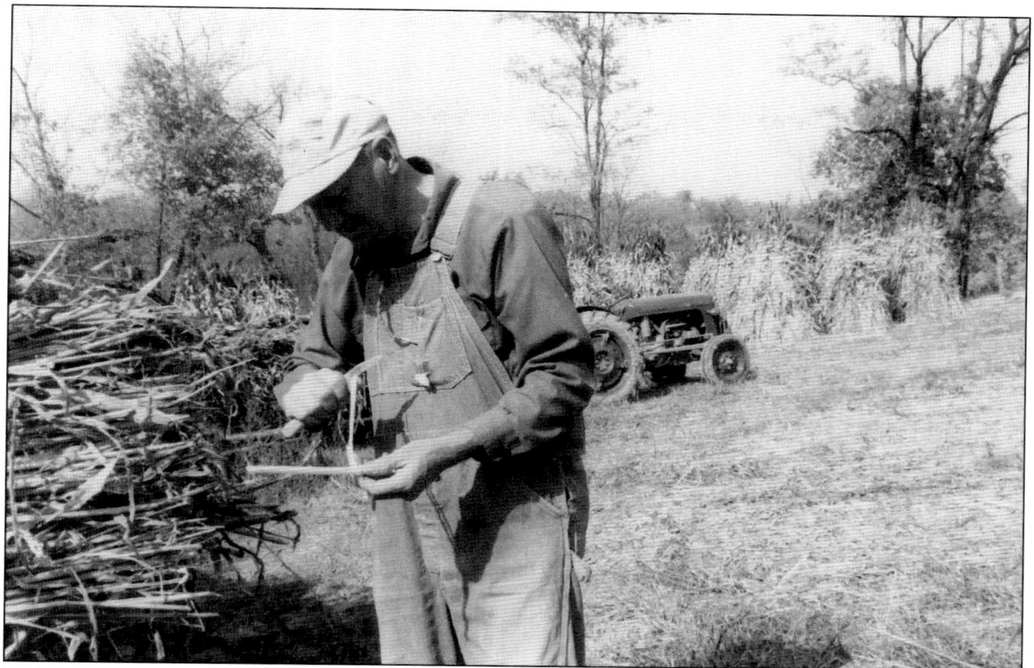

Early settlers found a steady, seasonably-provided supply of sugar available when they tapped for sap from the maple trees that grew in the woodlands and forests of Central Kentucky. Sorghum cane, a secondary source of sugar and molasses, increased in importance as the numbers of maple trees decreased. Avery Jenkins of the Leaning Oak Pike is shown stripping a small cut of cane for a sweet drink.

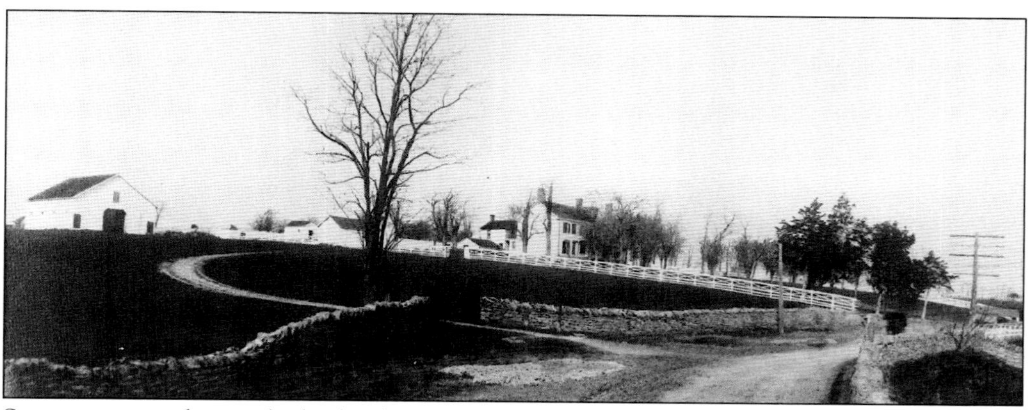

Sometimes one has to look closely to determine survivors of the turn of the last century landscape. In the 1930s, following a fire, the Bedford Browns replaced the early Kentucky Castle Ford (pictured) with the present Tudor Revival Stoneley. Remaining at the Cincinnati Road site are the winding lane, stone fences, the livestock barn (left), outbuildings including the spring house (far right), and the stone, back room of the older house.

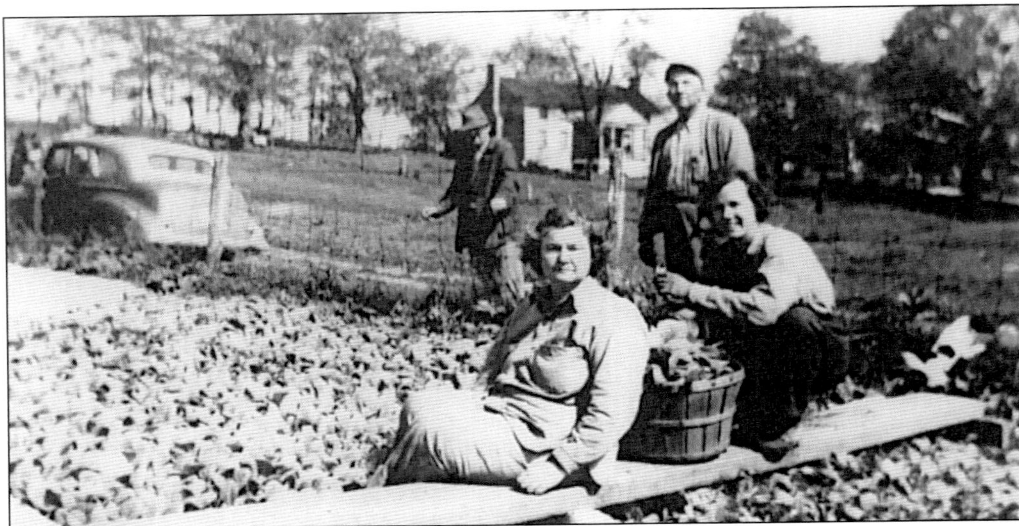

Around 1880, burley tobacco took over the countryside. On a portion of a Cincinnati Pike farm, which is now part of the Colony subdivision, stood a weather-boarded log house that is believed to have belonged to the Bradford family. Members of the Bruin family, seen here pulling tobacco plants, from left to right, are as follows: (seated) sisters Maudie Bruin Miller and Gertrude Bruin Covington; (standing) Will Bruin (father), and Charlie Bruin (brother).

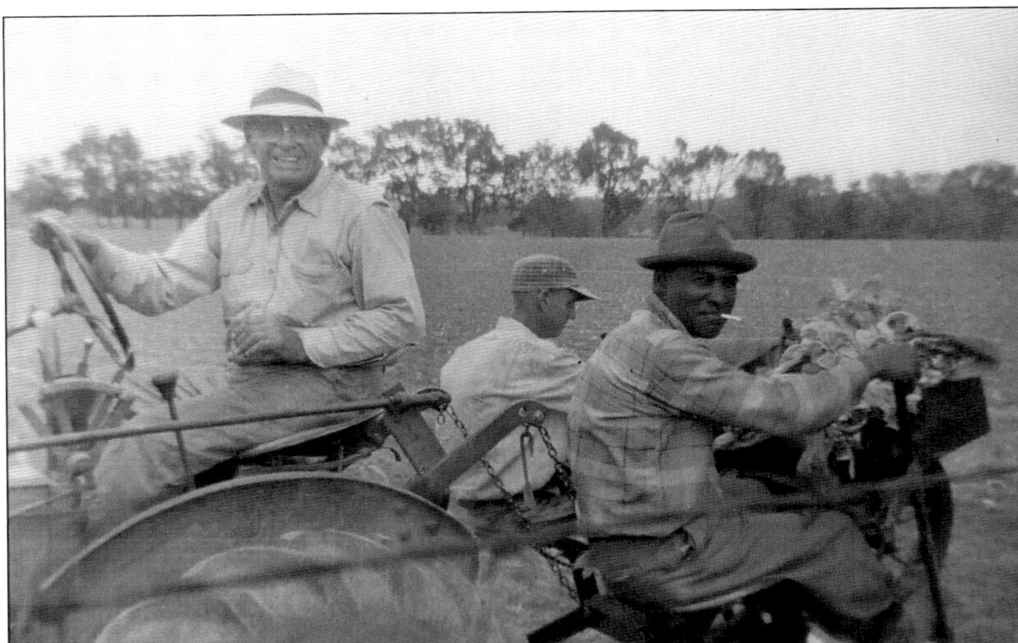

Tobacco cultivation began to increase in Scott County during and after the Civil War. Between 1876 and 1897, local cultivation of the new burley variety of the leaf increased from 156,300 to 4,008,557 pounds. Tractor-drawn, mechanical tobacco setters gradually replaced the old-fashioned hand setter. Above, Frank Williams drives the tractor while John Parker Wilson (right) and another farmer drop the plants into the mechanical setter.

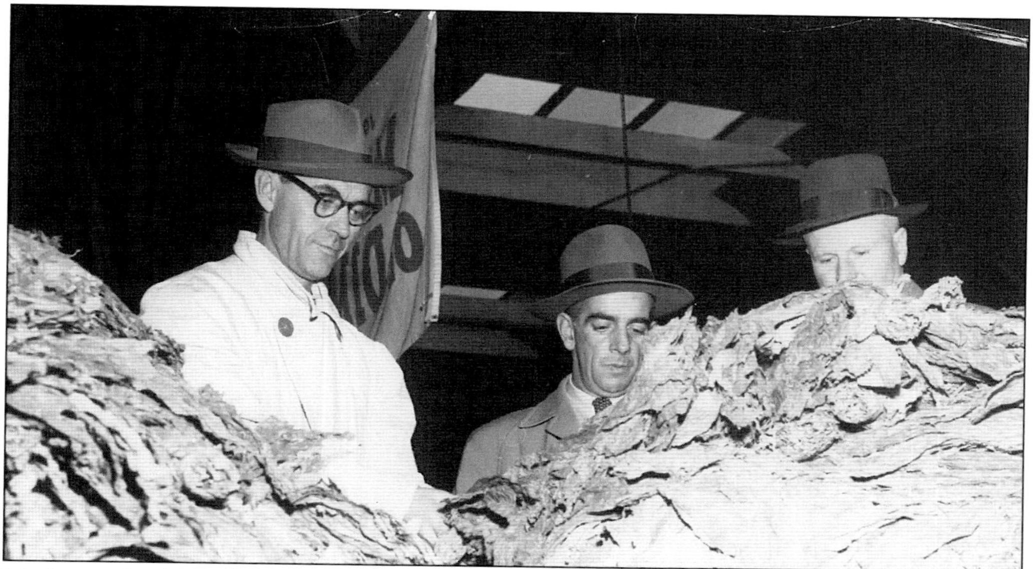

Marketing burley tobacco presented new problems. At first, tobacco companies sent buyers into the countryside to purchase farmers' crops. Toward the end of the century, the firms built receiving barns and warehouses at trade centers. Farmers, often economic victims of tobacco companies, organized the Burley Tobacco Growers' Cooperative Association and gained market equity, sometimes with violence. Above, Harold "Moon" Mullen listens as buyers bid on his crop.

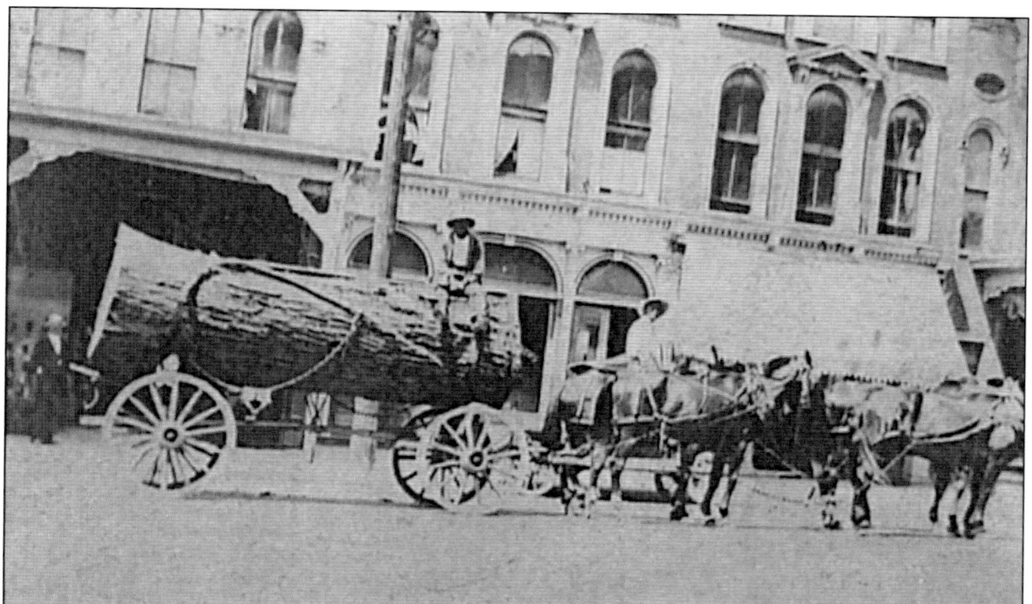

As cultivation of burley tobacco and huge crops of corn took over the landscape, farmers cleared more land and disposed of the prize hardwoods to national and world markets. Only a few farmers tenaciously held on to their historic woodlands. One of the biggest logs to be shipped out of Scott County was photographed in front of the Deposit Bank building, which is now Scott County Pharmacy. The rural landscape was thus changed forever.

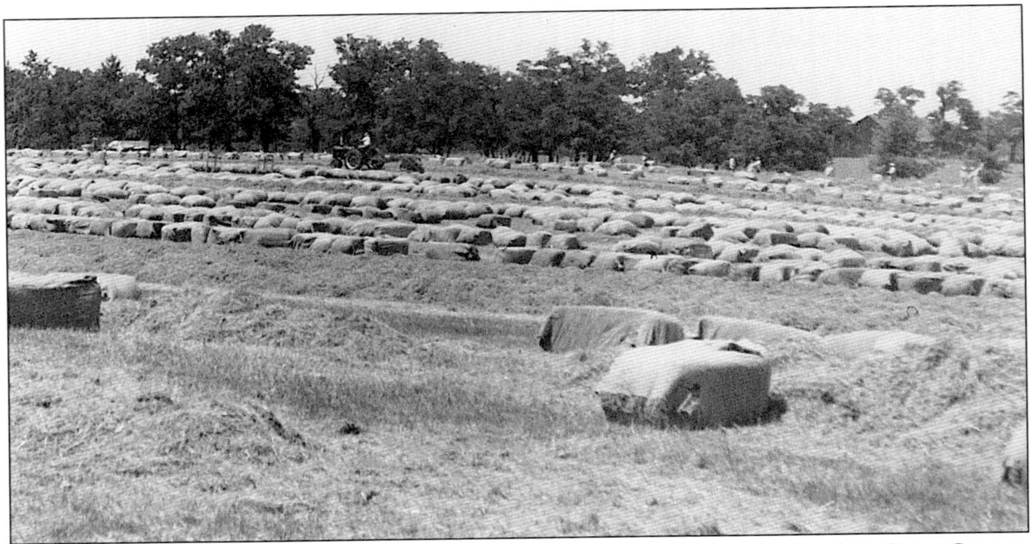

Production of clover and grass—especially bluegrass—seed peaked in 1912, when Scott County farmers produced 1,500,000 bushels of that product. G.M. Taylor and W.J. Askew merged their firms to become the major seed buyer in Scott County. The company led opposition to some producers mixing locally grown seed with inferior foreign seed. Production fell to 175,000 bushels in 1921 as competition from Europe and the Dakotas increased. Pictured above is a Taylor harvest.

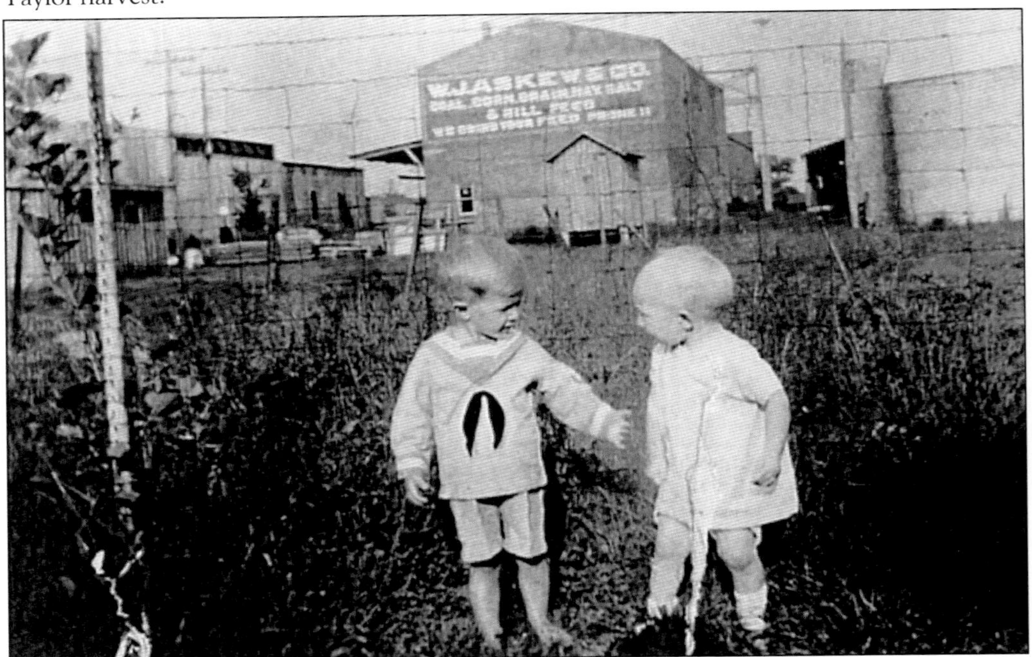

East Georgetown, located a short distance from the city's railroads, provided a significant industrial tract that included several businesses. They are, from left to right, as follows: a cannery, the W.J. Askew and G.M. Taylor mill and farm store, and the tobacco warehouse of the Burley Tobacco Growers' Cooperative. Posing in the foreground, in the garden of Kelly Linn, one of Georgetown's last master carpenters, are little J.T. Linn and neighbor Billy Blythe.

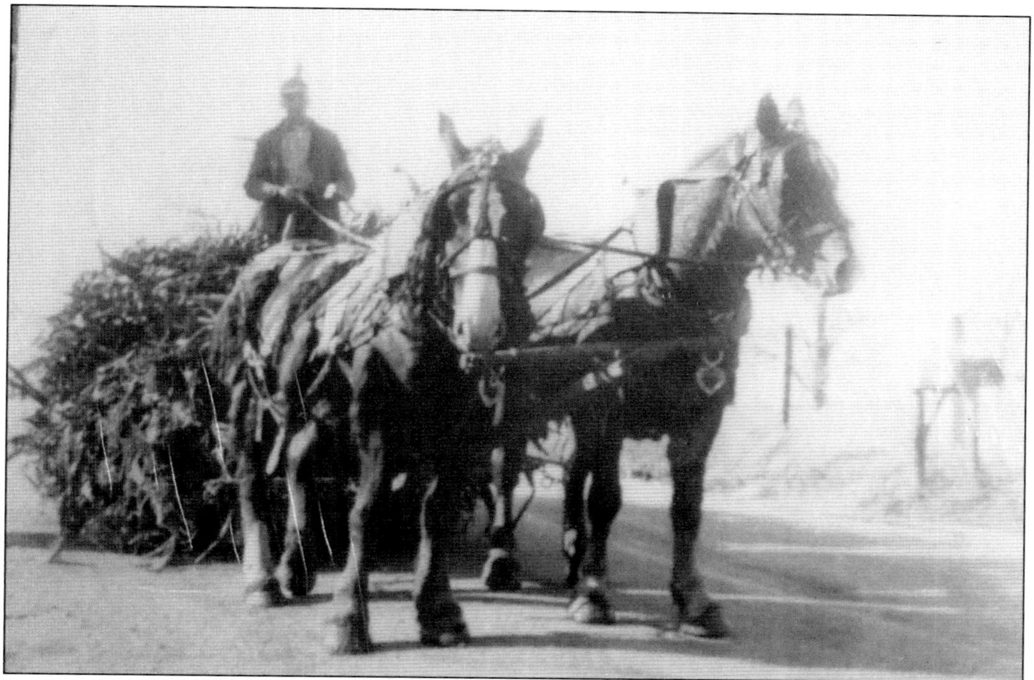

Mechanization of agriculture came slowly, with horses, mules, and oxen pulling most farm equipment until after World War II. Scott County's 1861 high of 3,052 mules and 696 jennies never recovered after the Civil War—there were 1,491 and 77 in 1871, 1,818 and 48 in 1873, 1,205 in 1900, and 1,461 in 1920. In this view, Billy Green operates a team of horses pulling a load of fodder as the age of beasts of burden in Central Kentucky came to an end.

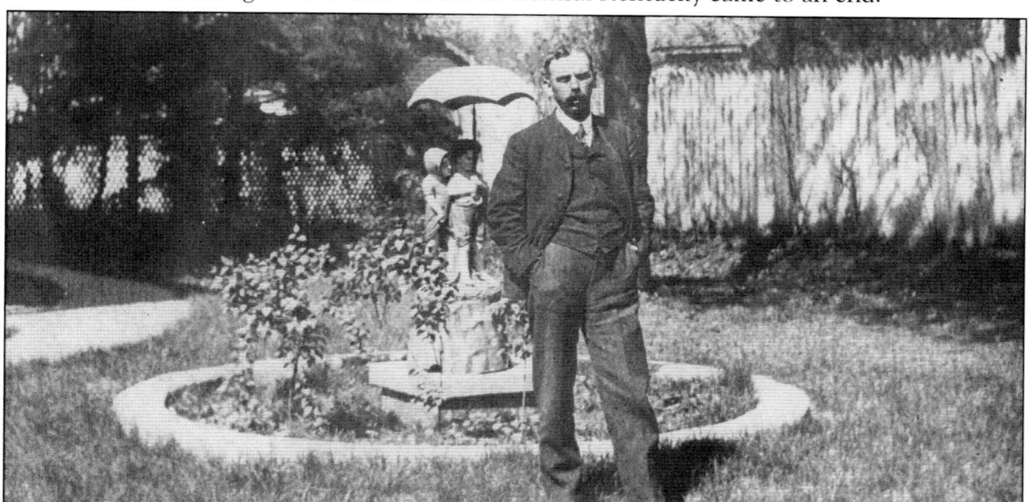

In 1906, eight farmers owned more than 1,000 acres each for a total of 20,599 acres—11.3 percent of Scott County's farmland. At the helm was John B. Graves with 4,561 acres. Much of Graves's land lay along Dry Run and North Elkhorn and Cincinnati Pike. On his multiple estate farms, he erected substantial granaries, corn cribs, and large mortise-and-tenon tobacco barns. He also maintained the fine, older homes. Graves is shown on the lawn of his East Main Street home.

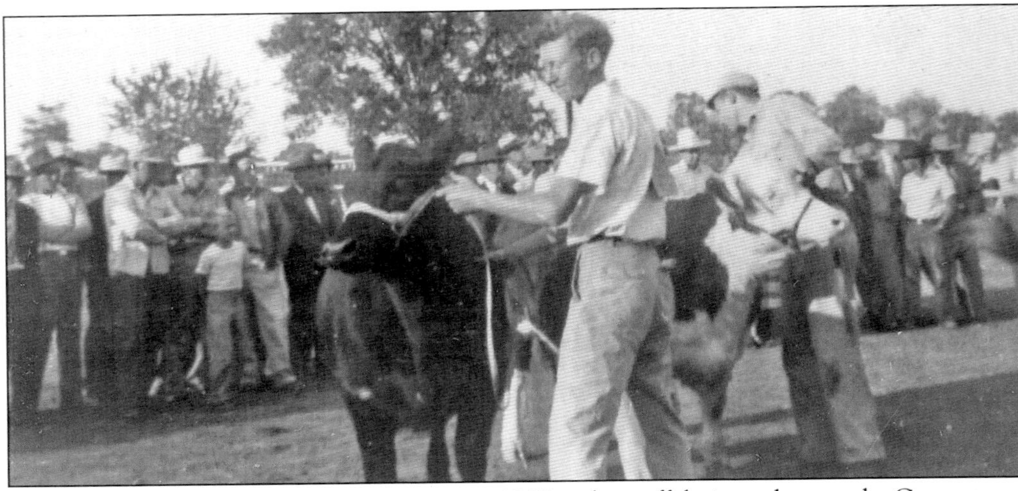

Farmers of all ages received the opportunity in 1947 to show off their products as the Georgetown Kiwanis Club reestablished the tradition of the county fair. The fair took place at Moss Park, a local recreation ground on the site of Lynn West's nineteenth-century racing track. West's and Moss's farm, in more recent years, provided land for the Peninsula subdivision. Young farmers Jimmy Stone and Ray Sharpe are shown in the cattle ring at the new fair.

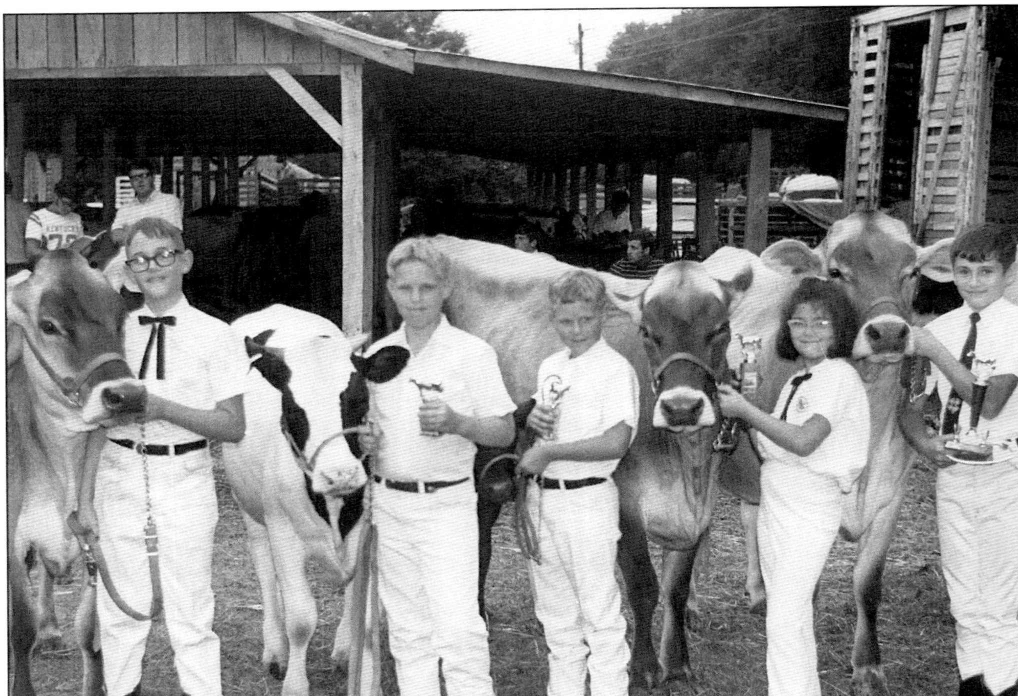

Dairy cattle declined numerically as beef animals became the dominant bovines on Scott County's rural landscape. Outstanding among dairy producers in the 1970s in the county's 4-H program were ribbon and trophy winners Herbie Zeysing, Chris and Jeff Blakeman, and Pat and Tommy Withers. Today, the county's sole dairy farmer, who thoroughly enjoys managing his herd, is Doug Brown. Brown's farm is located on Payne's Depot Road.

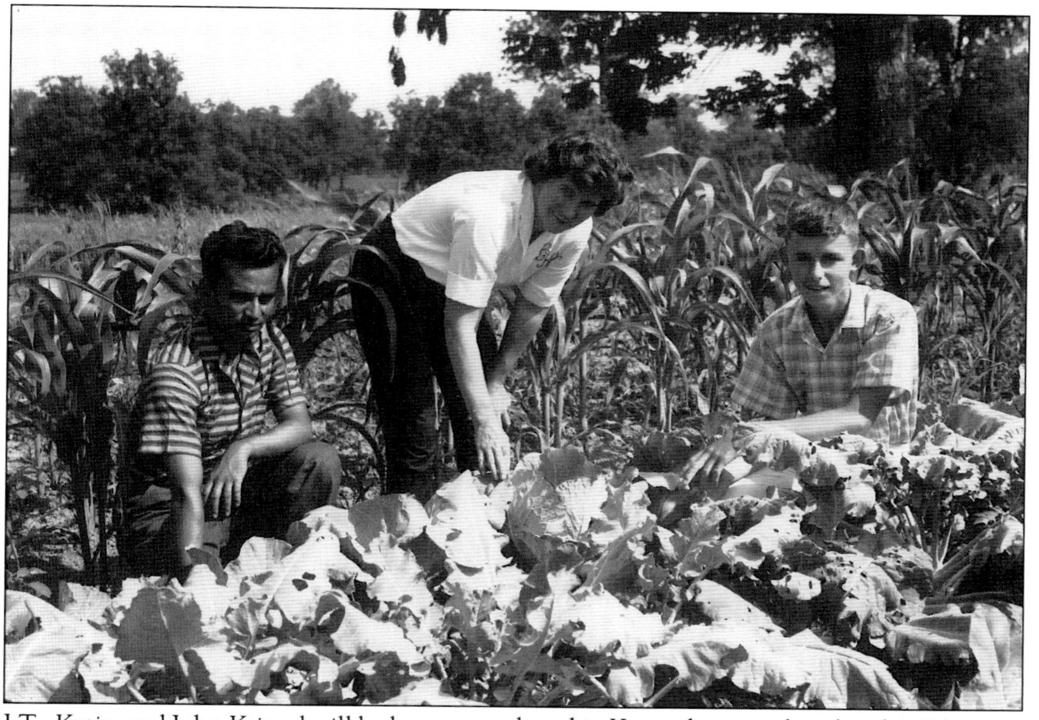

J.T., Katie, and John Kriegel will be long remembered in Kentucky agricultural and 4-H history. Between 1962 and 1981, one of the three Kriegels won overall and reserve horticulture honors at the Kentucky State Fair. John and Larry, the latter with tobacco honors, represented Kentucky at 4-H Congress in 1968. Katie and Johnny are pictured with 1962 houseguest Kasbah Pashar Shurma, a 4-H agent from Nepal.

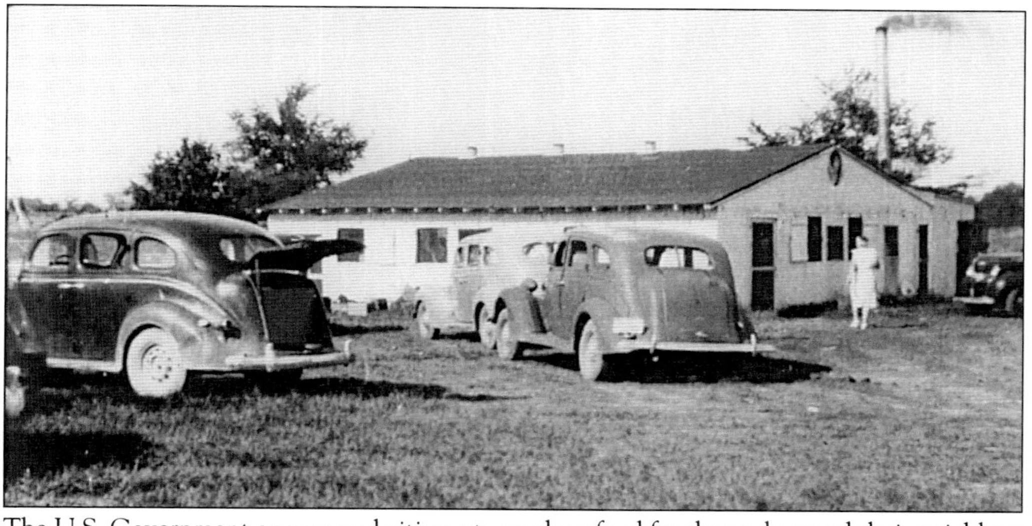

The U.S. Government encouraged citizens to produce food for themselves and their neighbors with "victory gardens" and community canneries in the difficult WW II years. Commercial canneries, as well as those operated through vocational agriculture and home economics programs, were popular summertime gathering places. The Stamping Ground Community Cannery, built by the community's national prize winning FFA chapter, dates from 1938.

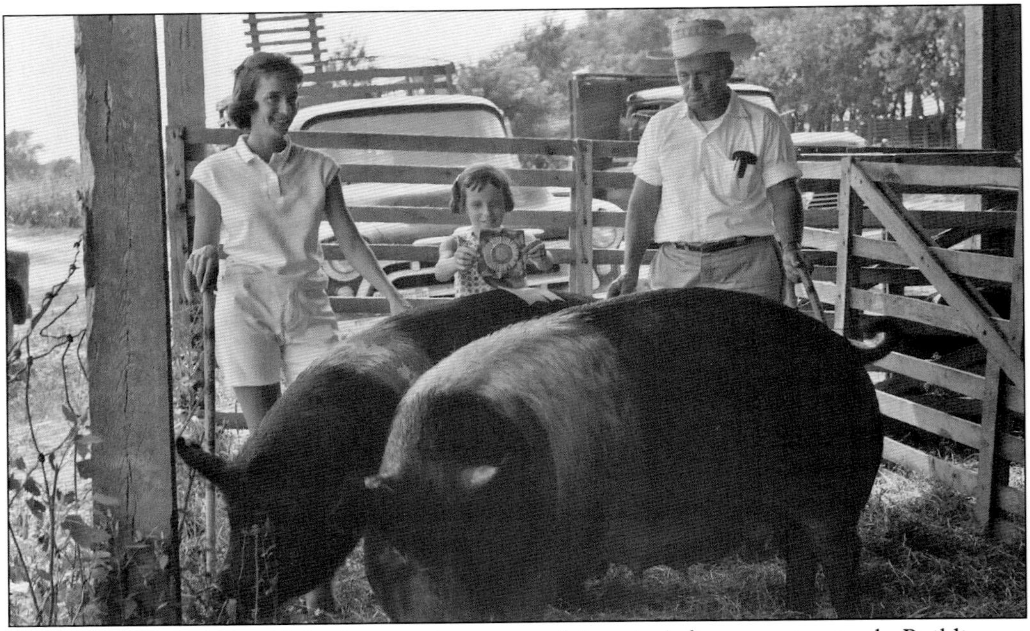

Kentucky hogs were established very early as some of America's finest meat animals. Building on this tradition in the 1950s and 1960s with prize-winning Hampshire stock were John McMullen and daughters Virginia (Penn) and Judy (Wiley). Virginia won a national 4-H achievement award in 1959, and Judy was a state champion in the next decade. The McMullen's farm was located on Stamping Ground Road.

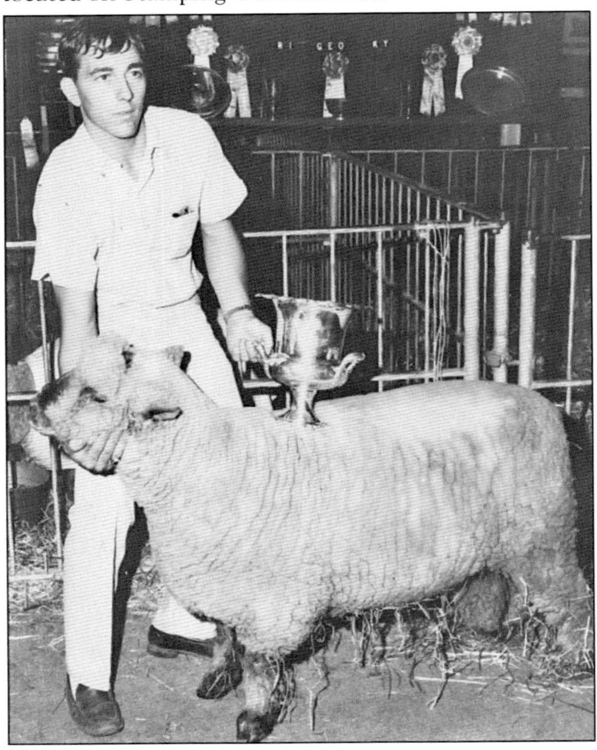

The challenge of raising sheep was often thwarted when roaming dogs attacked the docile flocks. Before the turn of the century, farmers such as Buford Hall and his son, Buford, grazed thousands of sheep. Scott saw its sheep population slowly decimated from the 1900 tally of 61,757 to 52,491 in 1910 and 29,853 in 1920. Pictured is 4-H and FFA exhibitor Ronnie Shrout of the Newtown club, who added the best sheep exhibitor's trophy to his family's impressive collection.

Two
Georgetown in Transition

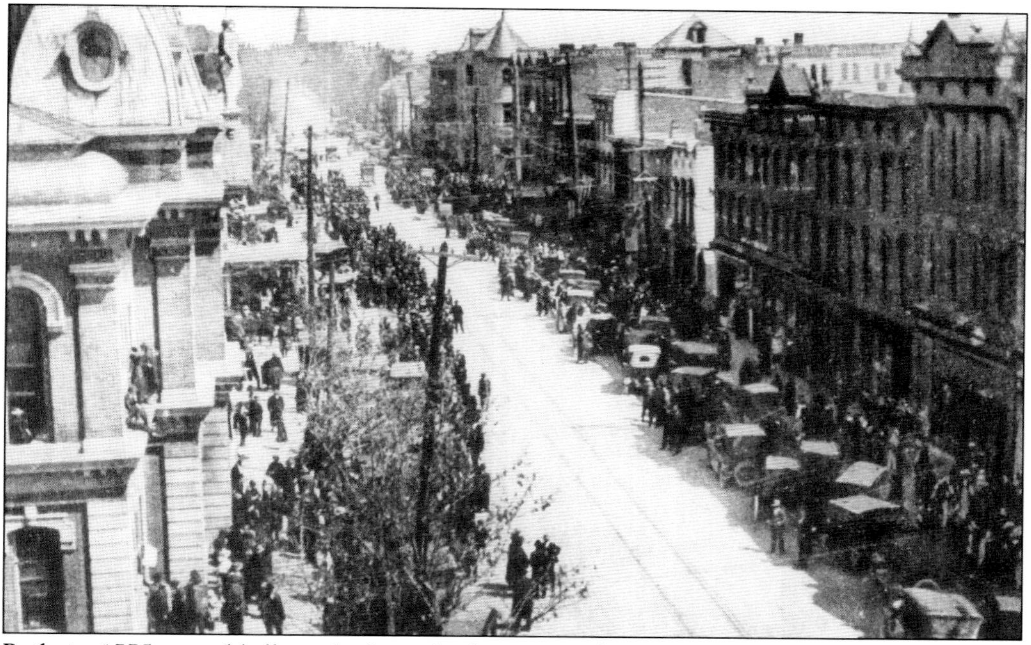

Built in 1775 on a bluff overlooking the big spring discovered by surveyor John Floyd the previous year, John McClelland's fort was abandoned in the early part of 1777, following an attack by Native Americans that resulted in McClelland's death.

Nine years passed before the Reverend Elijah Craig, a Baptist minister from Virginia, settled near the spring and began laying out town lots for the village he named Lebanon. In 1792, Lebanon, now renamed George Town, became the seat of the new county of Scott in the new state of Kentucky.

From a population of 380 in 1800, the small village of Georgetown has grown to a city of more than 12,000 inhabitants. Along the way, its focus has also shifted from a primary function as supply center and market outlet for a rural populace to a city more dependent upon an industrial and service economy. In an era of increasing urban development, this trend seems sure to continue.

Pictured in this view are citizens of Georgetown lining the streets during the 1920 Armistice day parade.

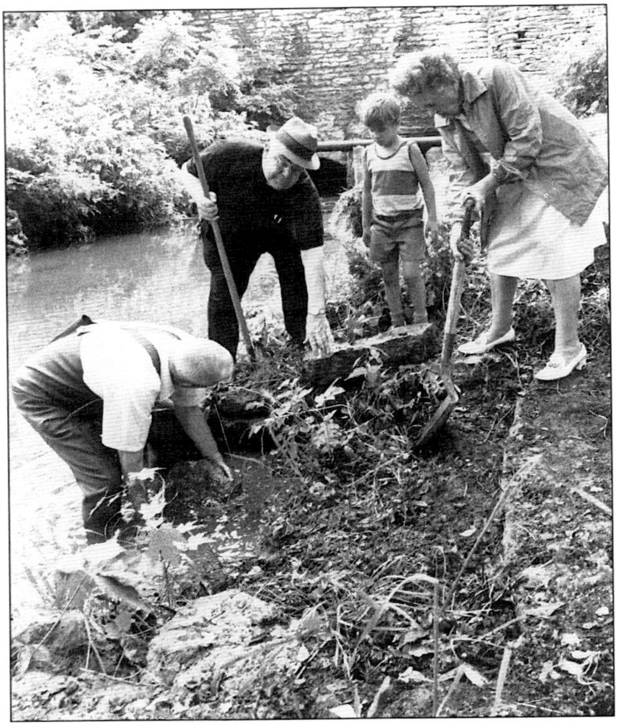

The reason for Georgetown's existence, Royal Spring, has provided a source of fresh water for the city since pioneer days. The stream also served as a site for baptismal ceremonies for many churches. Shown reworking the baptismal steps *c.* 1982 are Wallace Shropshire, Father James O'Rourke, Robert Bevins, and Lillian Jameson.

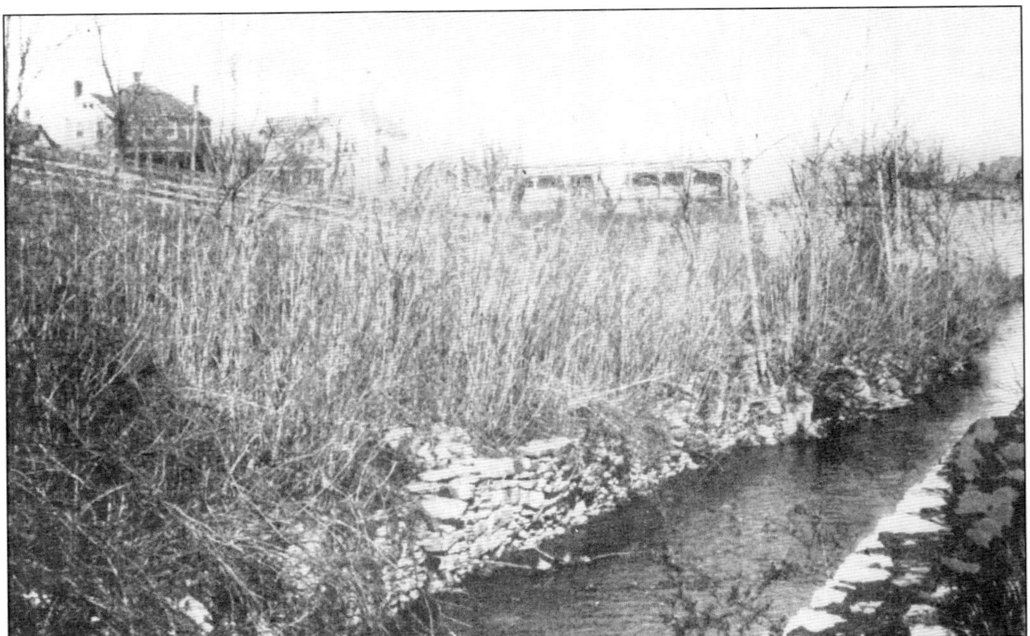

After years of controversy over water rights, the city settled the issue in 1922 by purchasing the neighboring landowners' rights to use the spring. This rather weedy-looking postcard image, taken from a point just east of the 1895 H.P. Montgomery home, shows, from left to right: the Albert W. Craig house, the Susan P. Long house, the old telephone exchange, and the cupola of the jail.

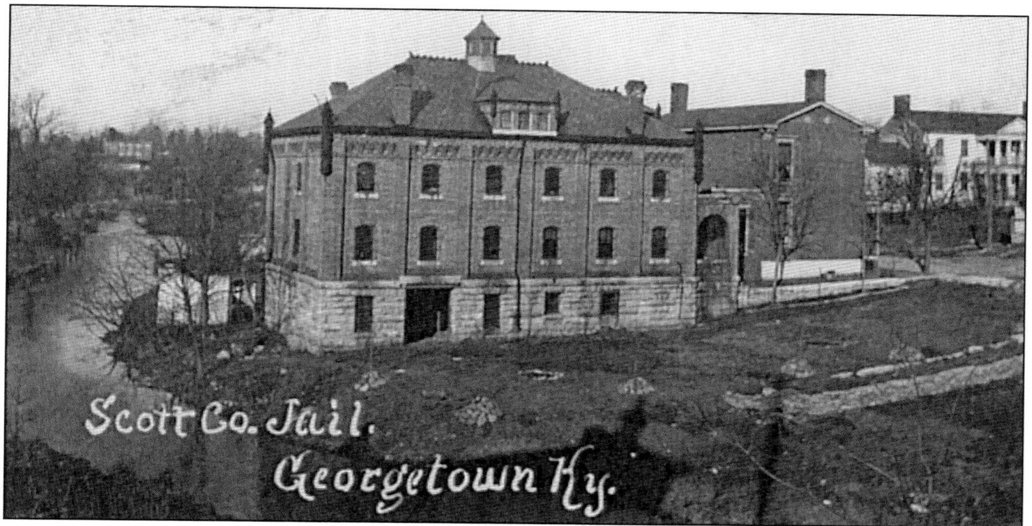

In 1892, Scott County entered the modern age of corrections with the opening of its new jail. Replaced in recent years by the Justice Center on North Hamilton, the old facility faced an uncertain future prior to its lease acquisition by the Scott County Arts Consortium. To the right of the jail stands the Stevenson/Bradley home, which was dismantled in 1973.

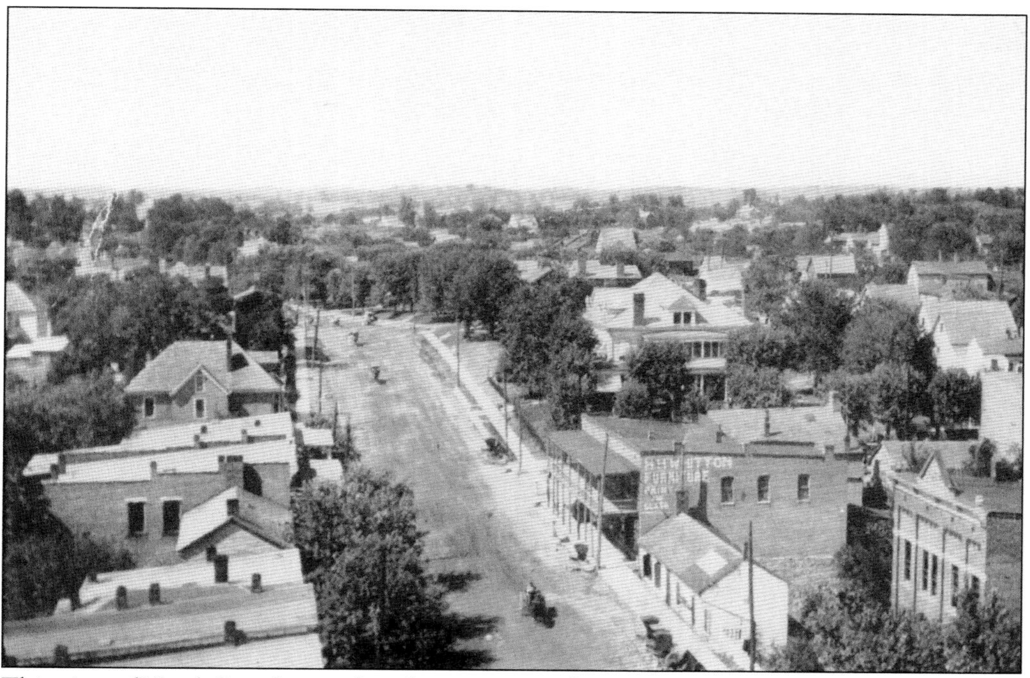

This view of North Broadway, taken from an upper floor of the Lancaster Hotel, is a reminder of the numerous changes of the last century. Among the lost structures is the large Italianate Johnson home at the corner of Washington Street, torn down in 1969. Buildings to the south were destroyed by fires in 1963 and 1964.

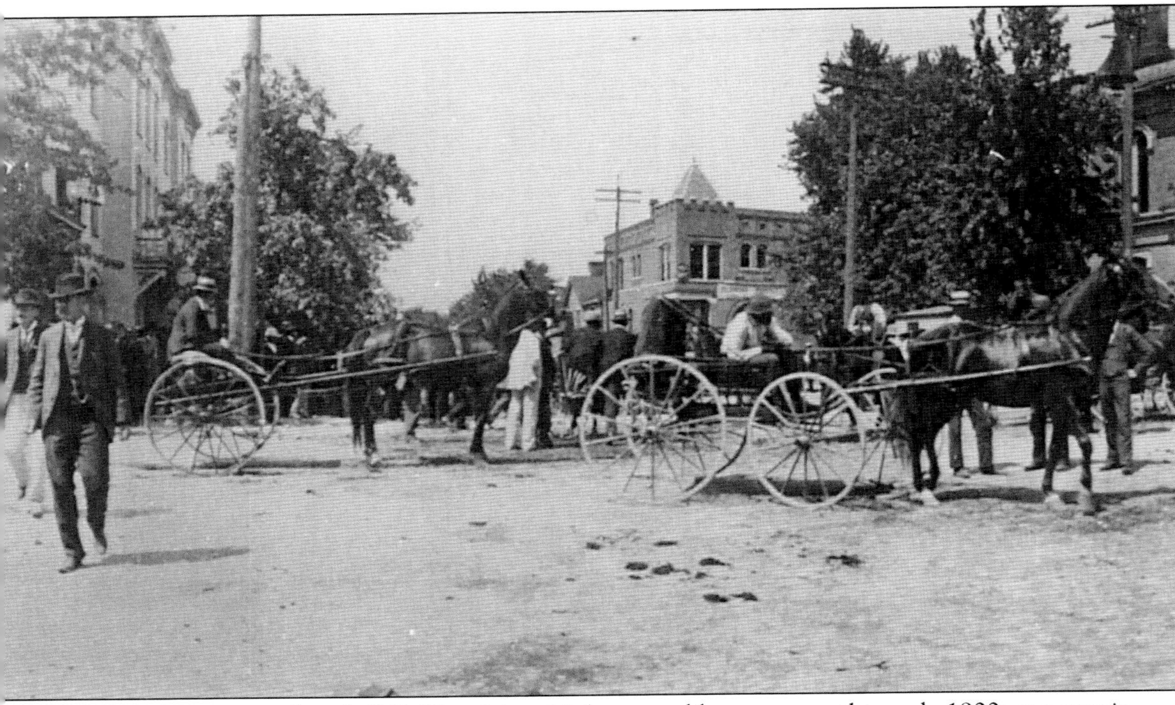

Georgetown resident Jeff Phillips drives his horse and buggy across this early 1900s panoramic view of downtown. Visible on the far left is the Lancaster Hotel facade. To the left of the

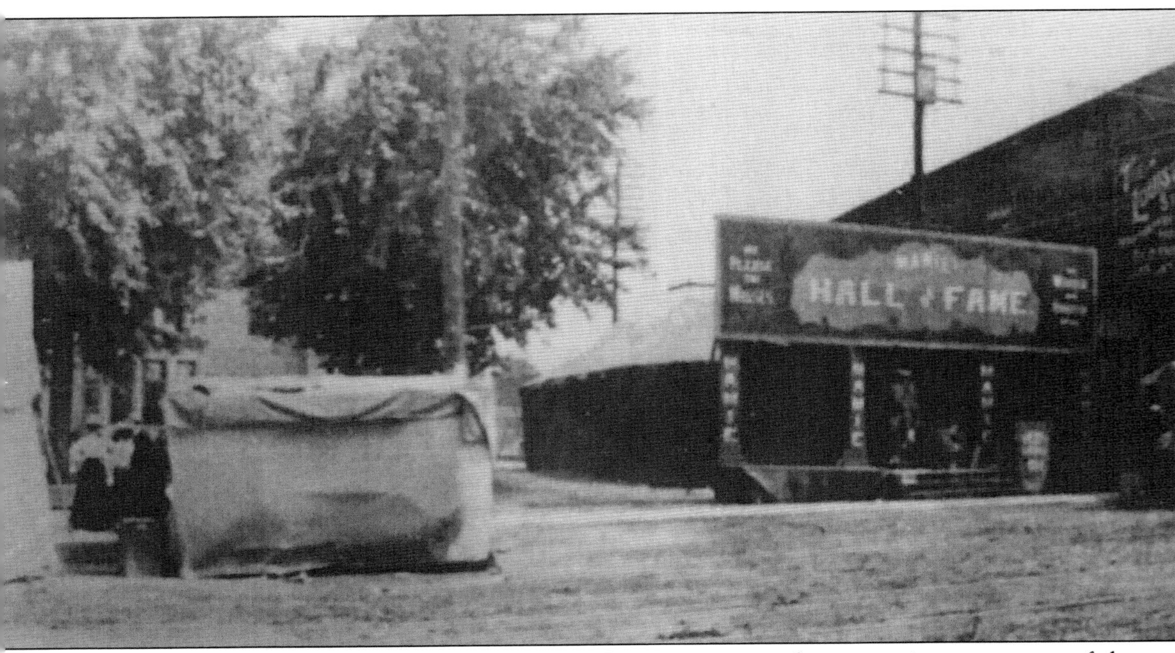

On Saturdays and the monthly Court Day, Georgetown was the entertainment center of the county. Court Day attractions included patent medicine shows, tightrope walkers, dancing bears, and the ever-present Blind Dave the Fiddler. This panoramic view shows Main Street

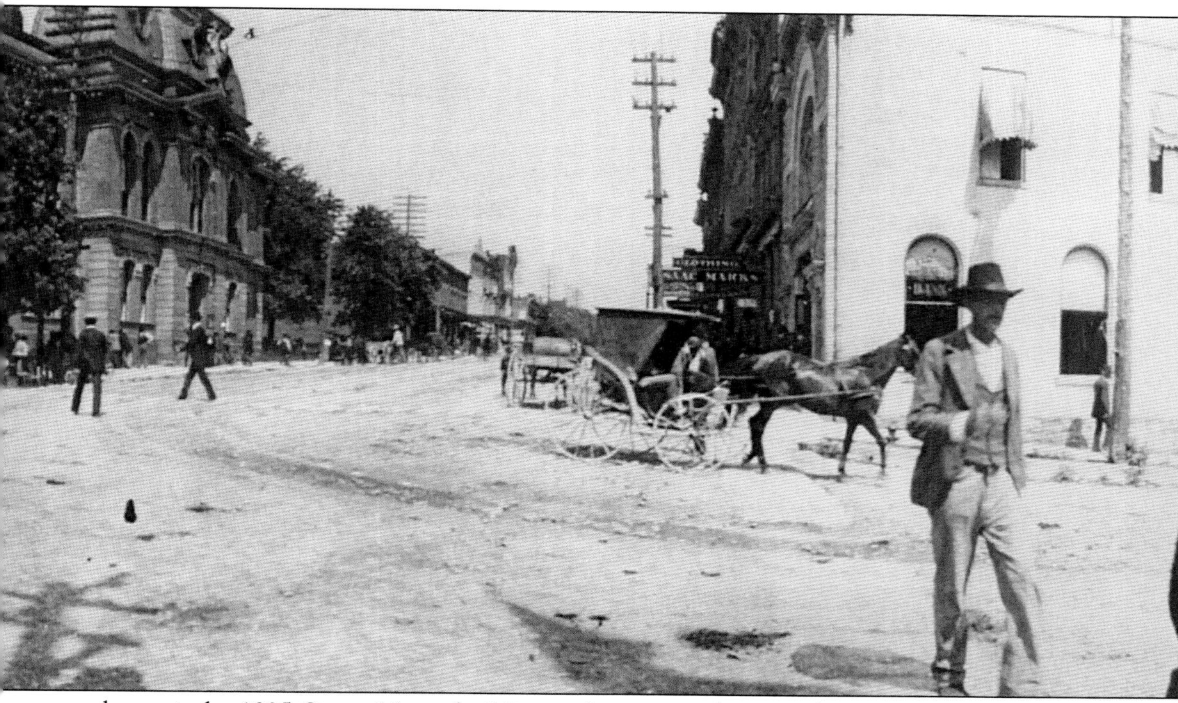

courthouse is the 1895 Carter Moore building with its original corner doorway, and on the far right is the Romanesque First National Bank building.

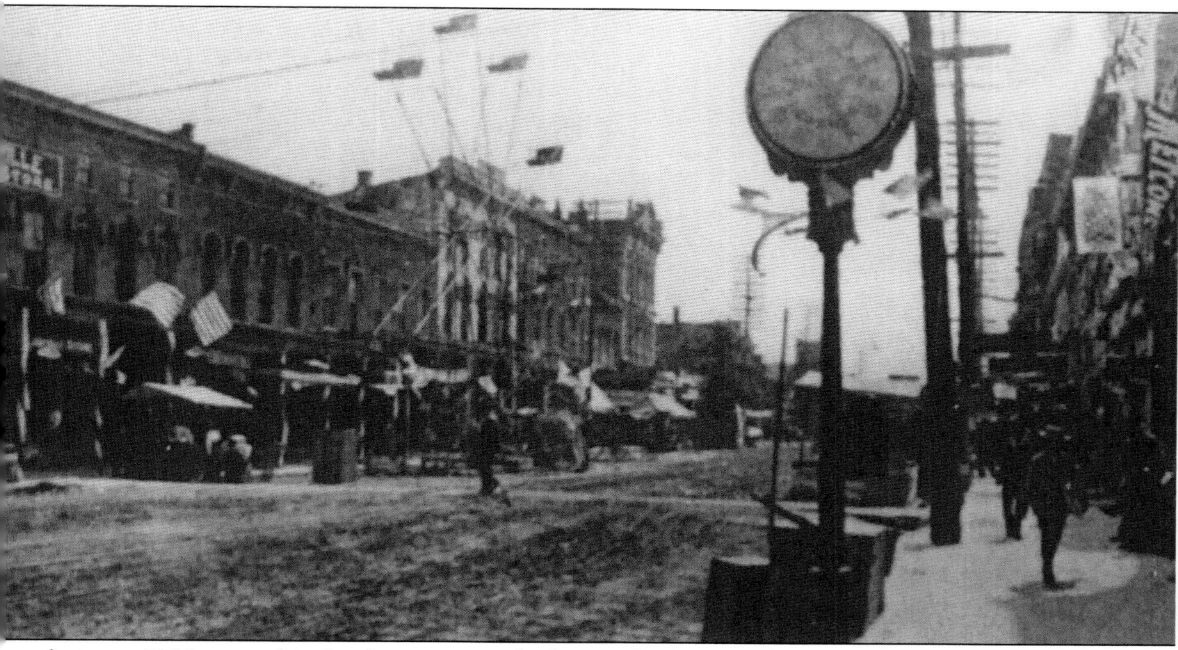

during a 1906 street fair. In the center is the Louisville Store, a dry goods chain store open intermittently from 1892 until its conversion to a drugstore in 1923. On the right is the large electric clock erected in 1895 by jeweler J.W. Keller.

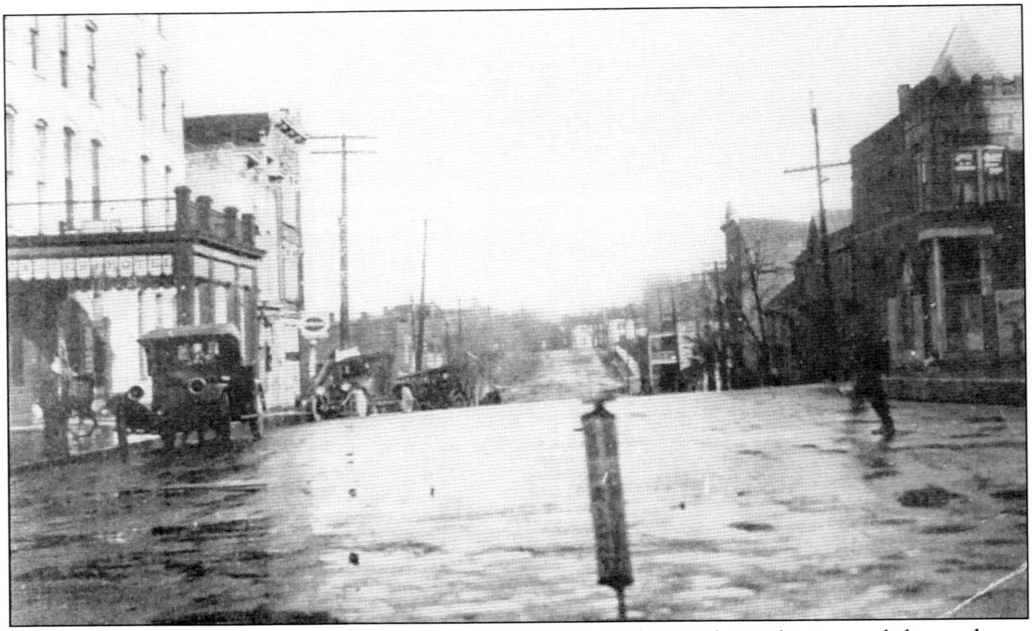

This view of the intersection of Main Street and Broadway during the early automobile era shows Georgetown's traffic cop: a marker warning motorists to "Keep To The Right." After numerous accidents, stop signs were placed at the intersection in 1924. Finally, in 1928, the intersection of Main Street and Broadway became the recipient of Georgetown's first stoplight.

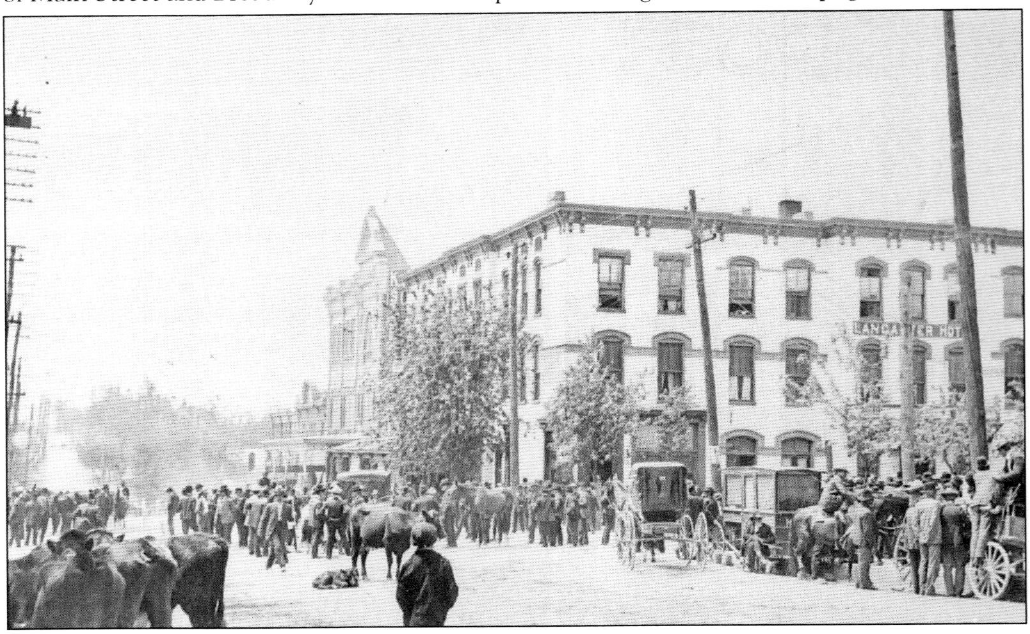

From pioneer times, the monthly meeting of the county court was the busiest day in Georgetown. Residents from rural areas came to town to buy and sell produce, trade animals, and argue politics. This Court Day scene shows the 1883 Lancaster Hotel prior to its 1910 enlargement. To the left is Kinzea Stone's elaborate 1892 grocery. Both buildings were demolished in 1963 for construction of the new First National Bank.

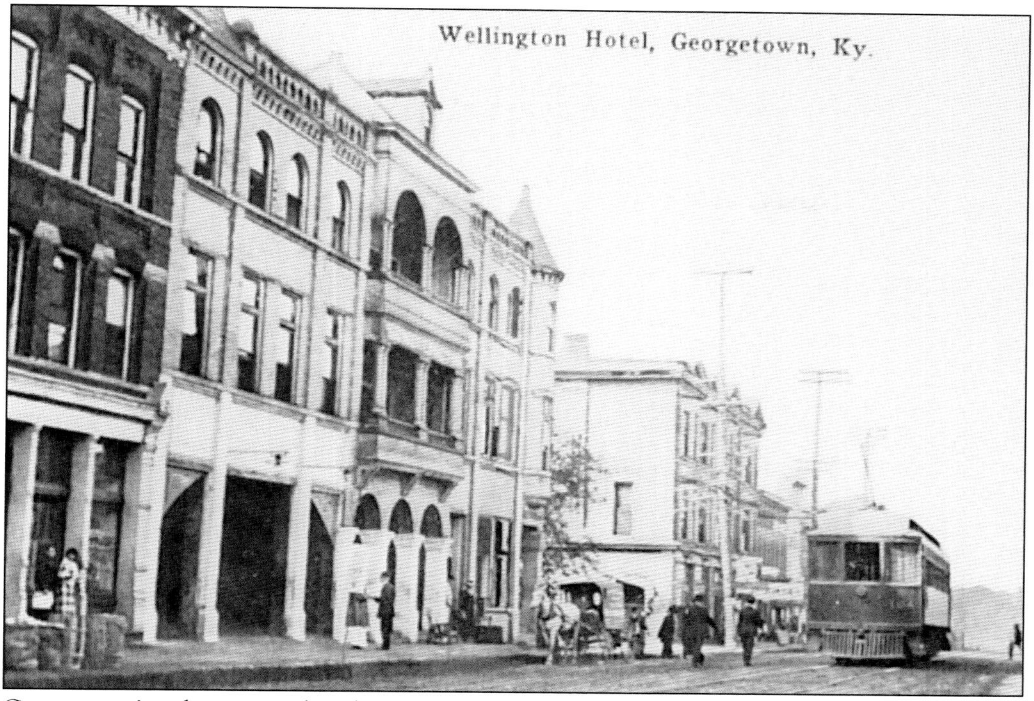

Georgetown's other major hotel was the Wellington, a 60-room structure built in 1896 by Simeon Wells to replace his Wells House Hotel across the street. It advertised steam heat, six bathrooms, and running water on all floors. The Farmers Bank occupied the corner room and eventually the rest of the building as well. The balconies were removed in 1926.

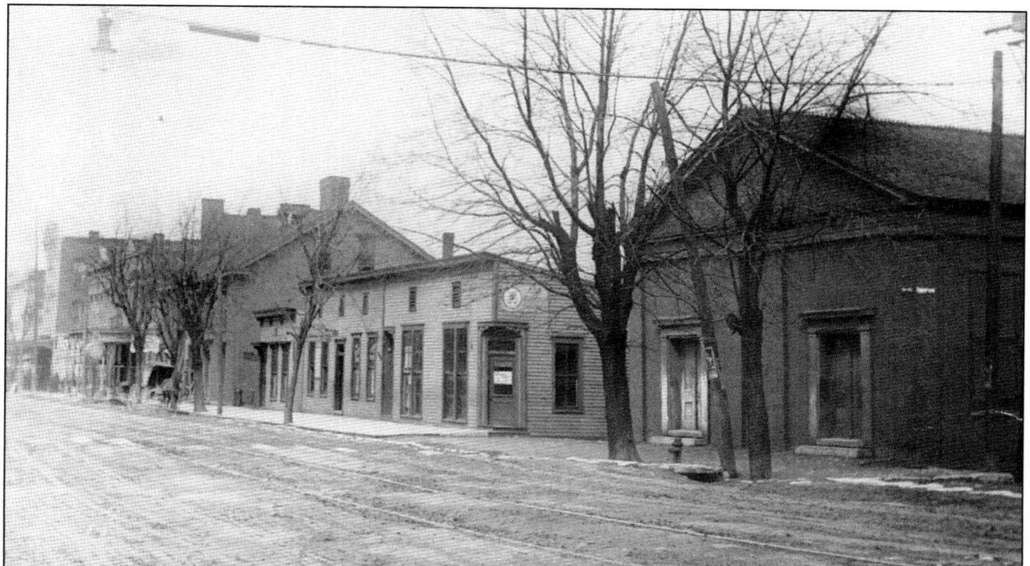

The former Georgetown Post Office, in use until 1998, stands on this site on the north side of Main Street west of Mulberry. On the right is the old Particular Baptist Church, torn down in 1912. The frame buildings (left) were moved to another part of town and were converted to residences. The first letter was mailed at the new post office in January 1916.

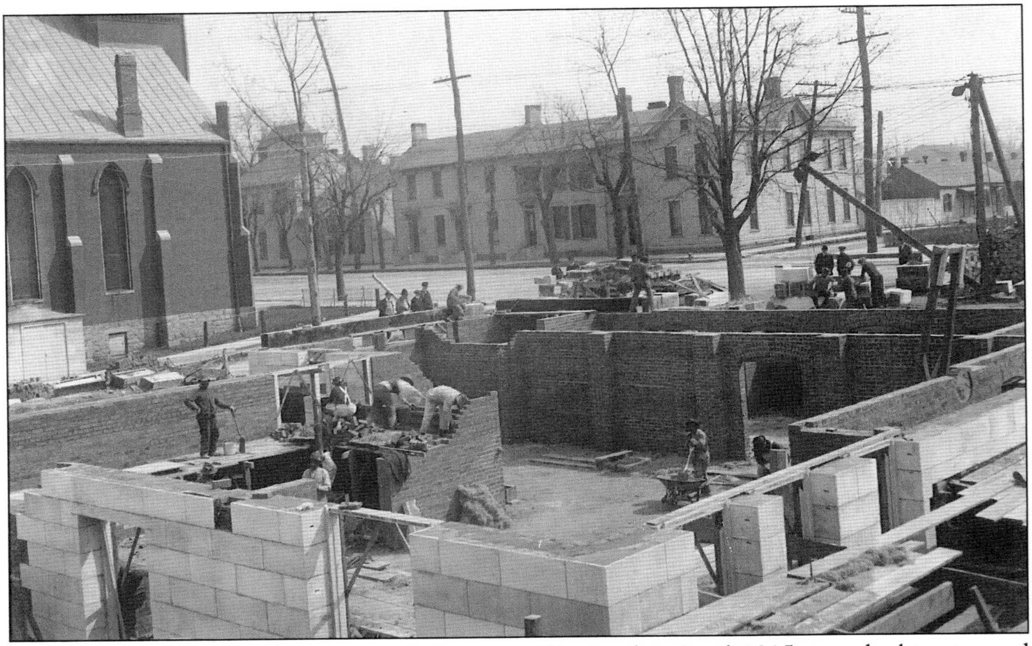

Workers construct the foundation of the post office in this April 1915 view looking toward the south side of Main Street. Visible in the background is the unusual tower of the Leo Tarleton house, prior to the home's conversion to the bungalow style. Through the influence of Congressman J.C. Cantrill, Georgetown secured a post office much larger than normal for a town its size.

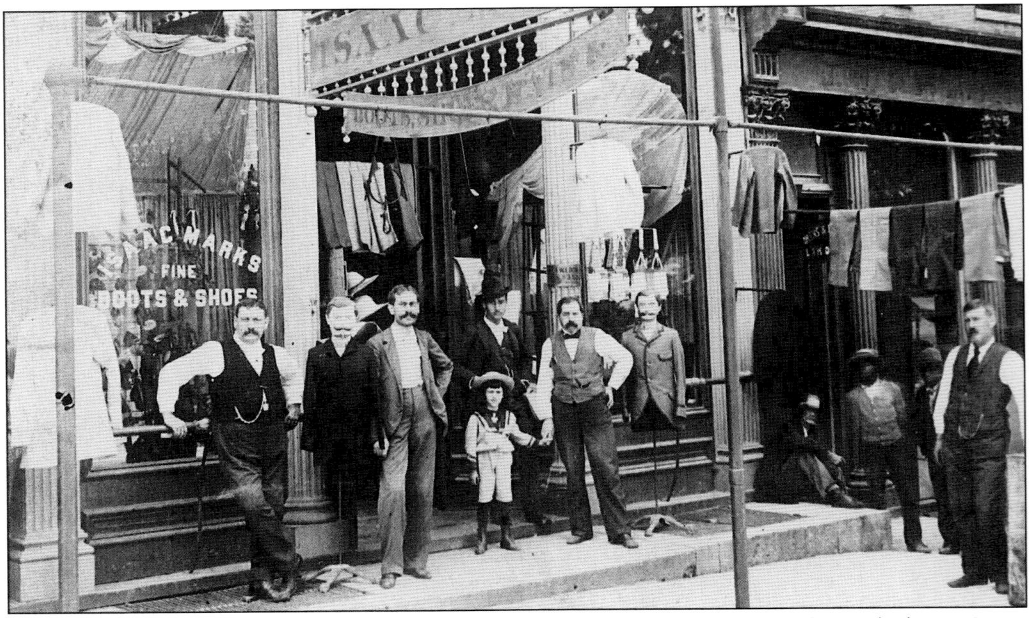

Isaac Marks, William Ehrlich, and M.A. Waterman pose outside Marks's Palace Clothing House on Main Street. Marks, born in Germany, was the premier dry goods merchant in Georgetown for over 30 years until his death in 1900. Active in numerous civic and fraternal organizations, he also served on Georgetown's first city council.

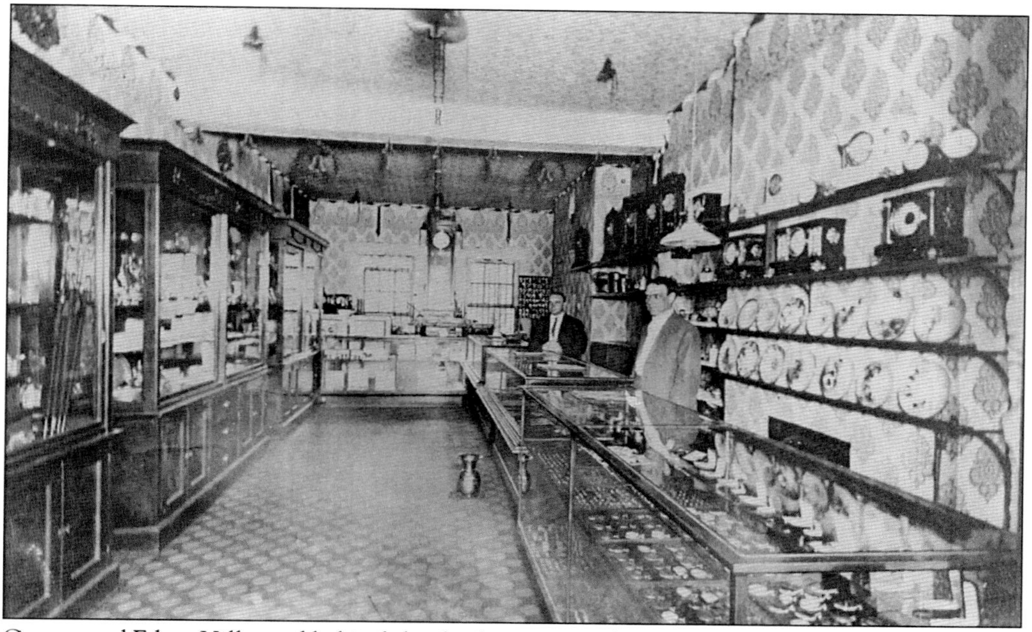

George and Edgar Hill stand behind the display cases in their jewelry store on East Main Street. The store had its beginnings in 1894 when 20-year-old George Hill, son of a school teacher from England, moved to Georgetown and opened a small watch repair shop.

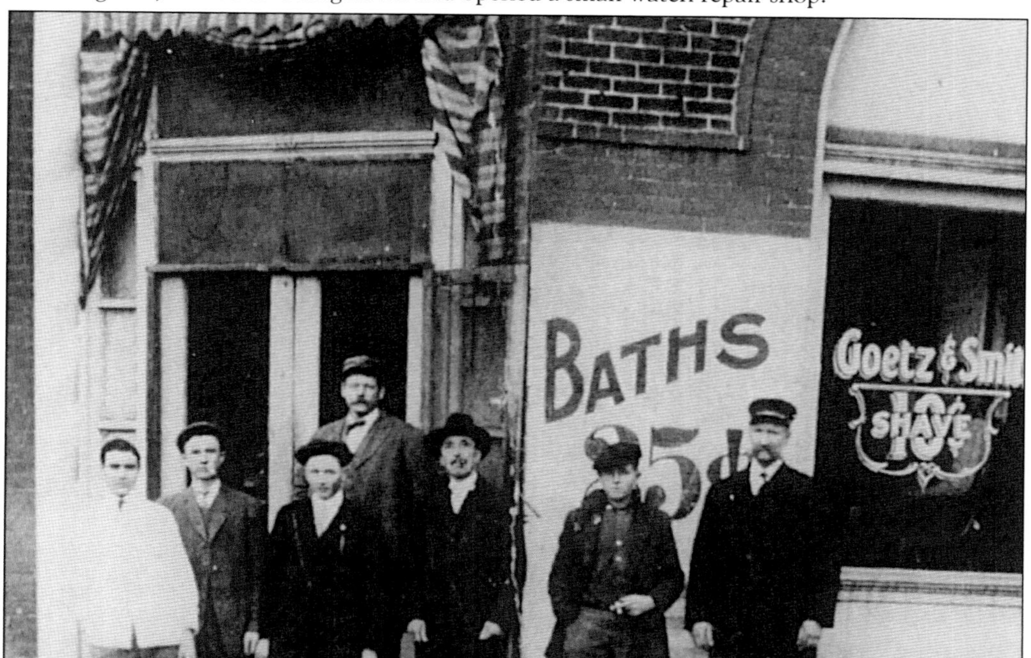

Peter Goetz, "Tonsorial Artist," was a native of Worms, Germany, and worked as a barber in Georgetown from 1873 until shortly before his death in 1915. Among those pictured in front of Goetz's former shop at the corner of Court Street and Broadway are dry goods merchant Robert Kravetz and Georgetown streetcar conductor Zip Lee (far right).

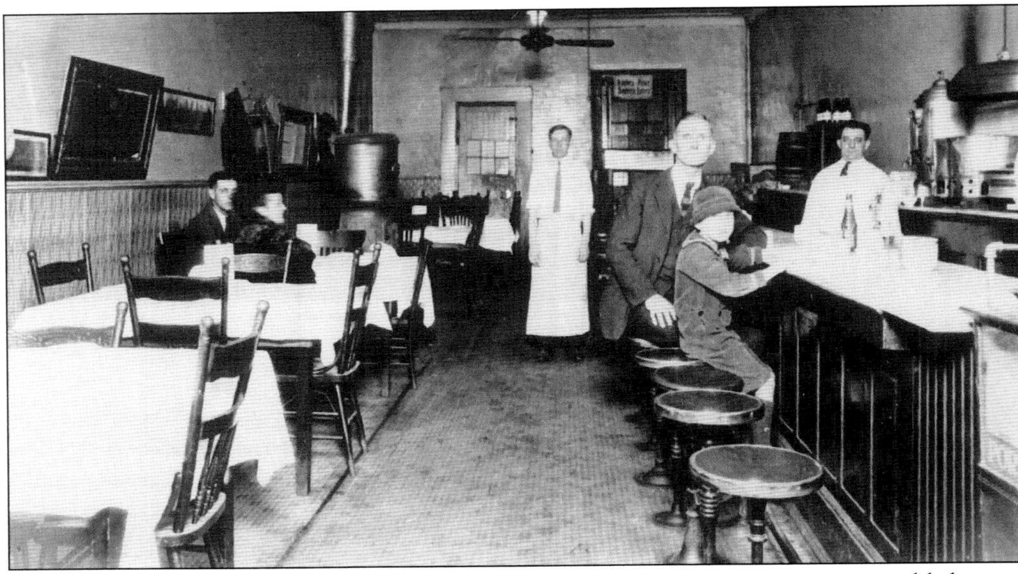

James Varellas watches from behind the counter of his popular Georgetown eating establishment. Known as "Jimmy the Greek," the 24-year-old immigrant leased the Lancaster Hotel dining room in 1914, and two years later purchased Gray's Restaurant on West Main Street. After serving in the first World War as a cook, he returned to Georgetown and continued in the restaurant business.

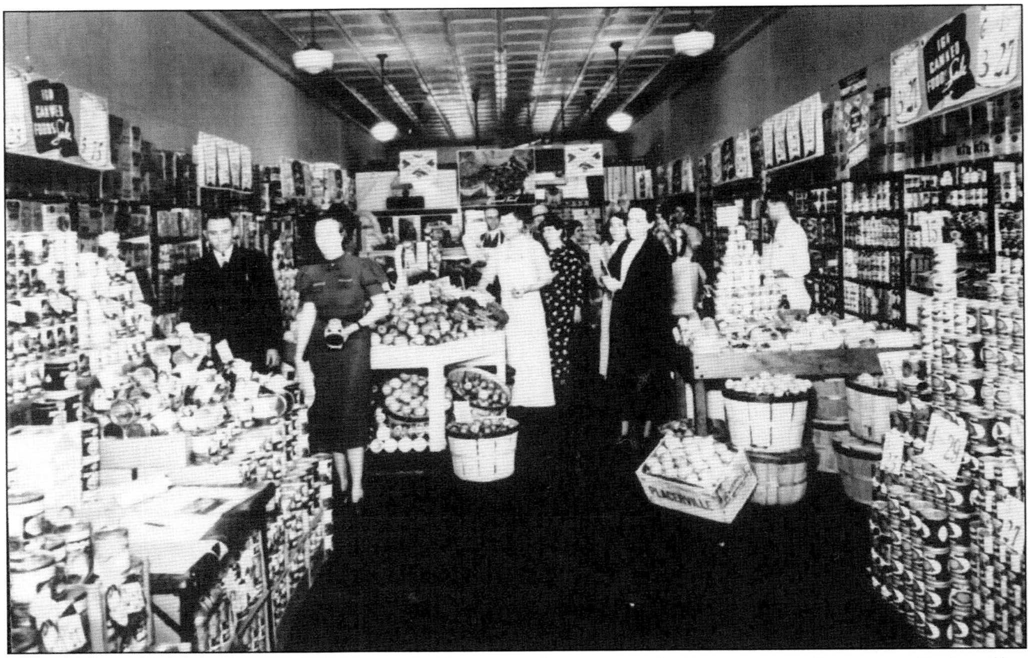

Prior to the domination of the grocery business by major chain supermarkets, small, locally-owned stores existed throughout Georgetown. Kemper's Grocery was a downtown destination from the mid-1930s until its destruction by fire in 1960. Pictured are Lonnie Kemper (center), Walter Zeysing, and Finley Williams assisting Saturday morning shoppers at the store's original location on the south side of Main Street.

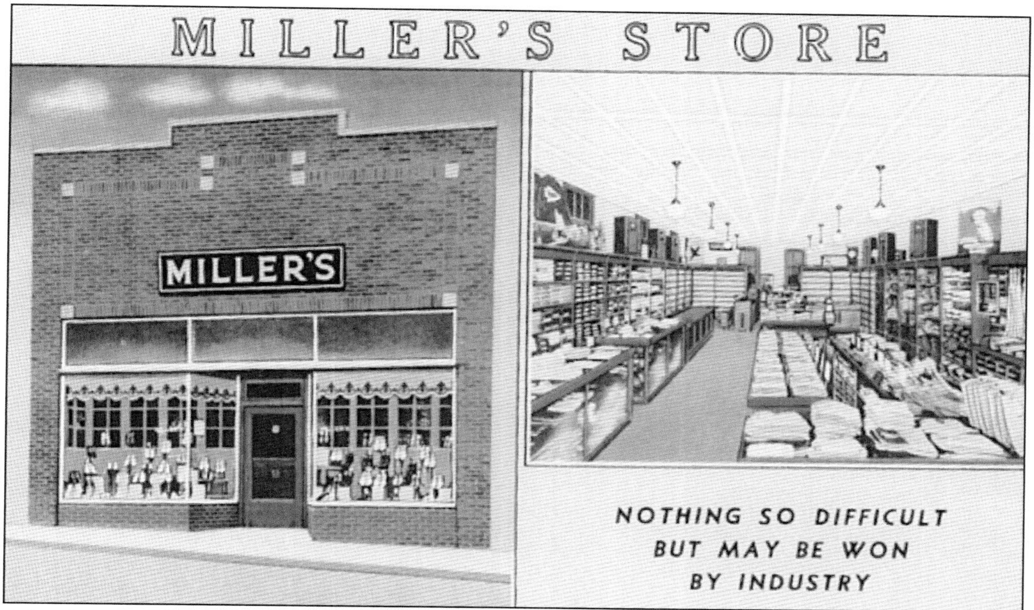

After being in business for 19 years in his father's old location, African-American businessman John Miller opened "the largest general store in Georgetown" on North Broadway in 1933. During the Depression, it had annual sales of up to $50,000. Miller remained in business at his new location until 1946.

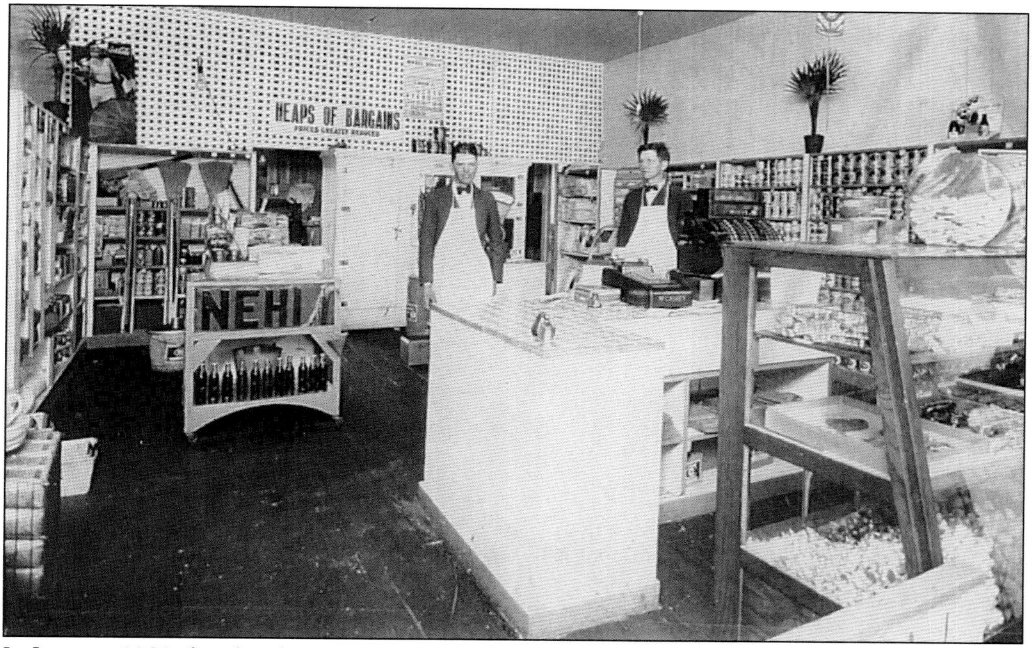

In January 1930, four local groceries reopened as IGA stores. Pictured above are Bill Gaines and Roy McFarland in McFarland's IGA on North Hamilton Street. From 1936–1945, McFarland also operated a store on Clayton Avenue, which was repurchased by his son Warring Davis McFarland in 1950. W.D. McFarland continued to operate the business as "Mac's Kentucky Food Store" until retiring in March 1998.

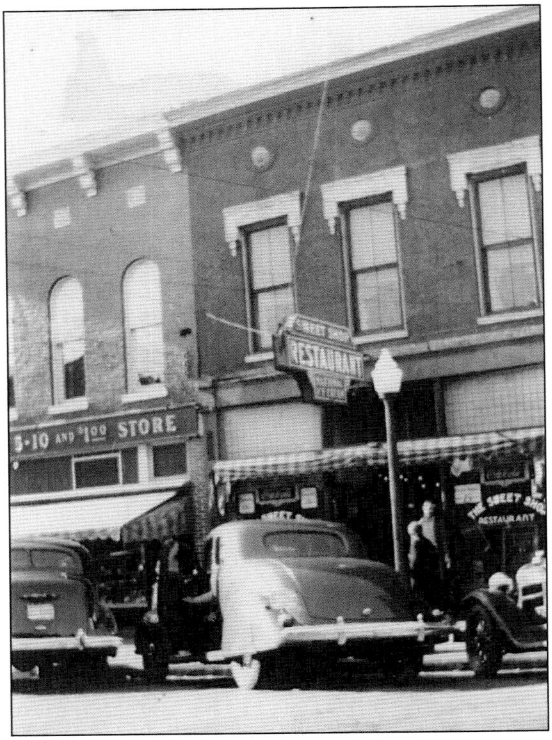

For nearly 50 years, the Sweet Shop was a popular gathering place for Georgetown's young people. Opened in 1919 by Lewis Finley and Travis Glenn in T.B. McCann's former confectionery shop, it became the meeting place for the local high school crowd. During the Depression years, a full meal could be bought for a quarter, and ice cream cost a dime.

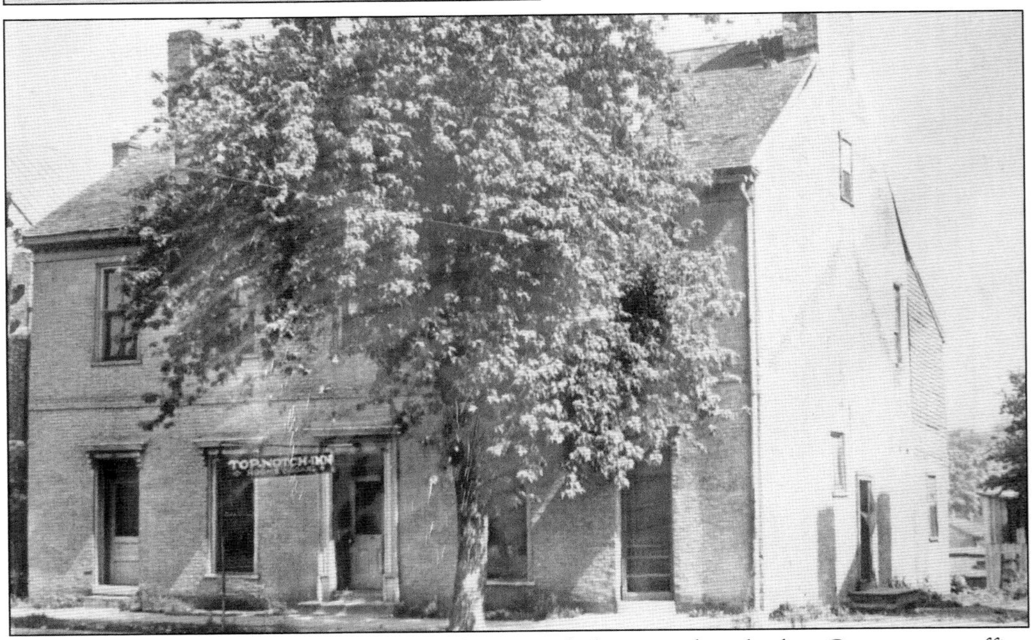

This early building housed the Top Notch Inn and also served as the last Georgetown office of the interurban railroad, which connected Georgetown and Lexington. After the demise of the interurban, the building was taken down in 1937 in preparation for the 1939 construction of the Art Deco-style Buick Garage. It is the present home of the city's Emergency Services Division.

Prior to the Main Street revitalization/beautification programs, large business signs dominated both sides of Main Street. This mid-1970s view shows the Scott County Pharmacy prior to its expansion into the former Jacobs Clothing Store. Also pictured is one of Georgetown's oldest businesses, Fava's Restaurant. It was founded in 1910 as a confectionery by Italian immigrants Louis and Susie Fava.

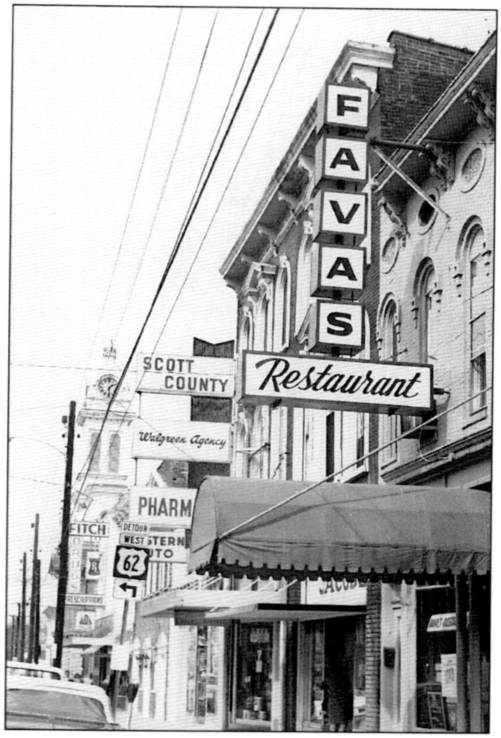

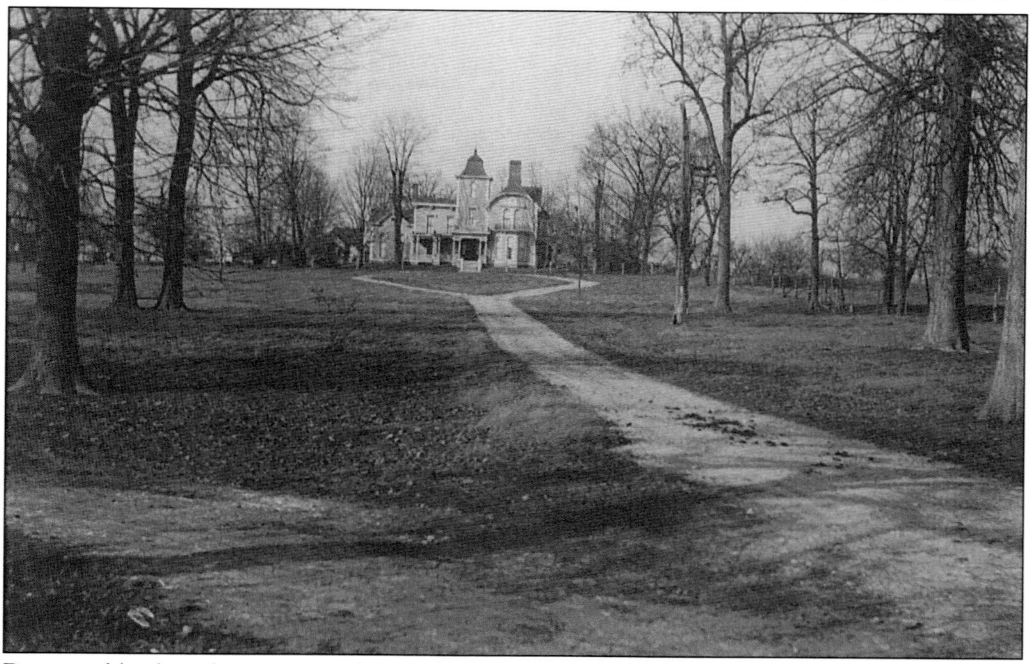

Destroyed by fire after a severe electrical storm in 1966, the old Hambrick home stood on the site of Hambrick Place subdivision on South Broadway. Purchased in 1846 by Georgetown College Professor Danford Thomas, it was remodeled extensively during the Victorian era. It remained in the Thomas and Hambrick families for 120 years.

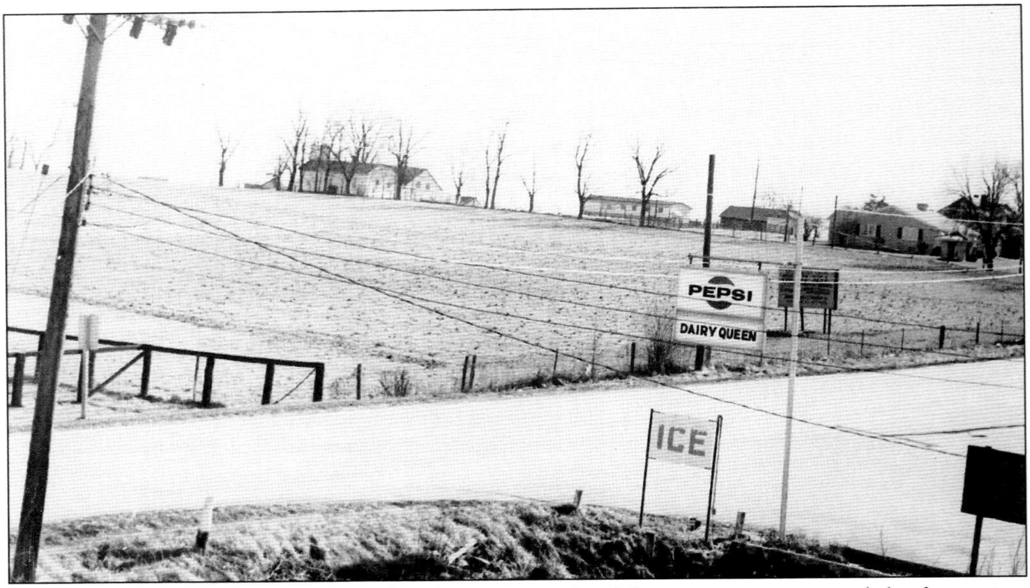

Rapid residential and commercial development south of Georgetown prompted the formation of zoning commissions in city and county government and also hastened the decline of the downtown business district. The above view shows the site of Washington Square Shopping Center before its development in the early 1970s. Dairy Queen opened on Lexington Road in 1955.

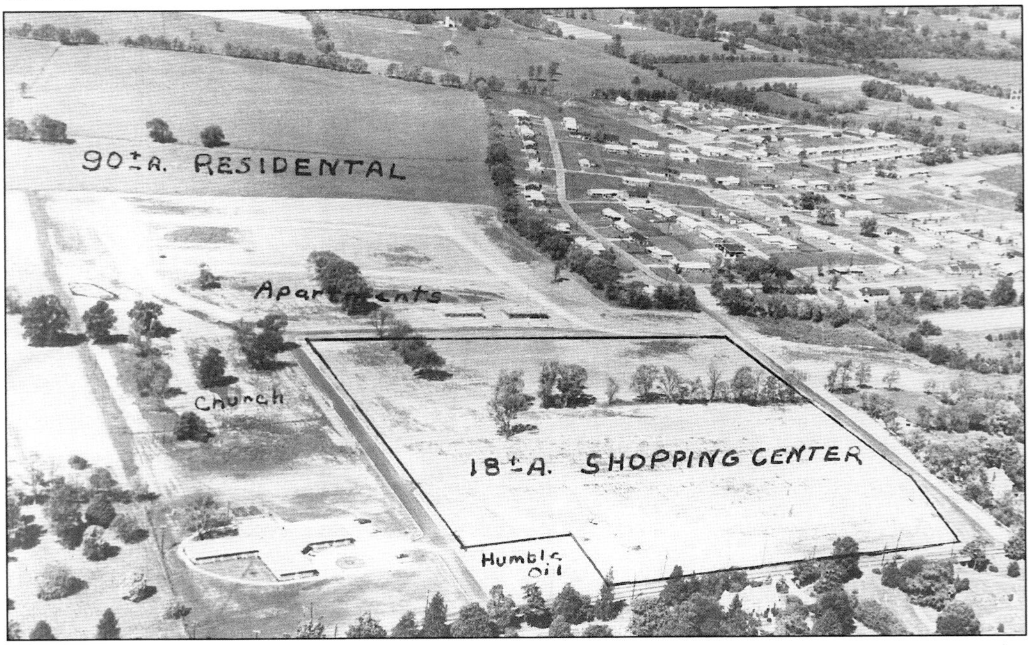

Georgetown began expanding significantly in late 1959, when construction began on the McMeekin Manor and Indian Hills subdivisions on the south side. This aerial view, looking west from Georgetown Cemetery, shows the first completed homes in Indian Hills and the future site of Indian Acres Shopping Center. Springhaven Nursing Home (bottom left) opened in early 1964.

Three
Stamping Ground and Sadieville

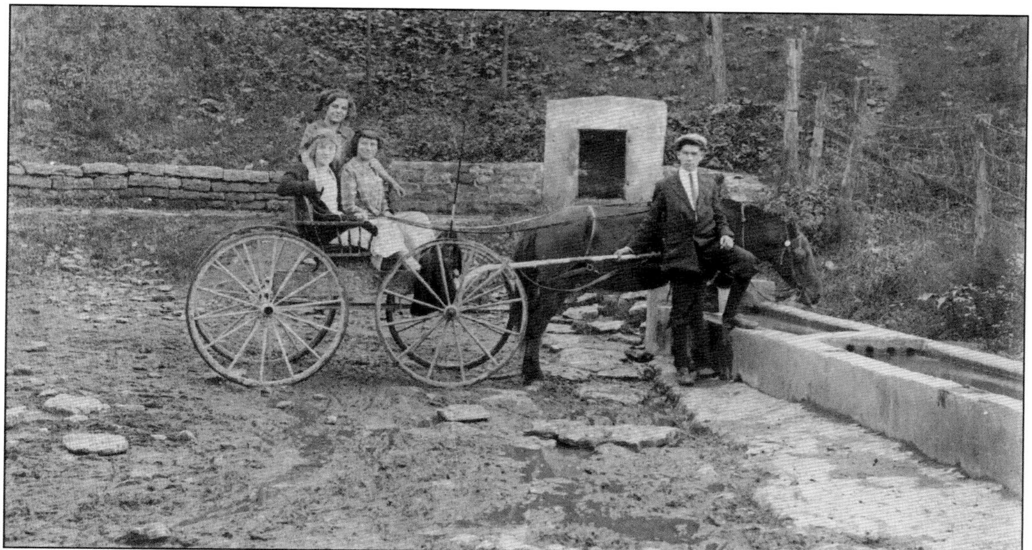

The right combination of location, roads, other natural factors, as well as social and economic influences, enabled a hamlet or village to become a town or city. Thus Stamping Ground and Sadieville grew into small cities while Oxford and Newtown achieved village status. Other communities, including Little Eagle, Big Eagle, Minorsville, Skinnersburg, Straight Fork (later known as Davis), Rogers Gap, Long Lick, Biddle, Porter, Hinton, Mount Olivet, Muddy Ford, Josephine, Zion Hill, and New Zion, thrived to a lesser degree.

By 1790, settlers occupied a variety of stations and early settlements in the vicinity of streams and buffalo roads and built new roads between significant points. By 1814, the community that became Stamping Ground had a tanyard, and later, a carding and woolen factory, distillery, and carriage factory. There were also taverns, stores, mechanics shops, and academies. Construction of Cincinnati Southern Railroad through northern Scott in the 1870s opened commercial opportunities there. In 1877, promoters S.T. Connellee, Richard F. Pack, and T.J. Burgess donated land and built a depot at the crossing of the Big Eagle turnpike to ensure the development of a brand new town to be known as Sadieville.

In this view, Lorenzo Bridges has stopped to water the horse at Stamping Ground's Buffalo Spring (*c.* 1920). In the buggy, from left to right, are as follows: Evelyn Perry (Crockett), Jessie Bridges (Jenkins), and Carmen Perry (Garner).

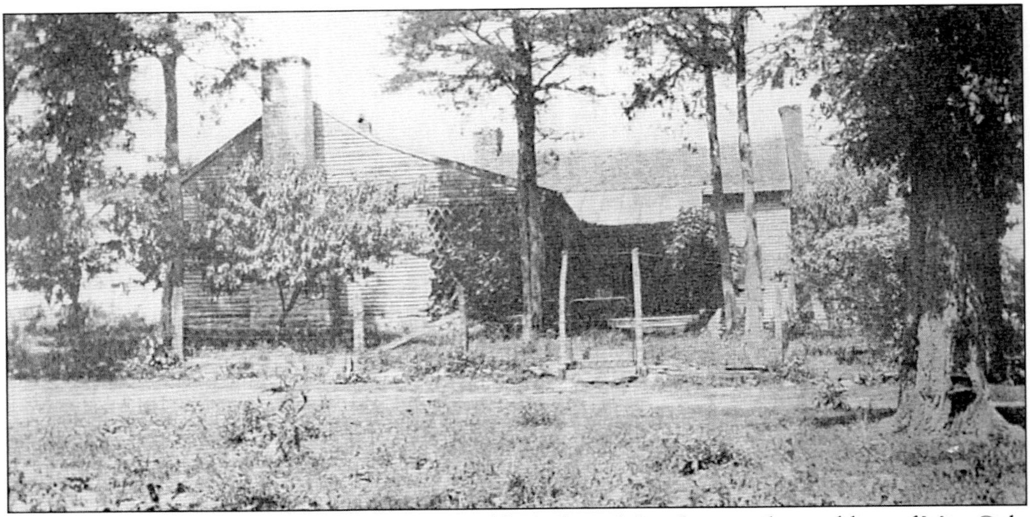

James Lindsay was uncle and guardian of Zerelda Cole and thus host to the wedding of Miss Cole and Robert James on December 28, 1841. James was a Baptist ministry student at Georgetown College. To the union were born Frank (1843) and Jesse W. James (1847) near Kearney, Missouri. They became famous as Confederate veterans turned outlaw. Pictured is the Lindsay house on Locust Fork Pike, the present home of Margaret Sprake.

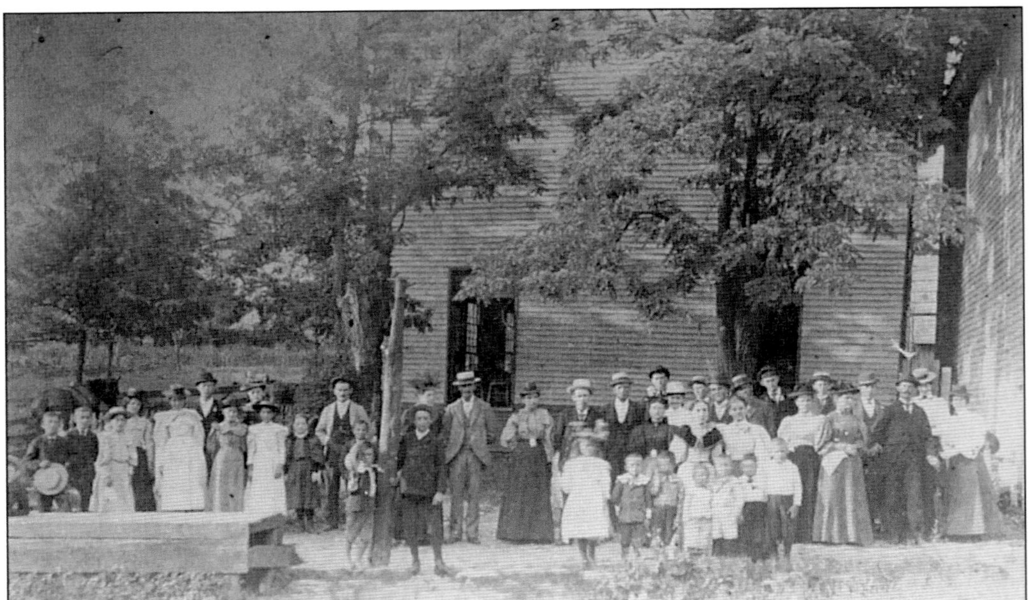

Stamping Ground Christian Church, organized *c.* 1826, met in a wooden downtown meetinghouse until 1899, when it was sold to the Masons for $280. The congregation added a second story *c.* 1851. The pulpit of the two-door church stood between the front doors. The photograph was discovered by Braddie Wiley while she was going through estate items of Alfred Easley. She discovered among the congregation members a picture of her grandfather.

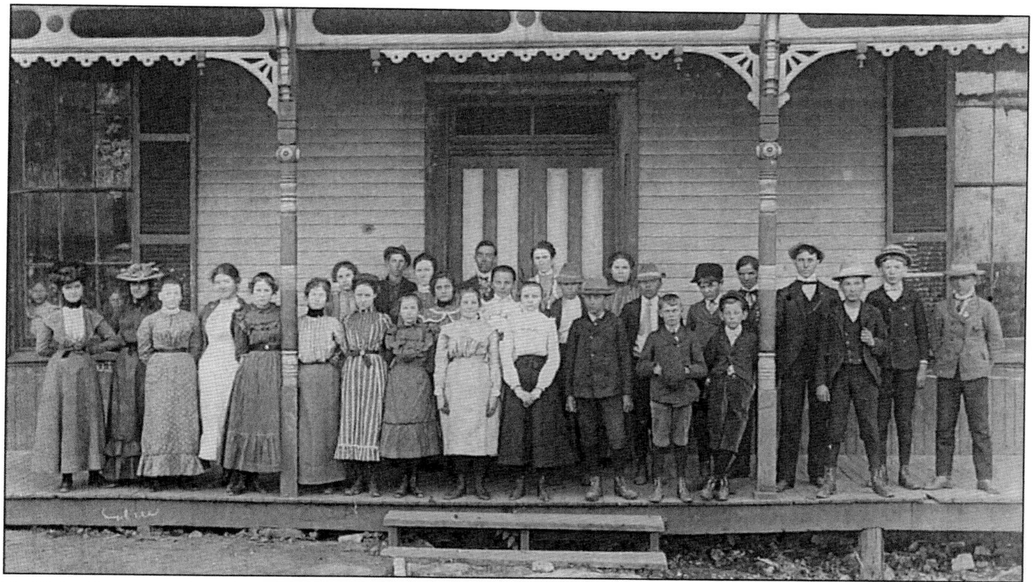

Buffalo Springs Academy was a private school that stood on the corner of Main and Burch Streets. Students of the upper grades, c. 1900, are shown dressed up in Sunday finery for the school photograph while other faces peer through the window (left). The front porch is very nicely finished with Victorian gingerbread trim. The grandmother of the photograph's owner, Pearl Wright Plummer, the tenth young lady on the front row, is wearing a white blouse and dark skirt.

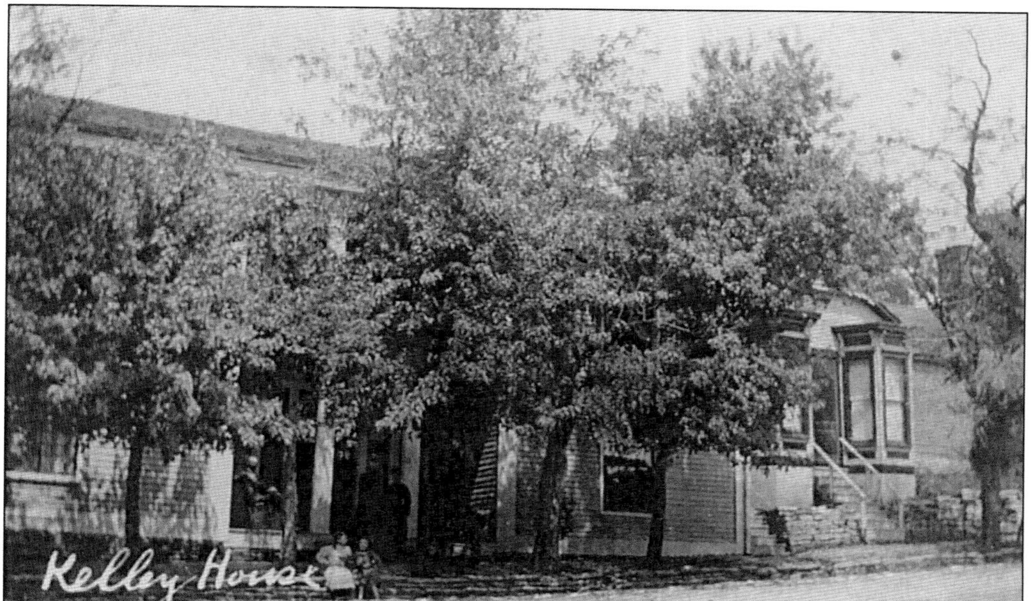

A green frame building occupying the present site of the Kentucky Forestry Service and popularly called "the green onion" is called "Kelley House" in the postcard reproduced above. It was destroyed by fire. At the side of a narrow alley (to the right of the hotel) was a building simply known as the "shotgun house." Older citizens have no recollection of the building having been called "Kelley House."

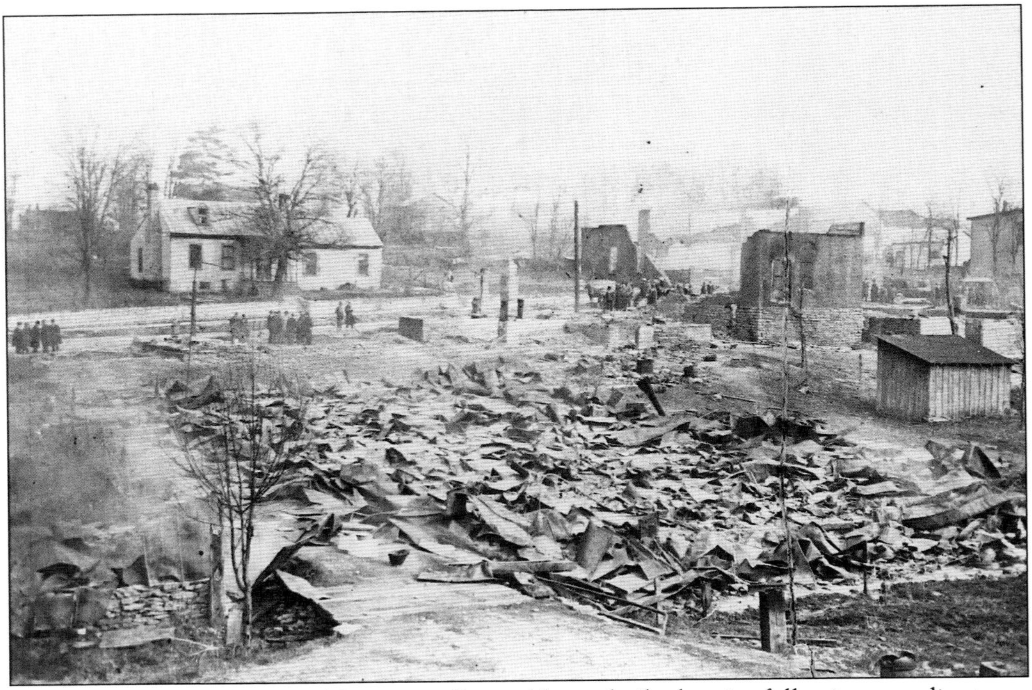

The persistent population of Stamping Ground has rebuilt the city following two disastrous fires and a tornado. The city is shown during the aftermath of an early 1900s conflagration. Townspeople in topcoats and top hats are shown surveying the damage. Before the 1974 tornado, several early Kentucky houses remained, lining the main streets. After the storm, the Alexander Bradford house (across the street at left) remained the sole sentinel to the various disasters.

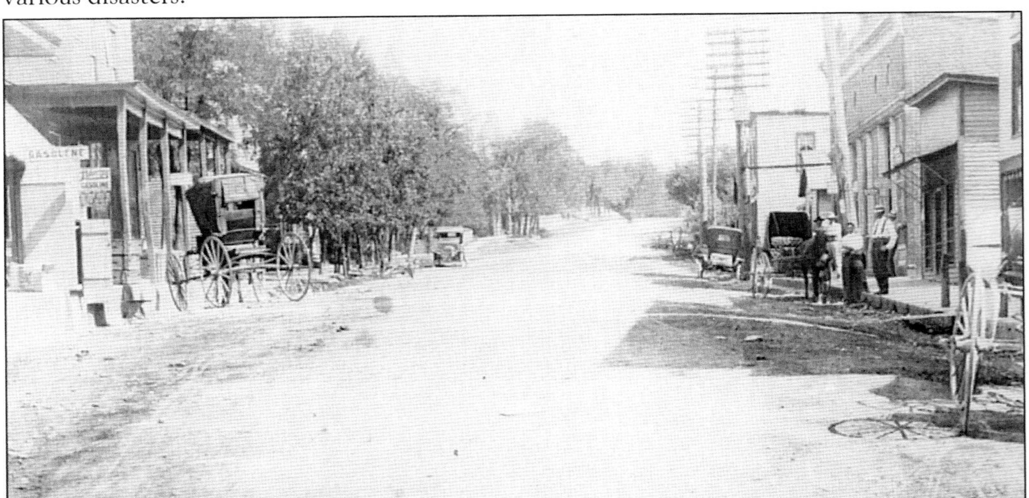

A postcard photograph stamped with a February 1915 date shows Stamping Ground. It was rebuilt after one of the devastating fires. The horse-drawn and motorized vehicles parked along the wide, dirt street date the photograph. Of special interest is the large buggy (left). Signs advertise both "gasolene" and "gasoline." There is a rock fence lining frontage near the center of the photograph on the left side of the street.

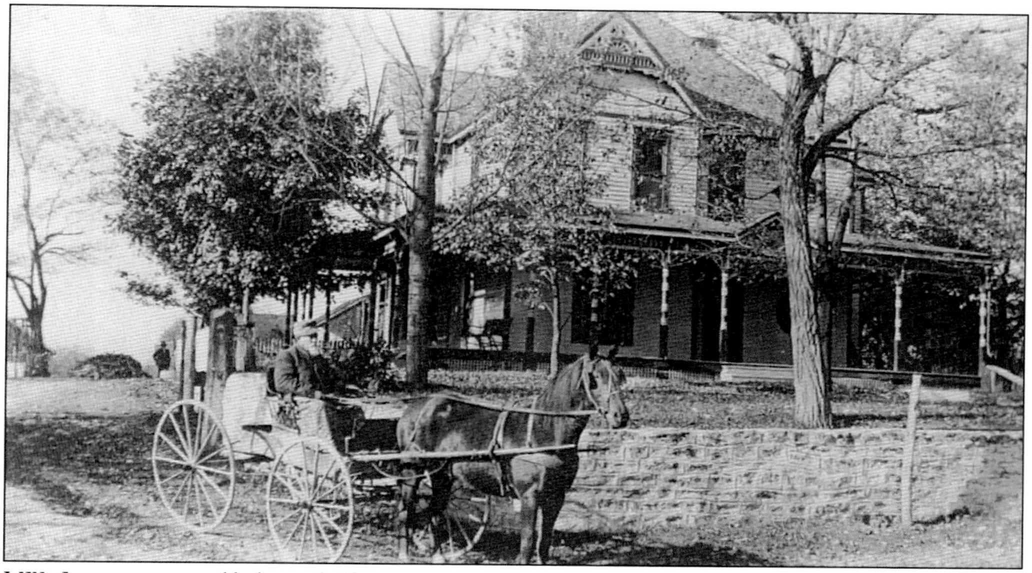

J.W. Jameson, grandfather of Clemmie Jameson (Mrs. Kirtley) Hall, is shown driving his rig from the driveway of his Stamping Ground home. The house fell victim to the 1974 tornado. Jameson, one of the county's largest tobacco growers, operated Jameson Brothers Store with his sons. He was also president of Citizens Bank. The Jamesons, with their four sons and two daughters, moved from Owen County to Owensboro before moving to Stamping Ground.

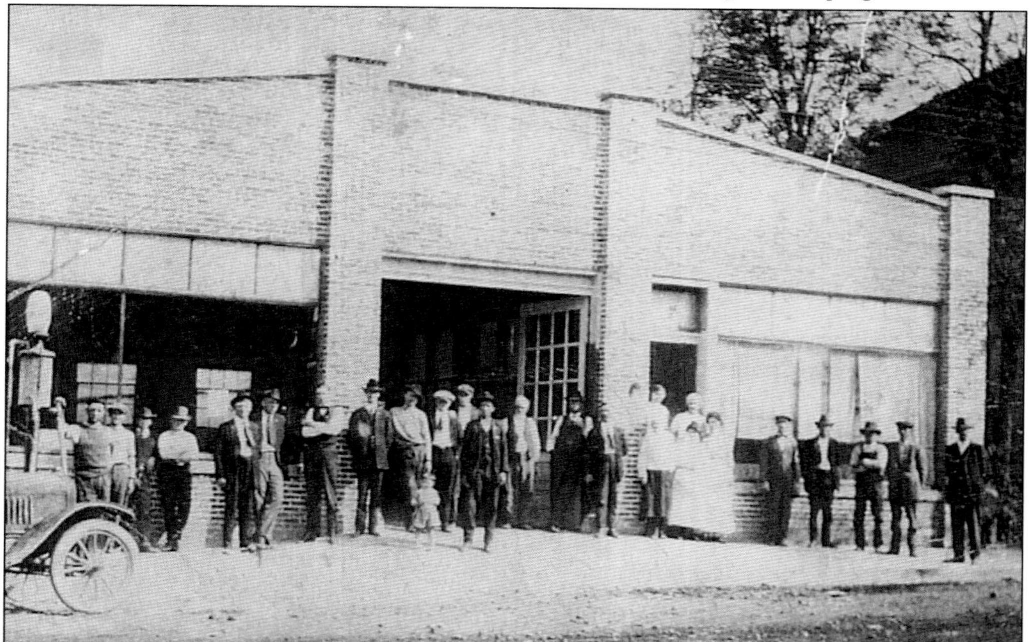

Stamping Ground residents associated with the Chevrolet garage on Main Street pose with an automobile in front of the establishment. On the left is Noel Gardner, father of Henry Etta Gardner Johnson (the photograph's owner). Fifth from left is F.E. Hall, owner of the garage and Mrs. Johnson's maternal grandfather. When destroyed by the 1974 tornado, the building housed the John Hall Grocery.

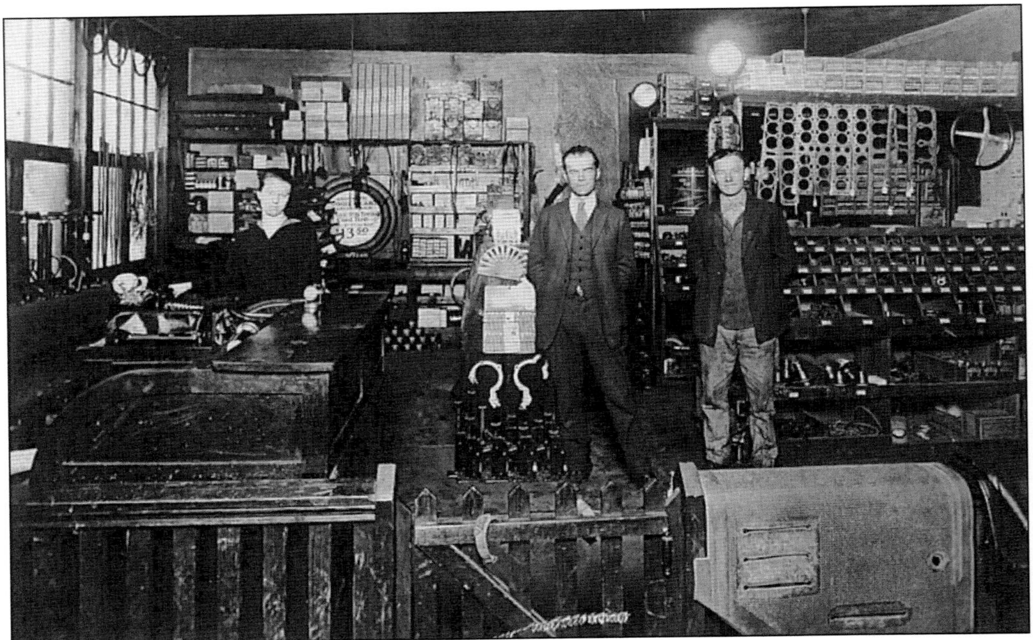

Elmer Davis (center) and George Gaines, owners of Stamping Ground's Davis-Gaines Motor Company, are shown inside their arts-and-crafts-style brick building with bookkeeper Mary Sinkhorn Wigginton. The photograph, owned by Gaines's son, G. Truitt Gaines, displays the variety of items used to service early motor vehicles. The business had a Ford franchise beginning around 1920. It closed in January 1970. The building was destroyed by the 1974 tornado.

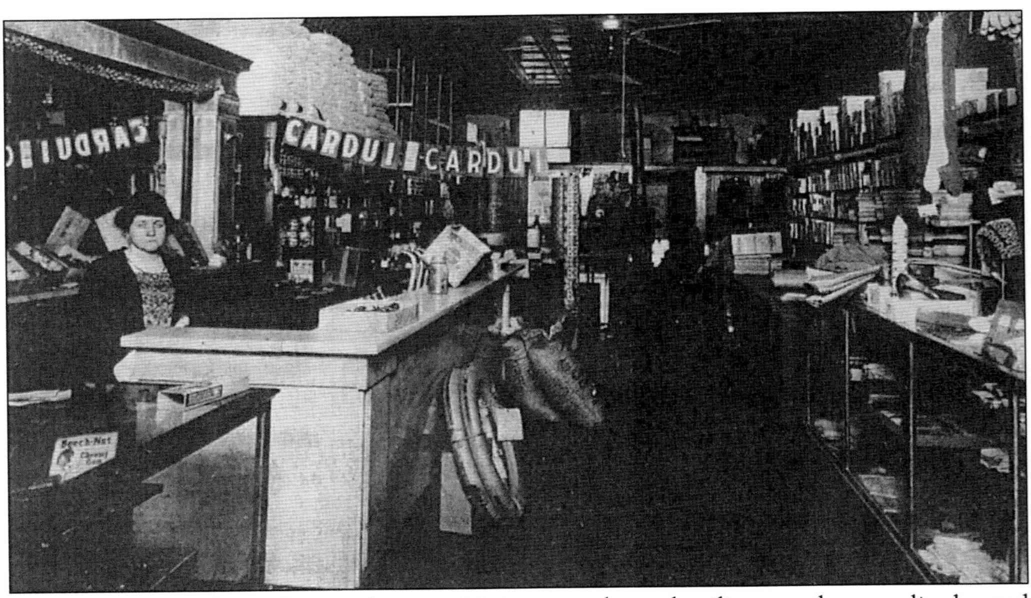

An old Stamping Ground general store with its pressed metal ceiling may have earlier housed a bar, as indicated by the large, elaborately framed mirror. Wares necessary or incidental to everyday life such as chewing gum, bicycle tires, clothing, linens, and bonnets are in the display. Behind the counter is Myrtle Wright.

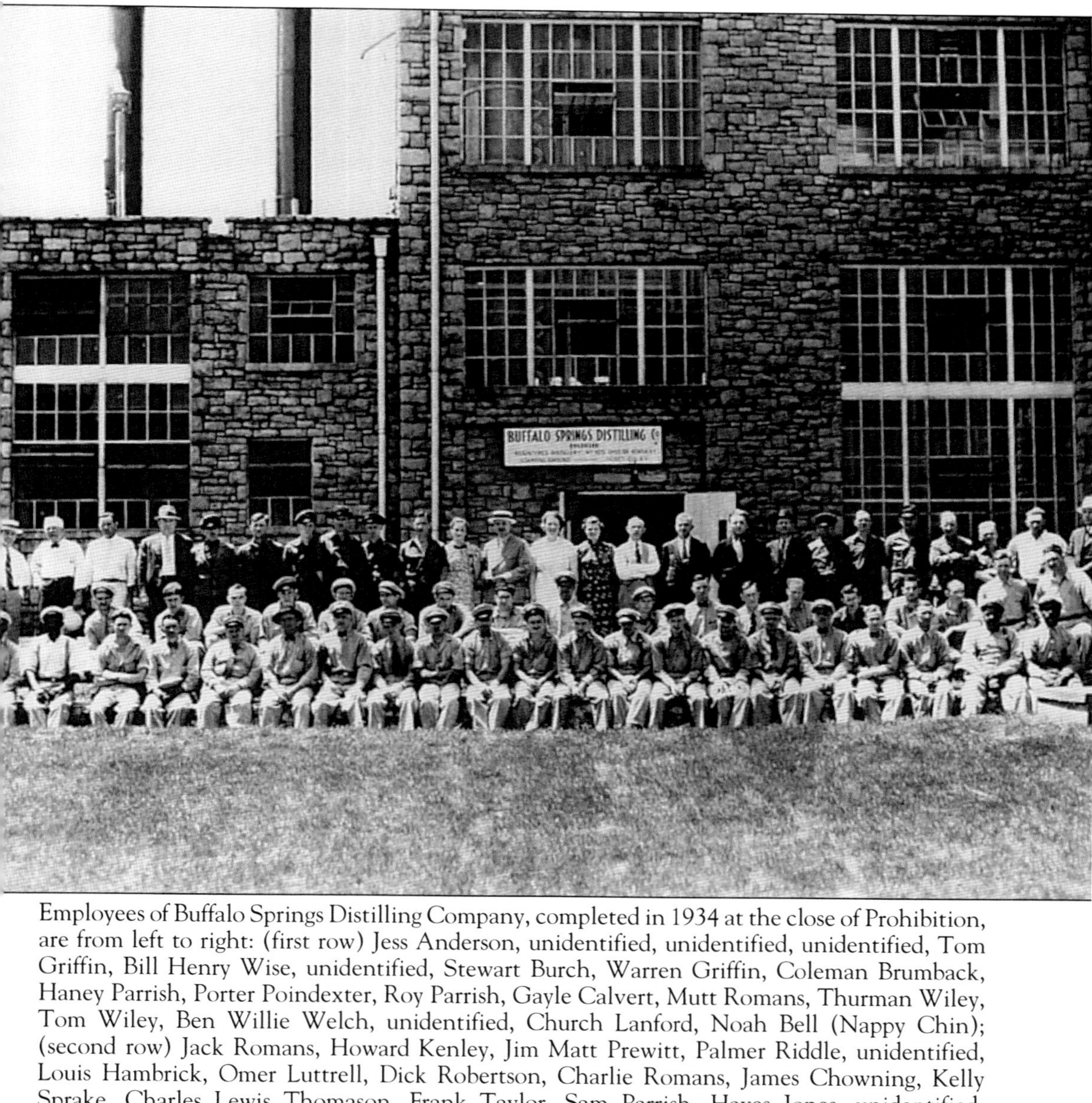

Employees of Buffalo Springs Distilling Company, completed in 1934 at the close of Prohibition, are from left to right: (first row) Jess Anderson, unidentified, unidentified, unidentified, Tom Griffin, Bill Henry Wise, unidentified, Stewart Burch, Warren Griffin, Coleman Brumback, Haney Parrish, Porter Poindexter, Roy Parrish, Gayle Calvert, Mutt Romans, Thurman Wiley, Tom Wiley, Ben Willie Welch, unidentified, Church Lanford, Noah Bell (Nappy Chin); (second row) Jack Romans, Howard Kenley, Jim Matt Prewitt, Palmer Riddle, unidentified, Louis Hambrick, Omer Luttrell, Dick Robertson, Charlie Romans, James Chowning, Kelly Sprake, Charles Lewis Thomason, Frank Taylor, Sam Parrish, Hayes Jones, unidentified, Harlan Wilson, Broadus Wiley; (third row) unidentified, Squire Willis, Ambrose Lathrem, unidentified, Charlie Baldwin, Ora Castle, unidentified, unidentified, Joe Sinclair, Buck Herndon, Louise Taylor, P.L. Wright, Susie Sharp, unidentified, unidentified, unidentified, unidentified, unidentified, unidentified, Carl Campbell, unidentified, Herbert Barber, Uron Snow, J. L. Parrish, and Tom Bixler.

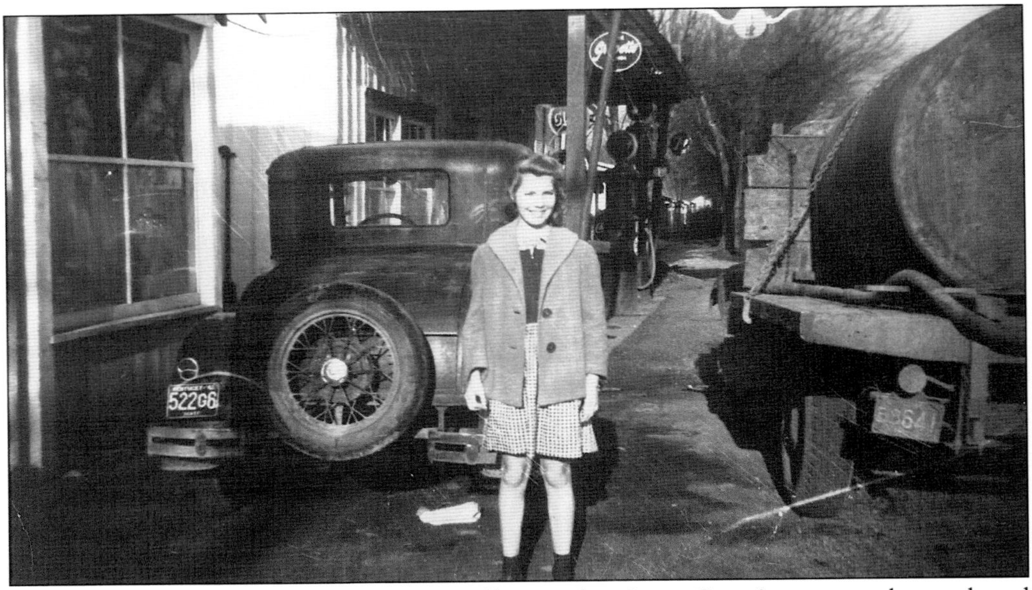

Jo Caula Gregg (Thiessen), posed in front of her mother, Jessie Gregg's, store on the north end of Stamping Ground on March 23, 1942. She stood between a coupe and a farm truck with a mounted tank used for conveying sour mash from the Stamping Ground distillery to farmers' hogs. The advertised soft drinks, including the one that "glorifies," continue in popularity at the end of the century.

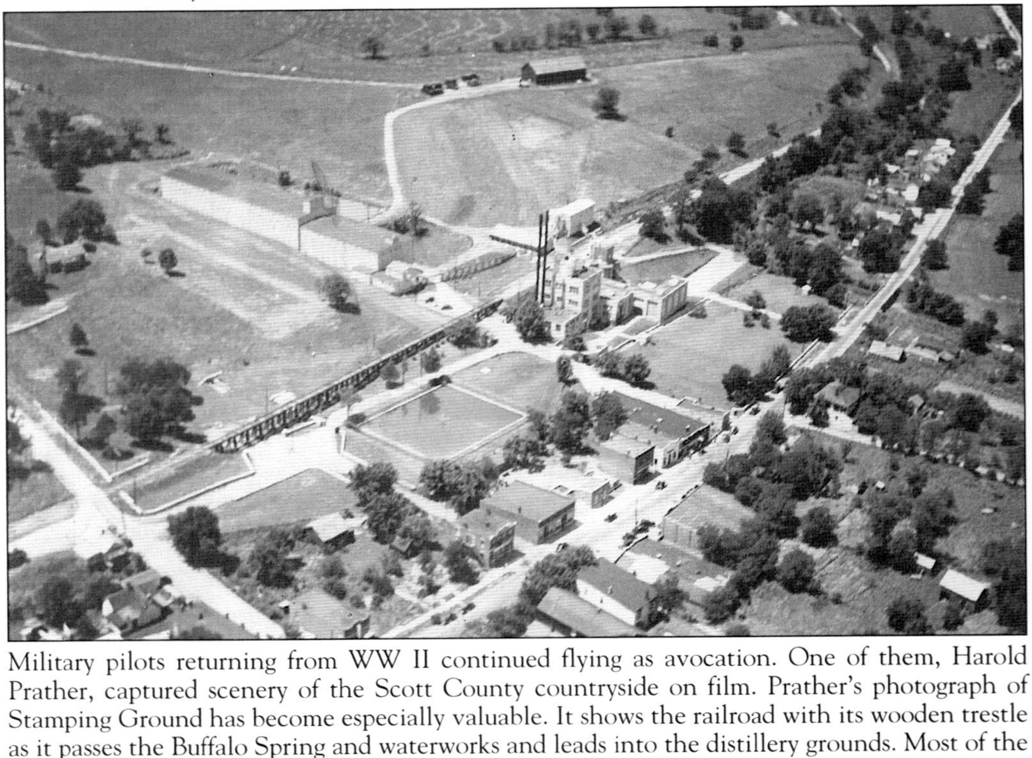

Military pilots returning from WW II continued flying as avocation. One of them, Harold Prather, captured scenery of the Scott County countryside on film. Prather's photograph of Stamping Ground has become especially valuable. It shows the railroad with its wooden trestle as it passes the Buffalo Spring and waterworks and leads into the distillery grounds. Most of the business houses along Main Street were lost to the 1974 tornado.

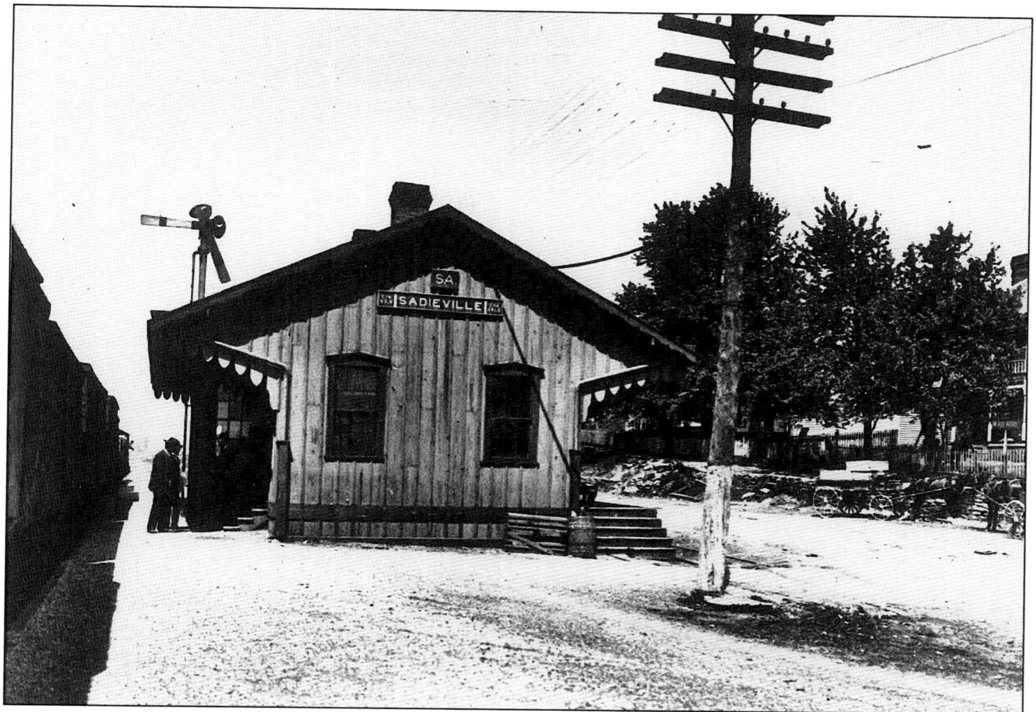

The real reason for Sadieville, of course, was the depot. A photograph from the collection of railroad historian and memorabilia collector John Farris shows the busy little station, a wooden battened structure with wide sloping eaves and interior chimneys. In the 1950s, Joseph Burgess acquired the old, abandoned depot and moved it to a lot on Pike Street. It remains today, awaiting reuse in commerce or public life.

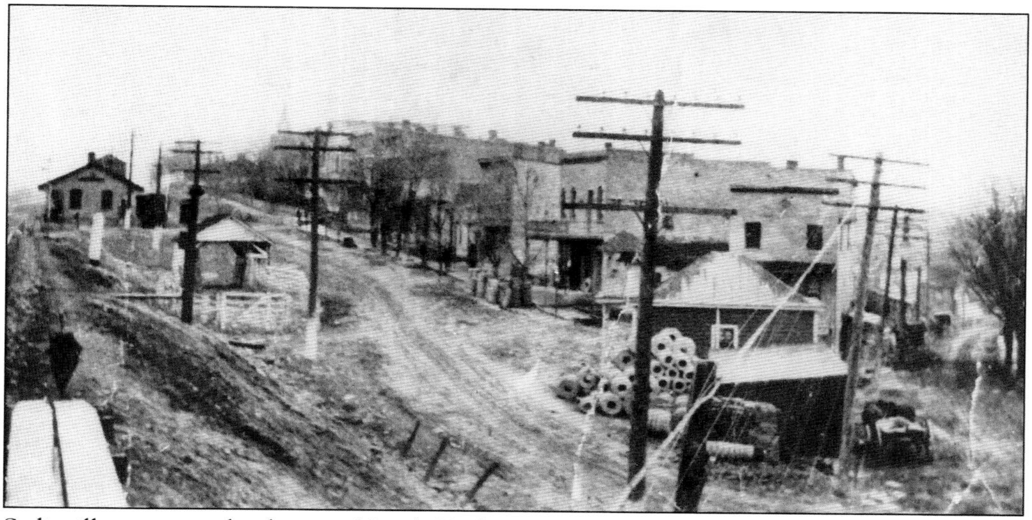

Sadieville was named in honor of Sarah "Sadie" Emison Pack, whose husband, Richard F. Pack, along with T.J. Burgess, purchased 20 acres of land abutting Cincinnati Southern Railroad from S.T. Connellee. By August 1877, Sadieville had a blacksmith and carpenter shop, a dry goods store, two groceries, one hotel, and seven dwellings. The above early-20th-century photo is from B.O. Gaines's *History of Scott County*.

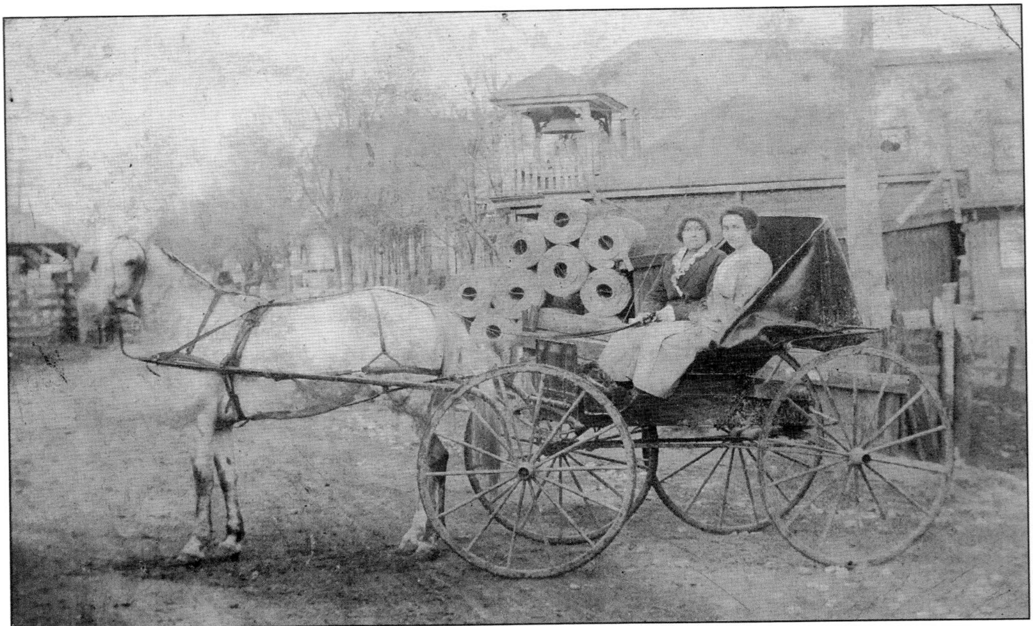

Some of the spools, possibly twine, shown stacked at the side of the Sadieville fire station in the previous photograph, made its way into the buggy of Dennie Truitt and Hetty Rose. The postcard photo was passed down from Mrs. Truitt to her son, George Marshall, and by him, to Eddie Marshall. A close-up view of the hip-roof fire station with cupola and bell, and the fence leading into the railside stock pens, corroborate the timing of the photograph with B.O. Gaines's likeness.

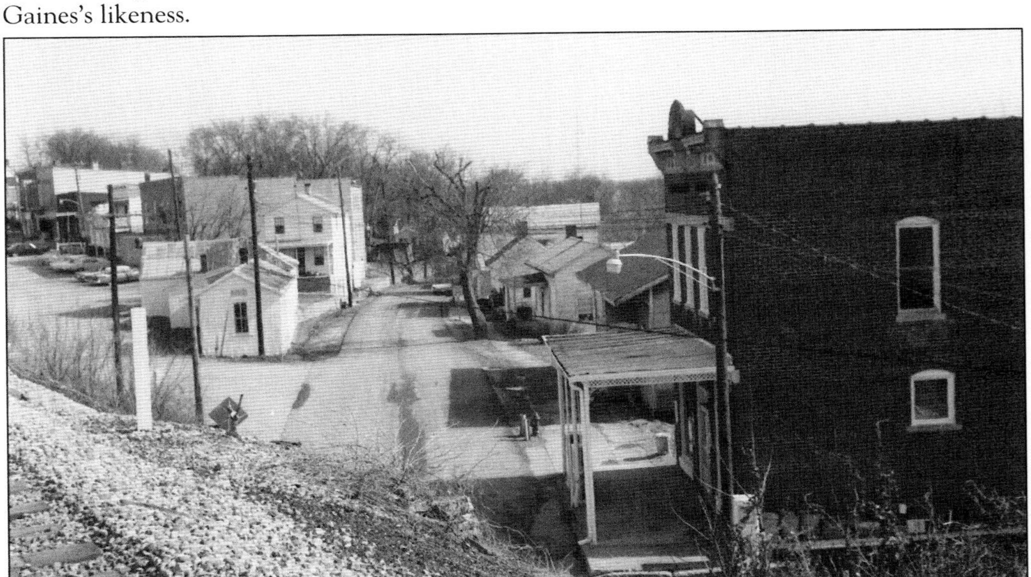

Sadieville's original Main Street, the Big Eagle Turnpike, became known as Pike Street. The earliest buildings of the city lined this thoroughfare. Photographed by the late historian W.A. Marshall from the top of the railroad overpass, the view shows, on the right side of the street, from left: Kaley Hotel, the post office and store, Jimmie Jones house and store, the relocated depot, and the 1905 Cornish Hall, the city's lodge building.

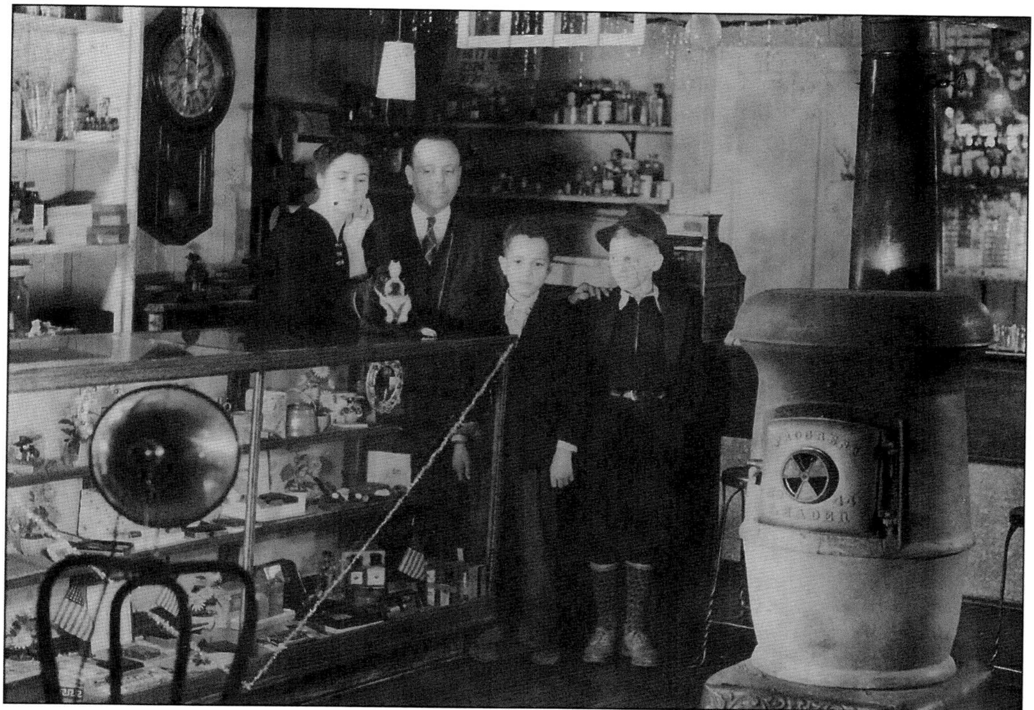

The drugstore on Sadieville's Main Street, much like today's pharmacies, carried numerous items in addition to the medicines displayed in bottles on the wall. Behind the counter are Katherine King Whitson and Ford Whitson, who operated the store, Junior Brooks, Eddie Marshall, and Taters, the bulldog. Brooks was a brother of Robert Brooks who, on December 8, 1941, became the first Scott County casualty of WW II in the Philippines .

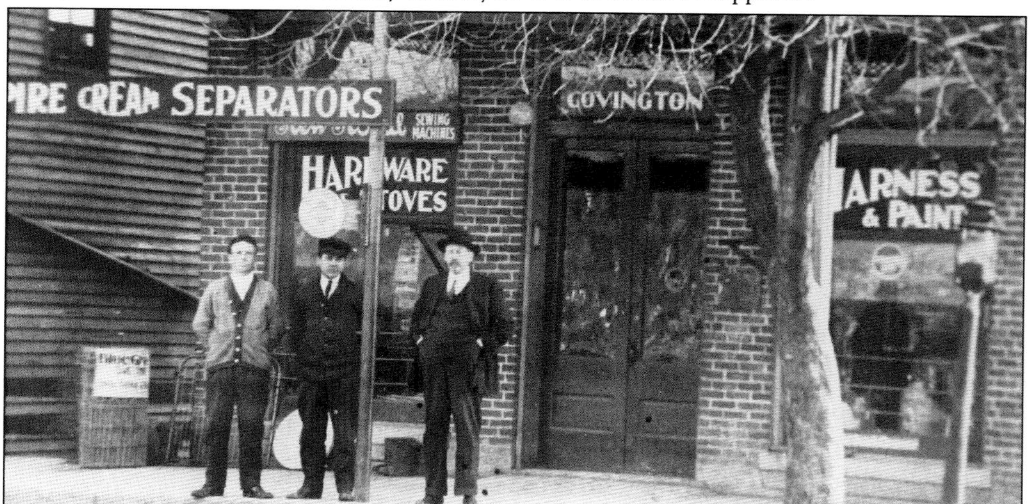

On Main Street, one of Sadieville's best preserved business buildings housed Jim Covington's Hardware Store. The building popularly known as Risk Hotel was built in 1890 by Leander Risk. It had two storefronts and a spacious upstairs. The photograph from the William A. Marshall collection also reveals the design of Sadieville's earlier street lights. The busy pattern of life in the very busy little railroad city declined once the rail system found it expendable.

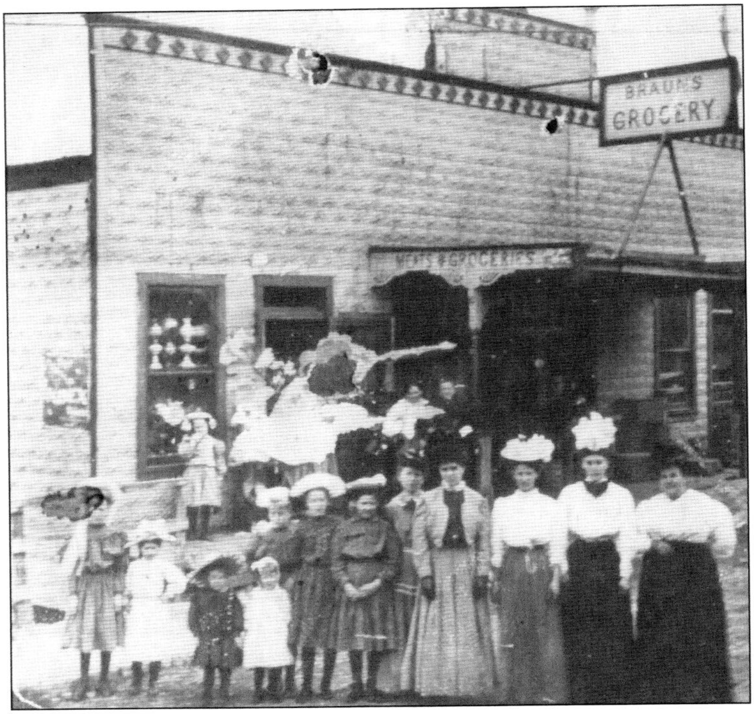

Emil Braun, a bachelor, came to America from Switzerland. He operated a general store built of molded concrete blocks in Sadieville, where he is listed in the 1910 and 1920 censuses. After the store closed, the building was used as a residence. The families associated with Braun's Grocery Store are shown here in their Sunday finery.

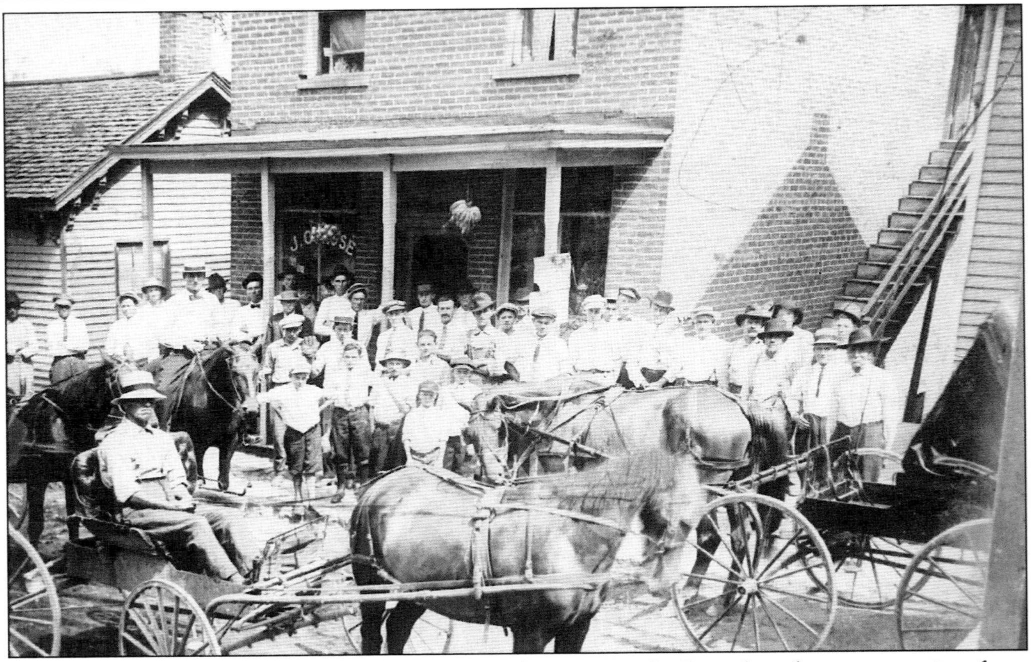

The J.O. Rose Saloon was already standing when Jasper O. Rose bought it at auction from Mary E. Barnes for $1,212. *The Georgetown Times* noted that, in 1907, Rose was operating in Sadieville "a first class saloon." Judging from the photograph, Rose's establishment was also a social center of Sadieville. The man in the buggy is Ed Burgess from Porter, who became the father of 21 children.

Four
Invention, Science, and Industry

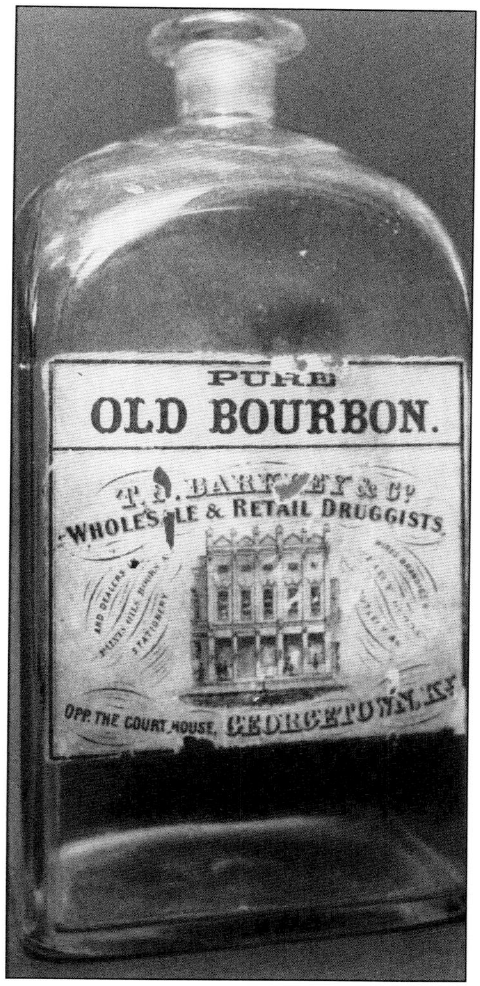

In all societies, there are individuals born with scientific minds that develop in a variety of directions. Some become interested in medicine, others become inventors, developing new technologies, and still others use those innovations to further the spread of industry.

Physicians were scarce during the frontier days but, by early antebellum days, Scott County was home to several university-trained practitioners. Beginning with the disease-prevention efforts of Dr. William L. Sutton during the 1849 cholera outbreak, local physicians have been involved in a multitude of endeavors to improve public health.

Whether Georgetown's founding father, the Reverend Elijah Craig, invented Bourbon whiskey is still a matter for debate, but in any case, he was the county's first major industrialist, owning at one time or another flour mills, a distillery, a paper mill, and a fulling mill and wool-carding factory. His were among the many industrial enterprises existing in the county during its early years.

Changing economic conditions eventually caused most of the older industries to die out, and local efforts to attract replacements met with limited and short-term success. Although some manufacturers have stayed and prospered, this trend has continued throughout the past century.

Pictured is a relic of one of the county's earliest industries. It is a view of one of the many local businesses destroyed during Georgetown's series of post-Civil War fires.

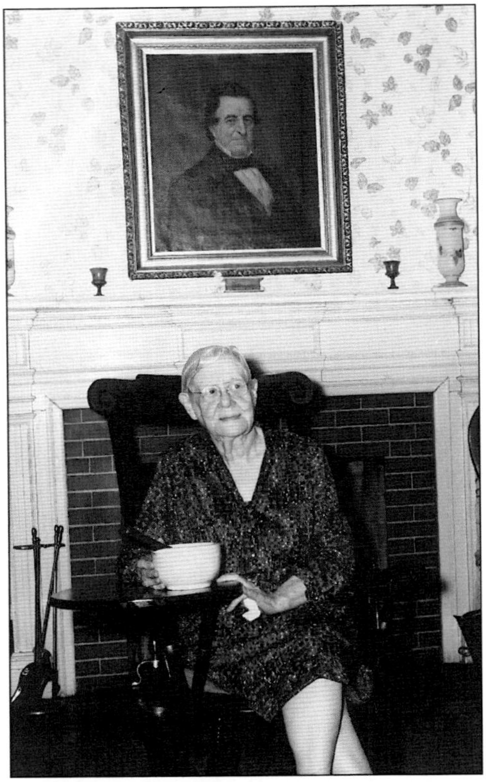

Scott County was the home of Dr. William Loftus Sutton (1797–1862), one of Kentucky's most progressive physicians during the antebellum era. Active in the organization of the Kentucky and American Medical Associations, he was also the author of the state's first Vital Statistics law. To the left, granddaughter Carrie Tarleton Goldsborough sits alongside his mortar and pestle beneath his portrait.

Pictured below, Dr. Harry Viley Johnson lectures the fiscal court on the history of medicine in Scott County. Dr. Johnson was a tireless worker in the fight to improve local health care. His efforts during the 1908 typhoid fever epidemic culminated in the construction of Georgetown's first water treatment plant. He was also a major influence in the establishment of the Scott County Health Department.

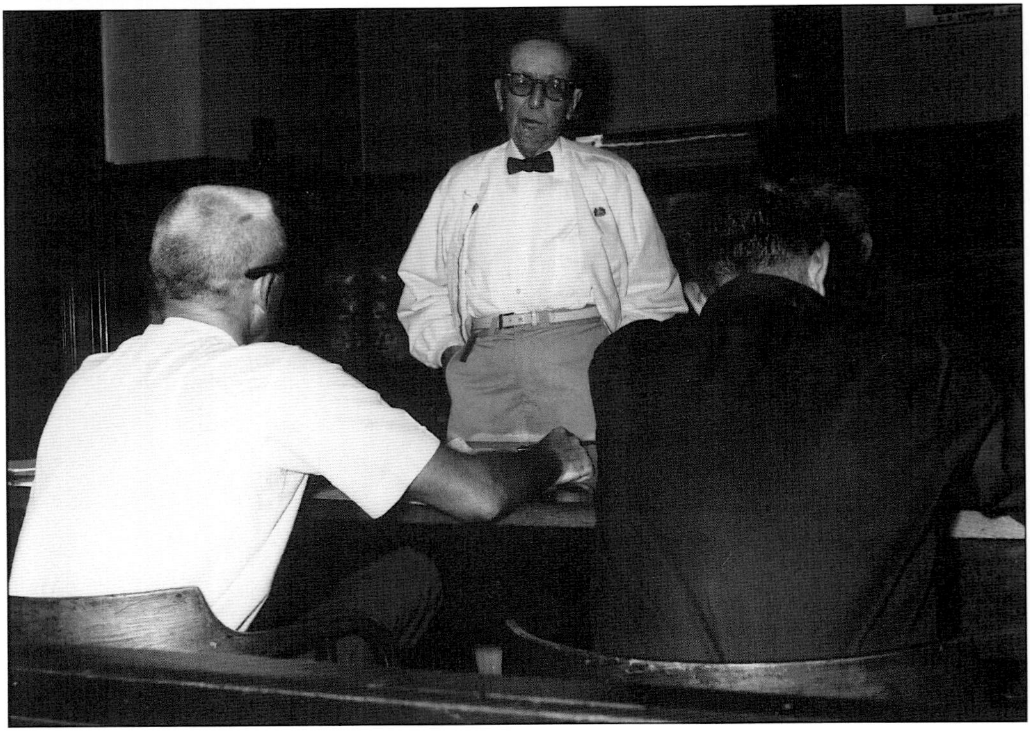

The death of 25-year-old John Graves Ford in 1916 hastened efforts led by Georgetown College President Dr. Arthur Yager to build a community hospital. In memory of her grandson, Mrs. Mary Jane Osborne Graves (pictured) donated a building site and made a substantial contribution toward the $30,000 facility. The John Graves Ford Memorial Hospital opened in September 1917.

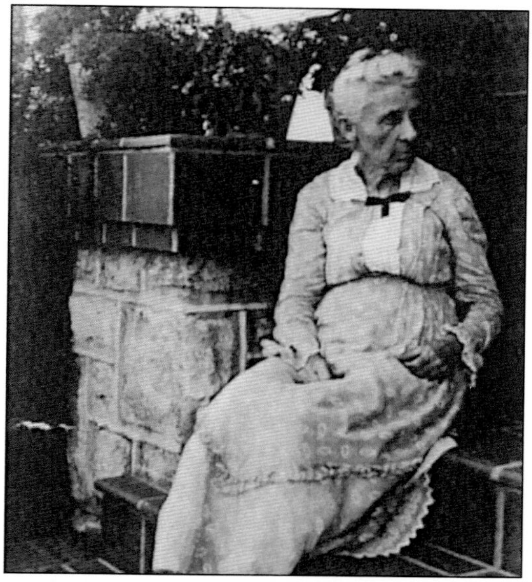

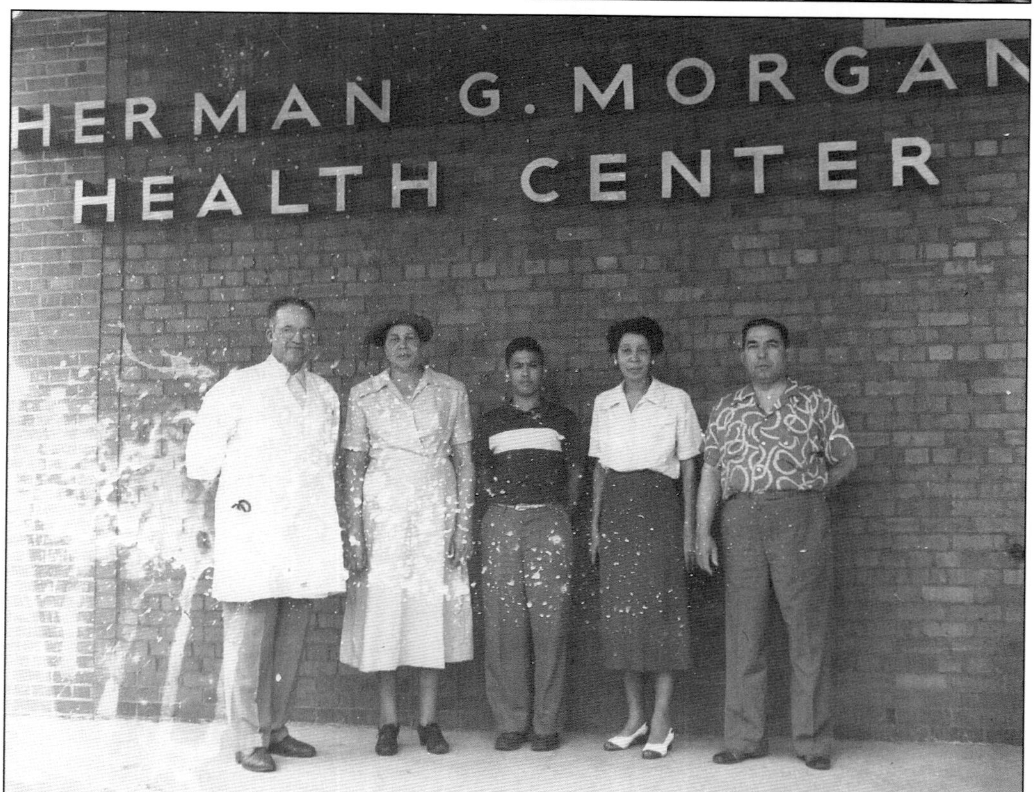

During the era of legal segregation, Dr. J.R. Dalton (far right), a 1918 graduate of Meharry Medical College in Nashville, operated a small hospital on Washington Street for the use of the African-American community. Pictured with Dr. Dalton in front of the Indianapolis Clinic run by Mrs. Dalton's brother-in-law, Dr. Walter H. Maddux, are as follows: Dr. and Mrs. Maddux, J. Rufus Dalton Jr., and Mrs. J.R. Dalton.

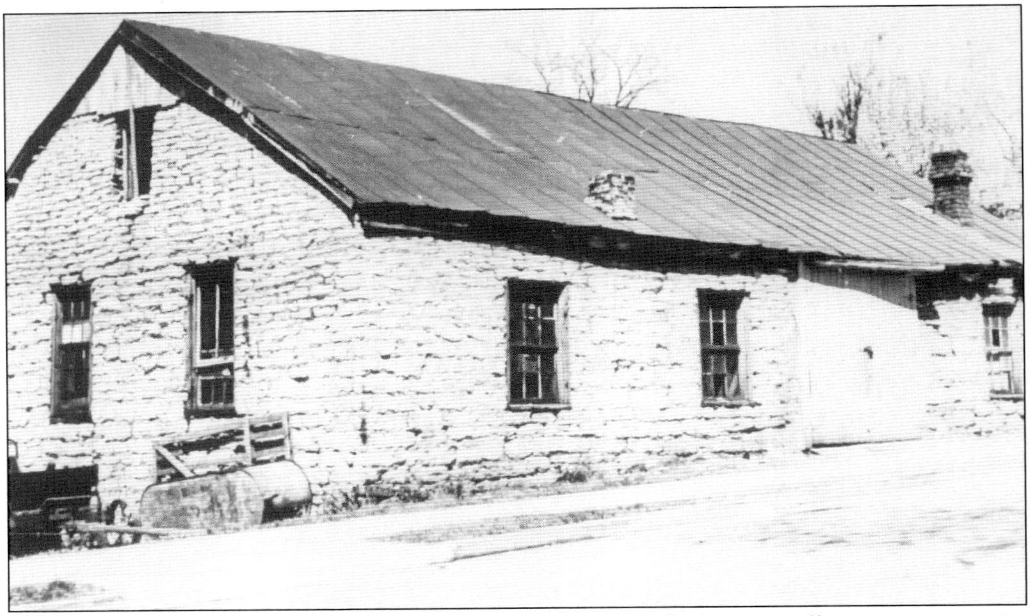

Blacksmith shops were common sights on city street corners and in every small county community from pioneer days until well into the automobile era. This old shop stood in Georgetown on the southwest corner of Washington and Hamilton Streets prior to construction of the Scott County Health Department in 1952.

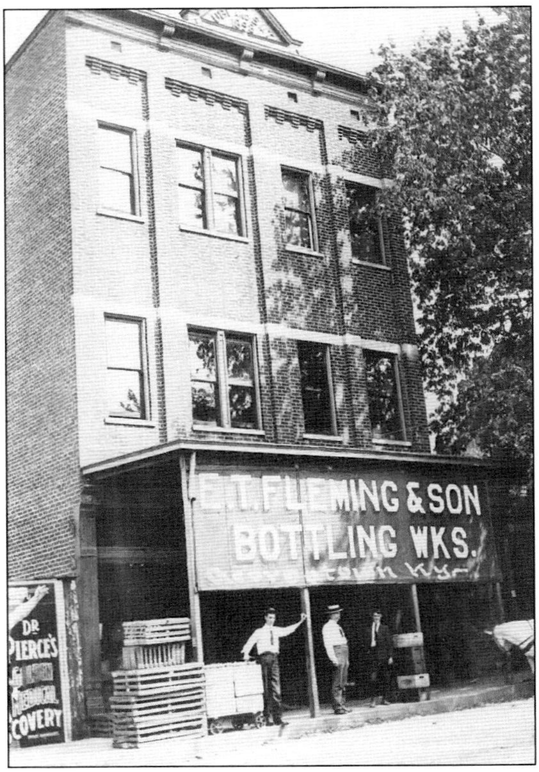

In 1891, the African-American United Brothers of Friendship lodge began constructing their meeting hall on the east side of South Broadway. Among its many later tenants was the E.T. Fleming and Son RoxaCola Bottling Works. RoxaCola was a product of Ale 8-1 creator G. Lee Wainscott of Winchester, Kentucky. He was a son of former Lancaster Hotel operator George Wainscott.

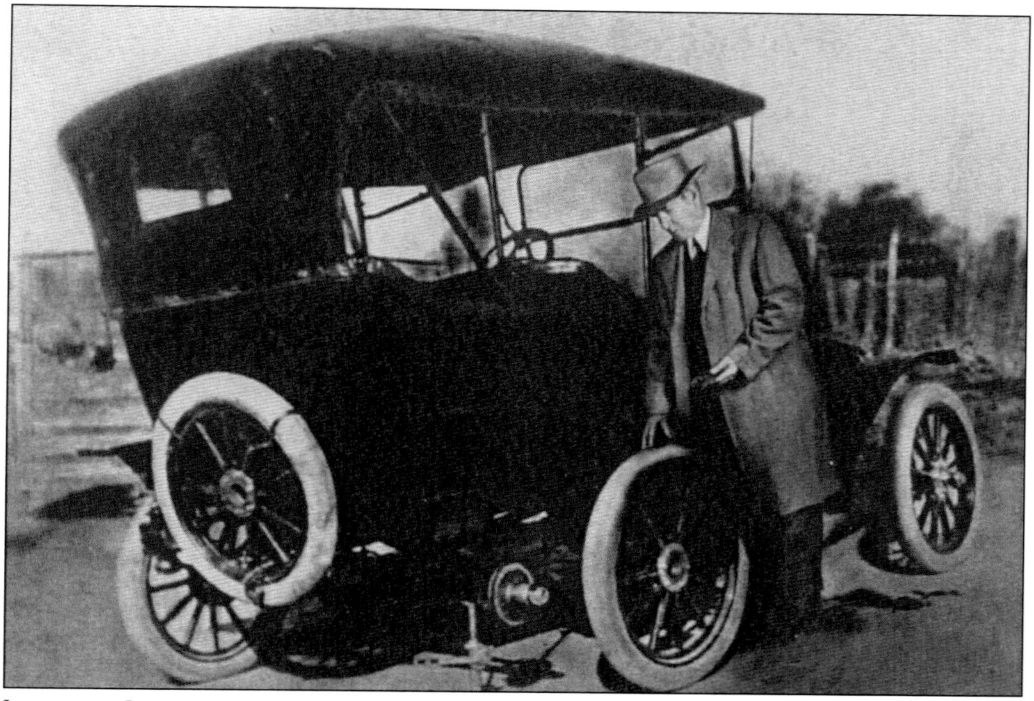

Longtime Georgetown mayor A.P. Prather inspects his invention, the demountable wheel, which greatly simplified the difficult task of changing a flat tire. The Prathers manufactured the wheel in Georgetown for two years but then sold the patent rights and repurchased their garage. Prather Brothers Chevrolet became a downtown Georgetown tradition for nearly 70 years.

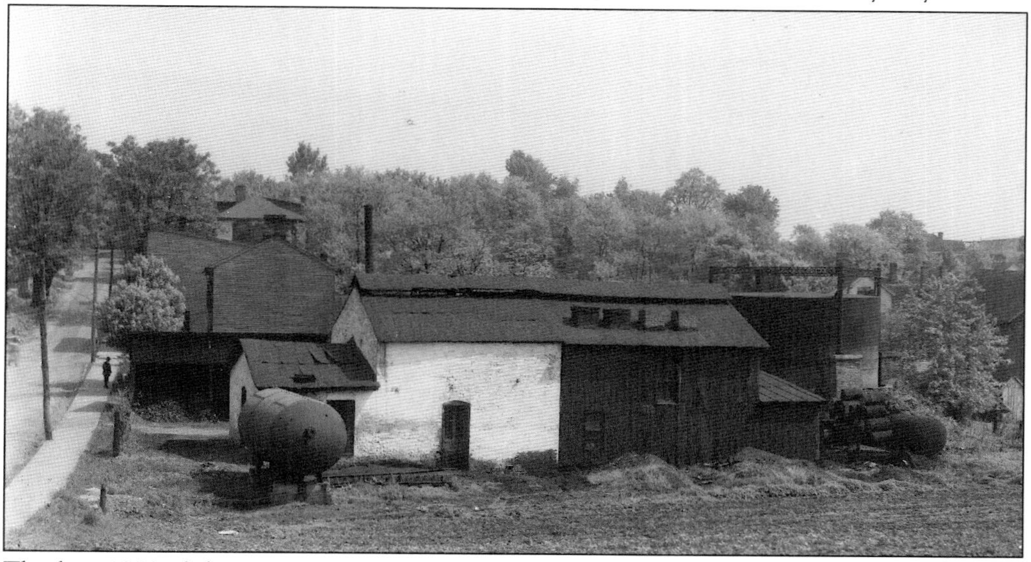

The late 1970s fight against a proposed coal gasification plant in Georgetown brought back long-forgotten memories of the town's original gas plant, which was built on North Mulberry Street in 1875. Financial and mechanical problems plagued the plant and the use of high-sulfur coal left downtown smelling like rotten eggs. Despite many attempts at refurbishing and reviving the plant, it was never a great success.

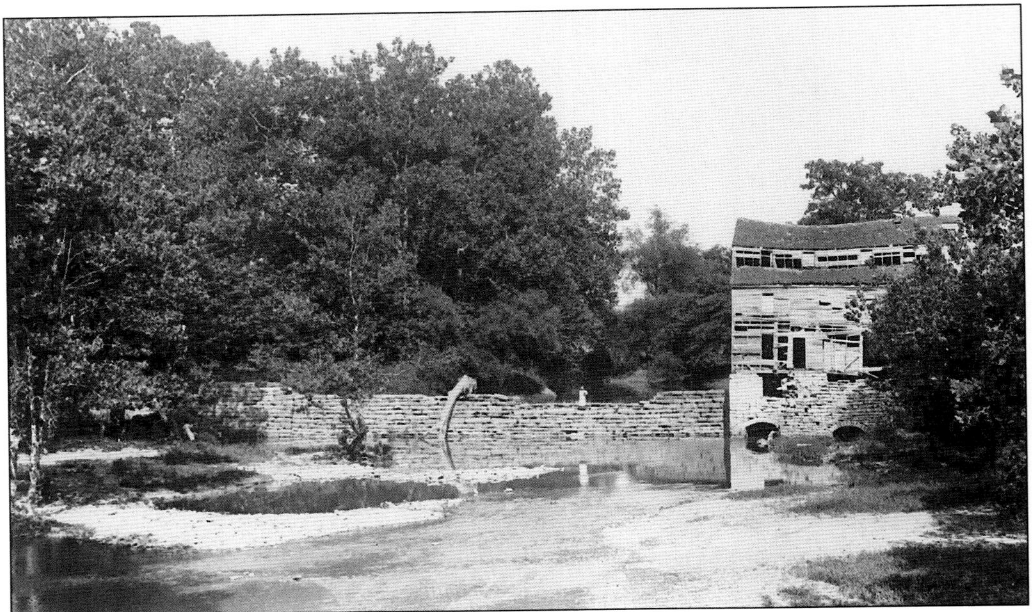

Gristmills were the most important of the early industries in Scott County. As soon as dams could be built, water-powered mills began production of flour and meal. Lemon's Mill, seen here, was constructed on North Elkhorn in 1838 and was the successor to the Reverend Joshua Leatherer's 1799 mill, which stood on the opposite bank of the creek.

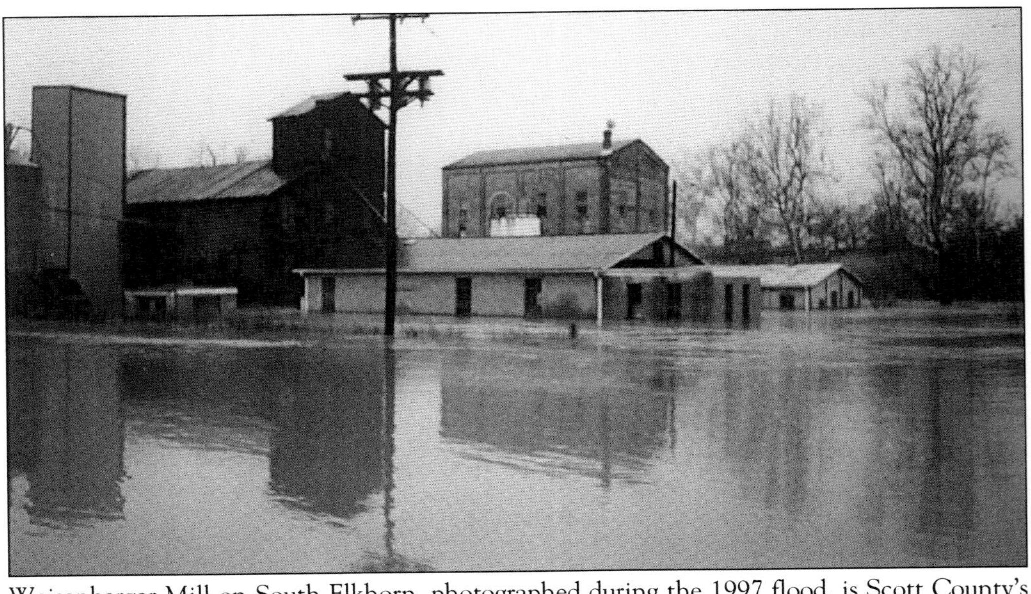

Weisenberger Mill on South Elkhorn, photographed during the 1997 flood, is Scott County's last operating flour mill. The 1913 concrete structure was built during a flood year that saw water reach the eaves of the office wing on the right. Stone from the original mill purchased by Augustus Weisenberger in 1872 was crushed and mixed with Portland cement to form the walls of the new building.

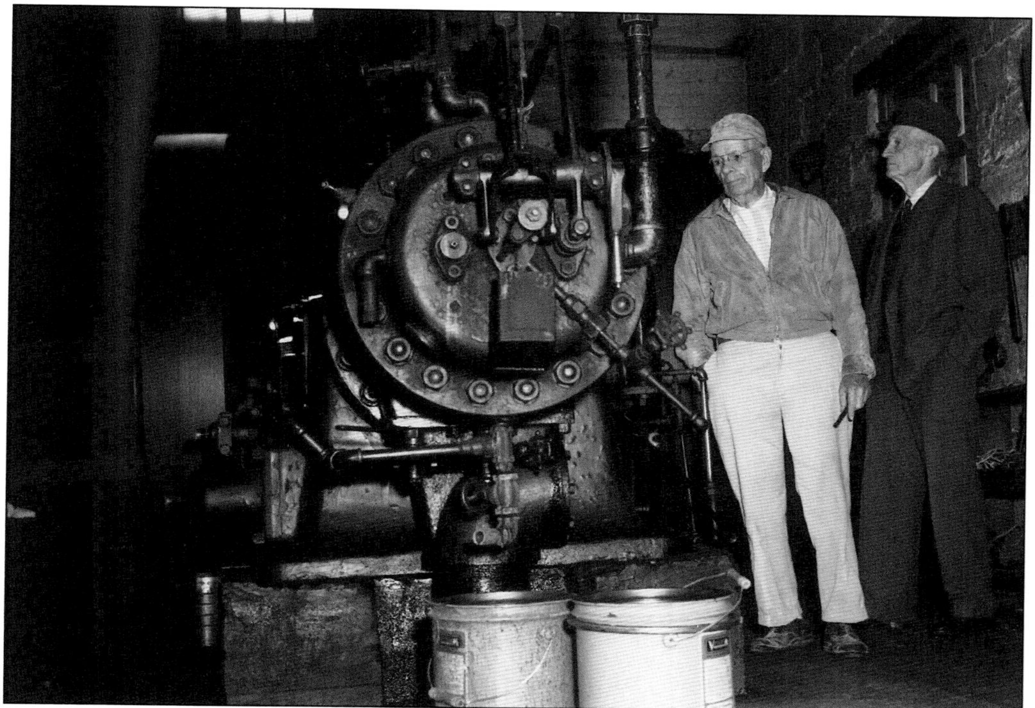

Third-generation miller Ben DeGaris and mill owner J.C. Ward inspect equipment inside Ward Brothers Mill, Georgetown's last operating flour mill. The successor to Elijah Craig's paper mill and Leander Stedman's woolen mill, it was built in 1895 by Richard Wolfe and Ben Stone to replace an earlier structure that had burned. The mill remained in operation until 1966.

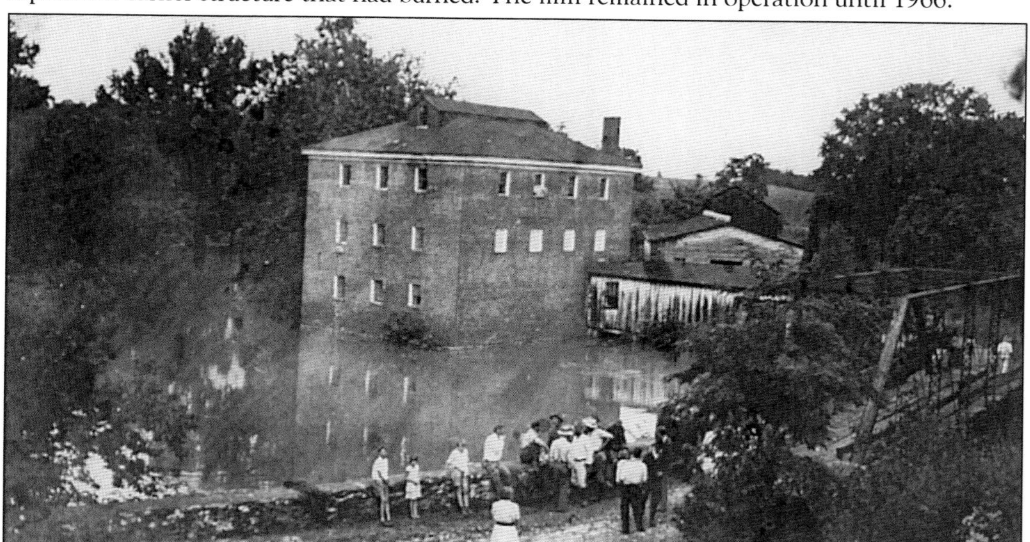

The picturesque setting of Johnson's Mill on Newtown Pike was the destination for many a Sunday afternoon excursion. During its commercial life, the antebellum structure served as a gristmill, sawmill, and distillery. Following the development of a huge crack in its northwest corner, the old mill was dismantled in 1979. The iron bridge was severely damaged by the 1997 flood.

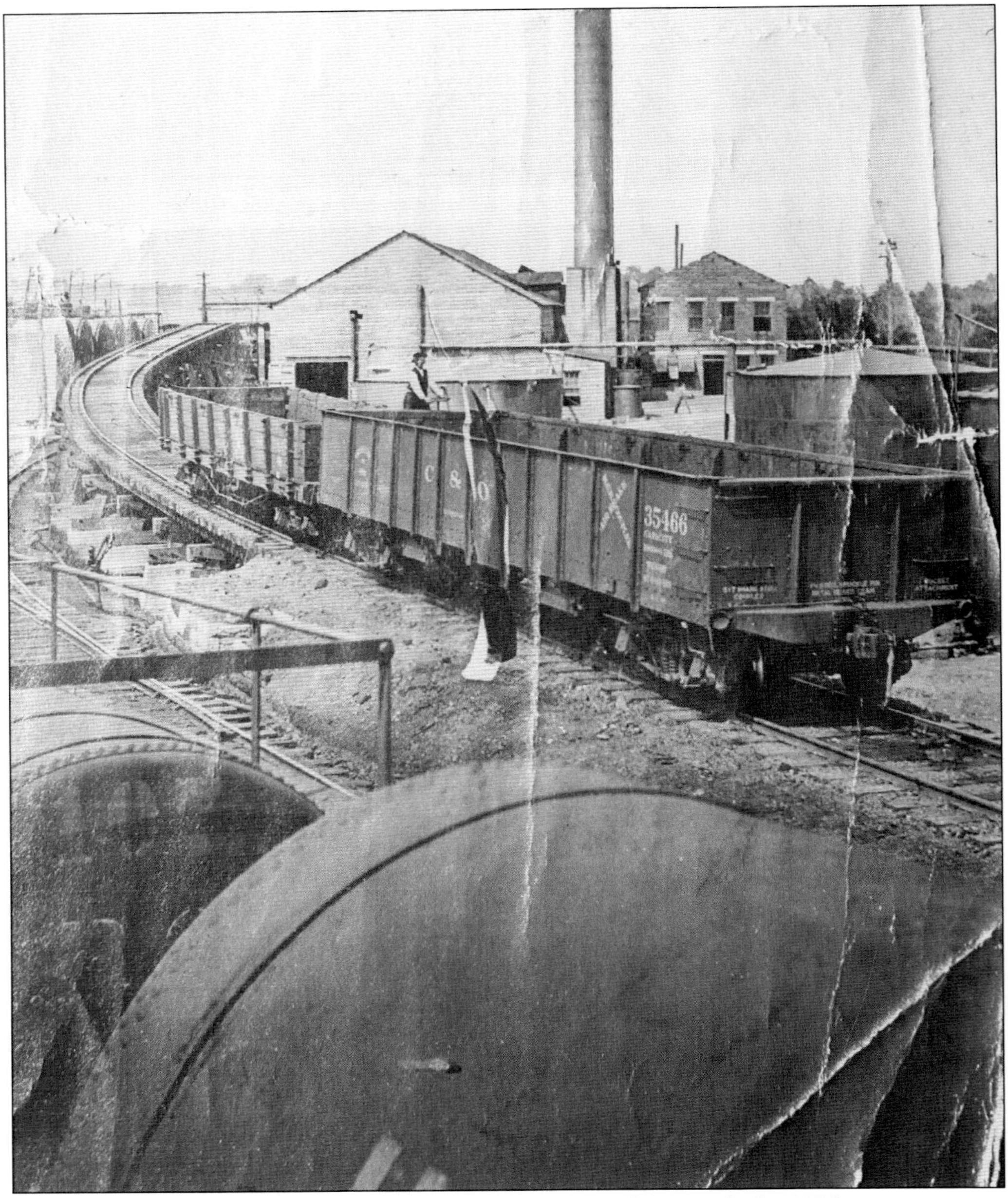

Georgetown seemed poised to become a center of heavy industry with the 1905 announcement by the Board of Trade that the Indian Oil Refining Company had agreed to move its plant to Georgetown. Construction began immediately, and by the end of the year, the plant was in full production on a 38-acre tract at the end of North Hamilton Street. By 1907, a wax plant and concrete block factory were also in use, over 300 people were employed, and over 3,000 barrels of oil were being refined each day. The plant's good relations with the community were marred, however, by the increasing problem of oil spills into Elkhorn, which resulted in several lawsuits and an indictment against the company. Partly due to this, but primarily because of increasing shipping costs, layoffs increased. By 1916, the plant had closed. Georgetown's hopes of industrial prominence came to an end.

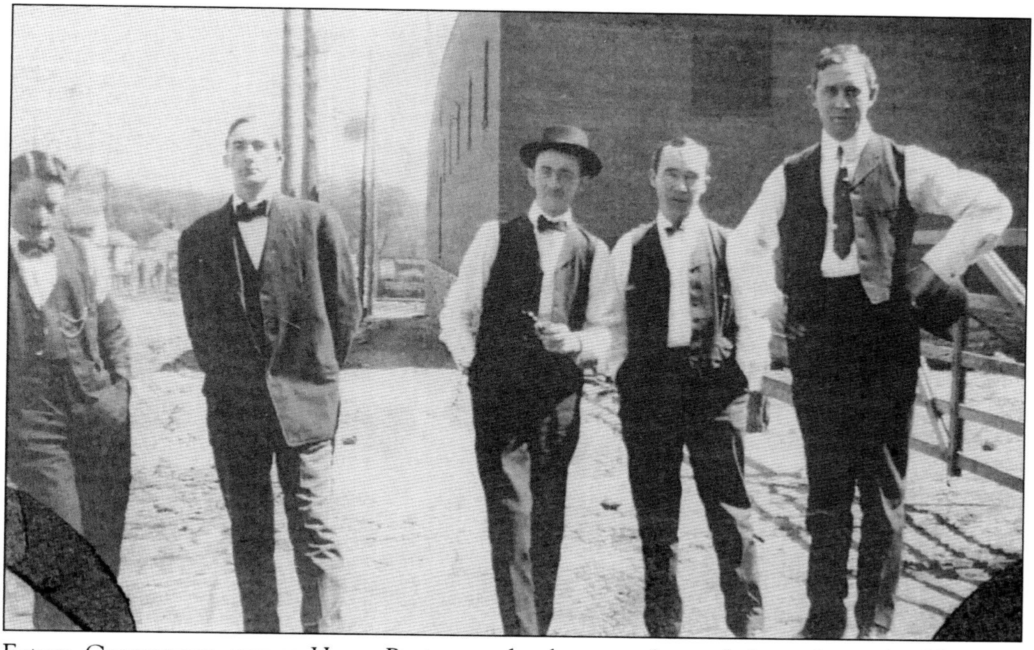

Future Georgetown mayor Harry Paxton and other members of the refinery bookkeeping department pose beside one of the company warehouses in April 1908. Among the amenities enjoyed by refinery employees were tennis courts, a baseball diamond and company team, and company-sponsored picnics.

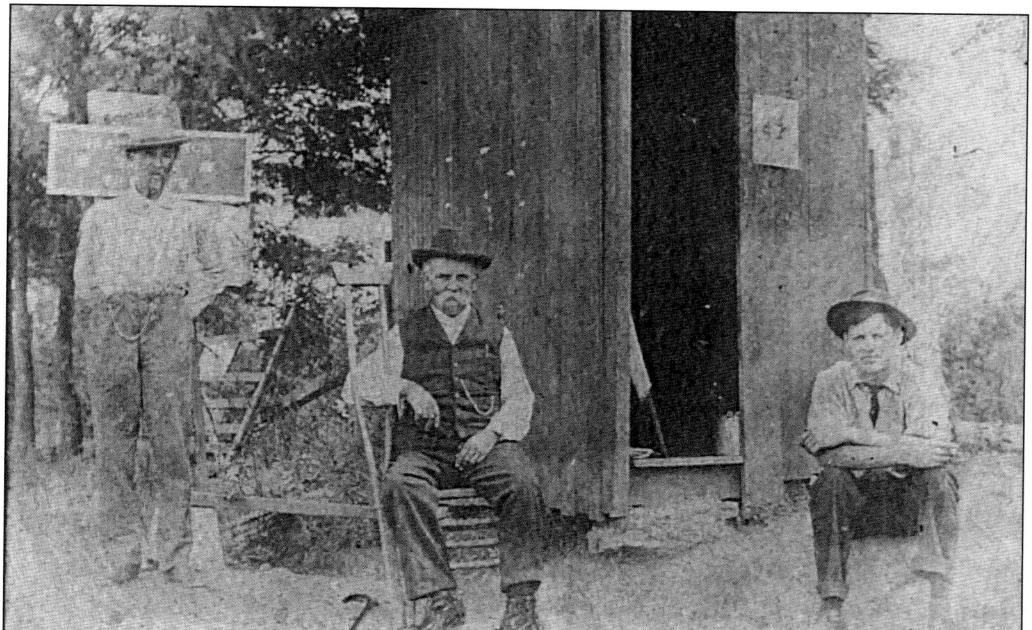

Refinery gatekeeper Jimmy Curtis (1850–1922) sits next to the guardhouse at the entrance to the Oil Company grounds. With the closing of the plant, scores of men like him found themselves unemployed. Georgetown went into an economic depression which was dismissed by the *Lexington Leader* as a "false depression" since, in its view, it was based on false prosperity.

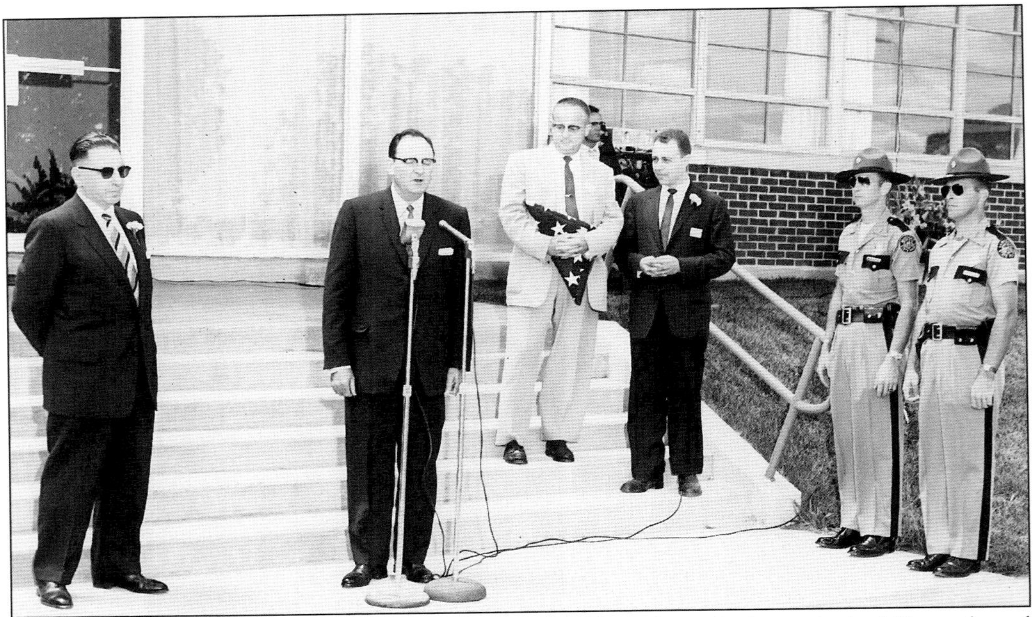

Georgetown's modern industrial era began in the mid-1940s with the arrival of Czarnek and Czarnek (the future Carbide Products) and Mallard Pencil Company. In 1955, Electric Parts announced its intentions to build on Lemon's Mill Road. Shown at the dedication of the factory in June 1956 are owner Ralph Theodore, Lt. Gov. Harry Lee Waterfield, Joe Johnson, and Henry Theodore.

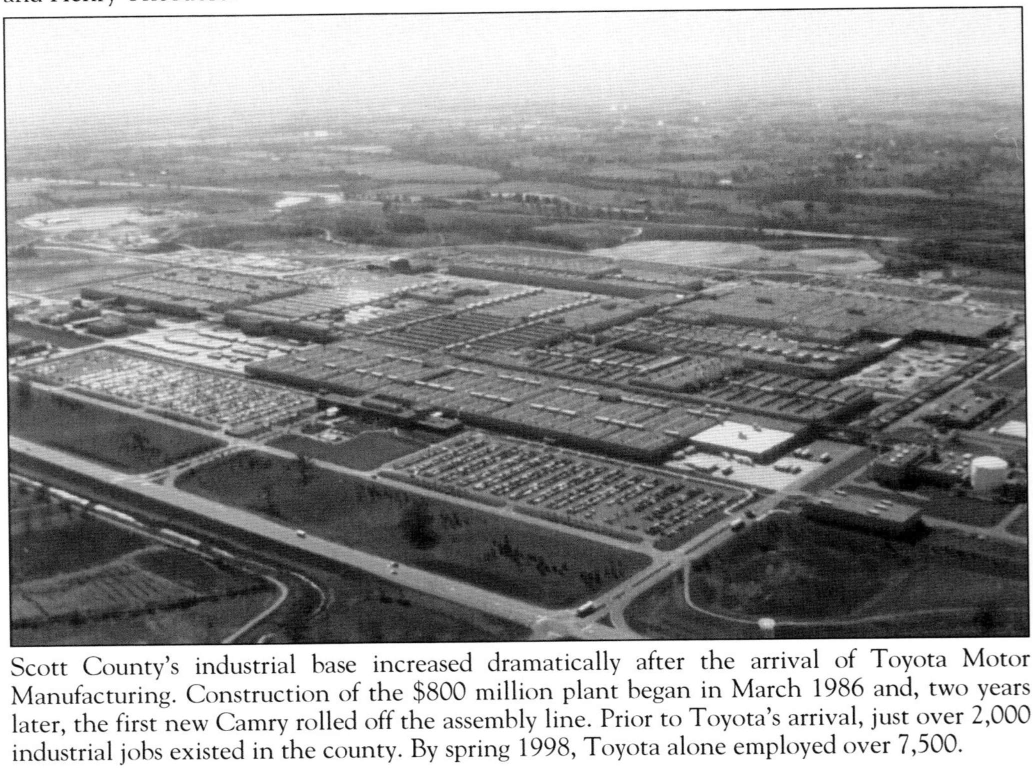

Scott County's industrial base increased dramatically after the arrival of Toyota Motor Manufacturing. Construction of the $800 million plant began in March 1986 and, two years later, the first new Camry rolled off the assembly line. Prior to Toyota's arrival, just over 2,000 industrial jobs existed in the county. By spring 1998, Toyota alone employed over 7,500.

Five

TRANSPORTATION

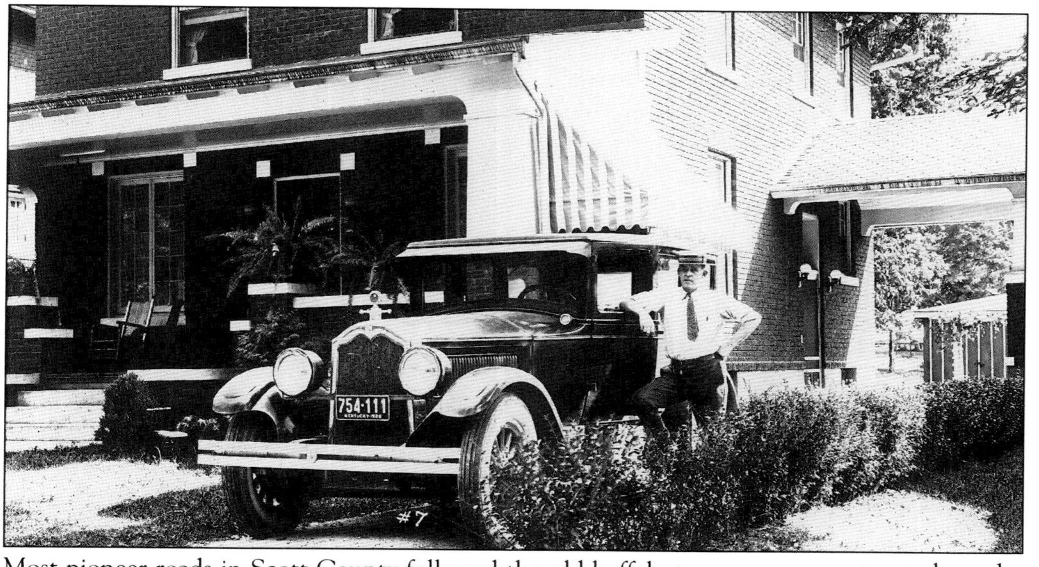

Most pioneer roads in Scott County followed the old buffalo traces or were cut out along the lines of the first land grants. Early improvements included removal of tree stumps, construction of bridges across mill dams, and the widening of more important routes to accommodate wagon traffic. By the mid-1800s, many local roads were in the hands of private turnpike companies that graded and macadamized the more important routes, built covered bridges, and constructed stone-retaining walls. By the end of the century, however, public dissatisfaction with high tolls and declining road maintenance led to the takeover of the turnpikes by local government.

After the appearance of automobiles, demands for improved roads accelerated. Construction of five U.S. highways through the county gave better access to rural areas and brought increased business. Better cars and better roads revolutionized personal mobility, just as the arrival of local passenger rail service had done decades before.

Although Payne's Depot lay on the route of Kentucky's first railroad (built during the mid-1830s), the rest of the county remained isolated until the opening of the north-south Cincinnati Southern route in 1877. Railroad fever ran high, and within 30 years, four more lines were in use. Rural hamlets such as Newtown and Rogers Gap were connected to the world by rail. The age of railroad travel, however, proved short. As competition from other means of transport increased, rail service declined, and passenger service disappeared altogether.

Above, Georgetown pharmacist David L. Parry poses with his new Buick in front of his home on Jackson Street. Demand for new automobiles remained high during Georgetown's pre-Depression years.

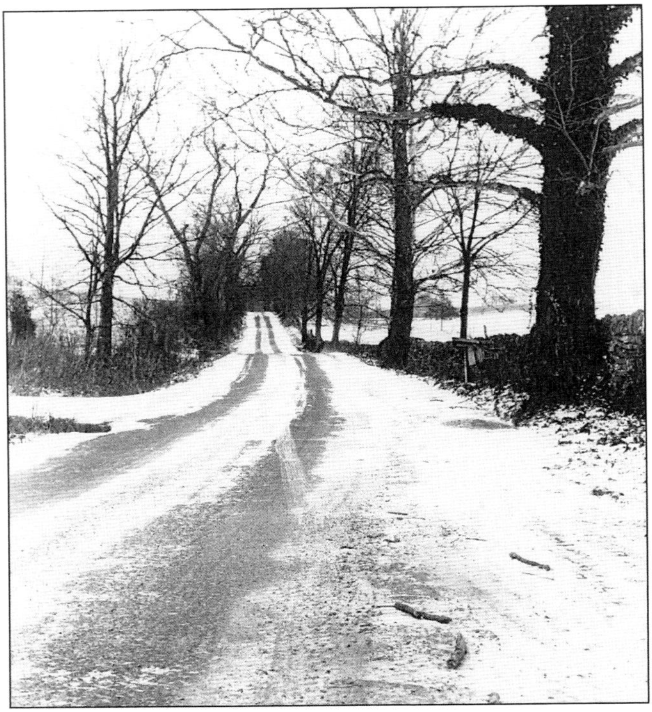

During the mid-nineteenth century, turnpike companies hired scores of stonemasons, many of whom were refugees from the famine in Ireland, to build retaining walls along the edges of the many local toll roads. Few of these walls survive today. Pictured here is a rare example of a rural road with its stone fences intact on each side.

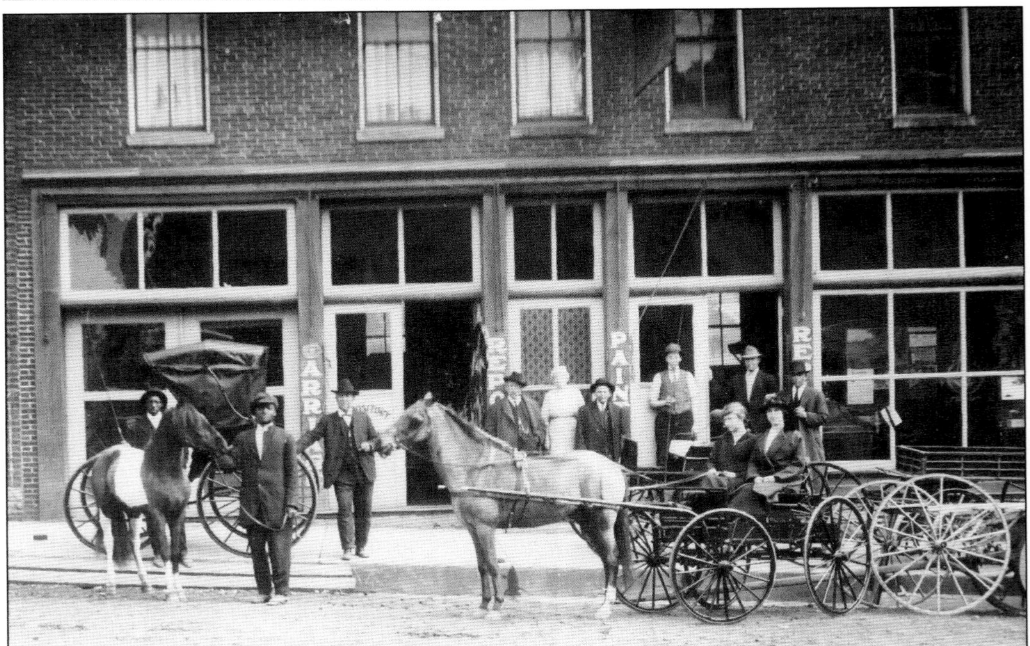

During the era when the horse was king of the local roads, carriage manufacturing became an important industry in Georgetown and in some of the smaller communities, including Stamping Ground and Newtown. In this view, Carriage Manufacturing and Repair on Georgetown's West Main Street displays some of its work.

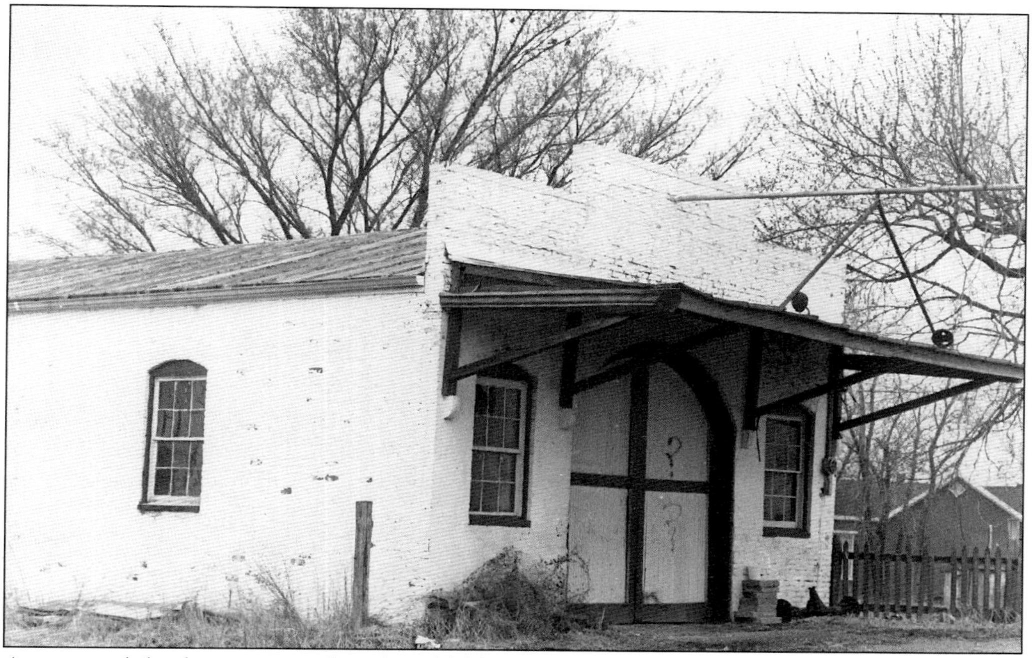

As automobiles became popular, the old blacksmith shops and livery stables disappeared or were converted to other uses, as was this shop at White Sulphur, near the Iron Works Road intersection. Built by P.J. Craycraft in 1907, this old structure later served as a garage and machinery dealership before being enclosed within a new metal building.

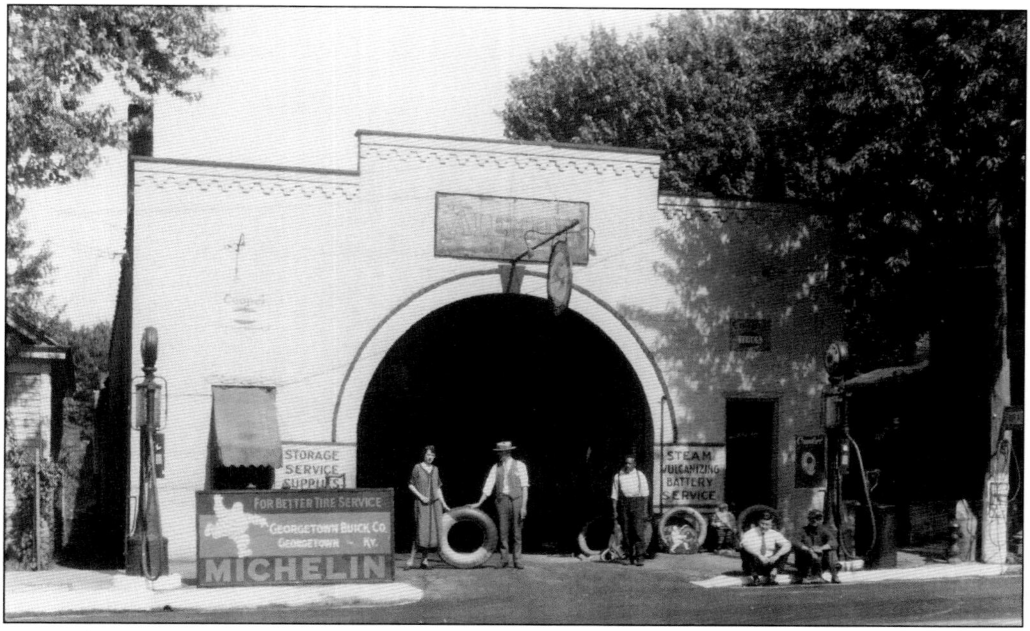

Pictured is G.H. Nunnelley's 1885 livery stable, located on South Broadway. It is one of the few surviving examples. In 1925, it became home to L.S. Odell's Buick Sales Agency. It is presently used as the Georgetown Decorating Center.

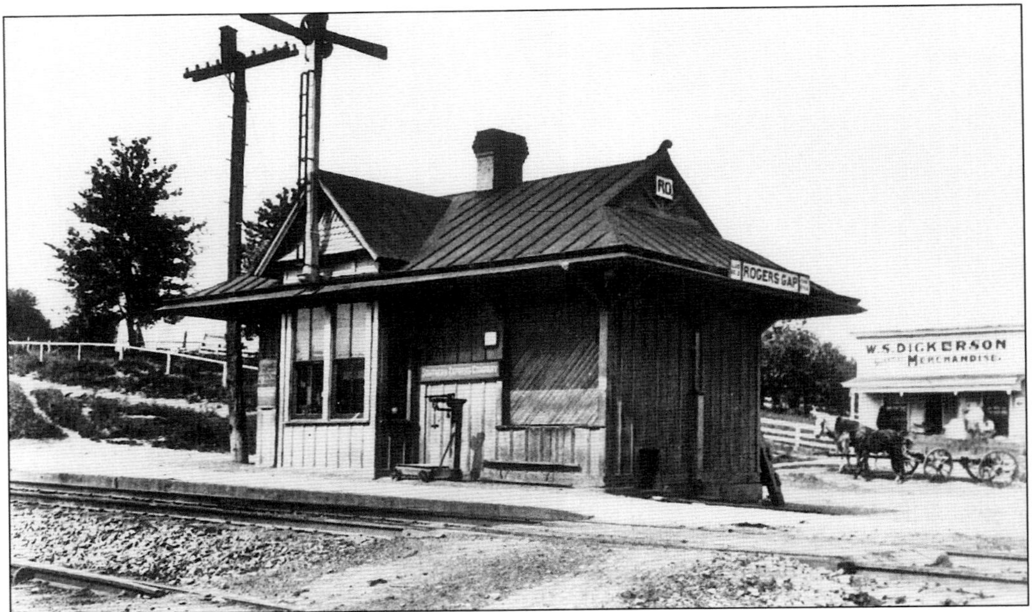

The 1877 opening of the Cincinnati Southern Railroad through Scott County provided rural residents with unheard of access to Georgetown and other cities. Depots were built at several rural road crossings including Rogers Gap, so named by the railroad surveyors for a local family. The depot above replaced an earlier structure that burned in 1900.

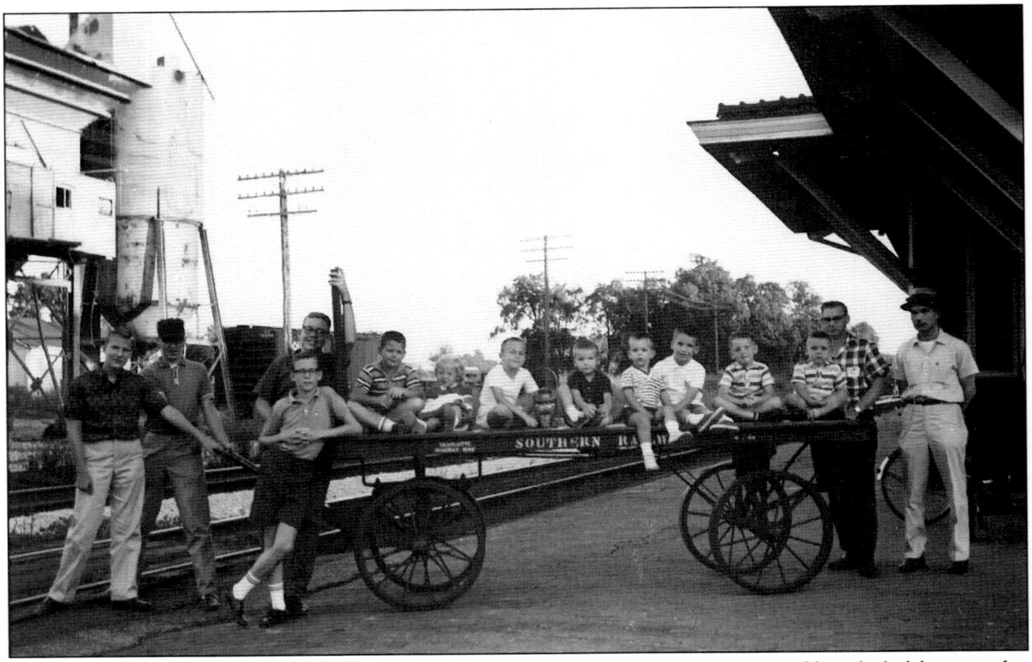

Georgetown railroad historian Flem Smith (far right) poses with a group of local children at the Southern depot. Smith, great-grandson of *Georgetown Times* founder John A. Bell, was such an authority on railroads that travelers were known to call him for scheduling information, finding his knowledge superior to that of the ticket offices.

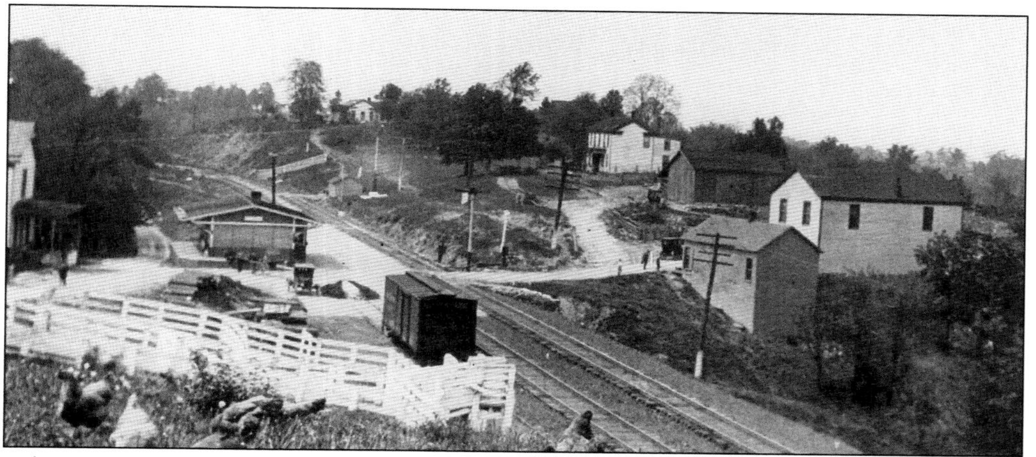

"The principal business done at the station on Saturdays and Sundays is drinking, quarreling, and fighting," complained the Hinton correspondent to the *Georgetown Weekly Times* in 1878. Hinton, like Sadieville, was a child of the Southern Railroad, and with the loss of its depot, became a much quieter place.

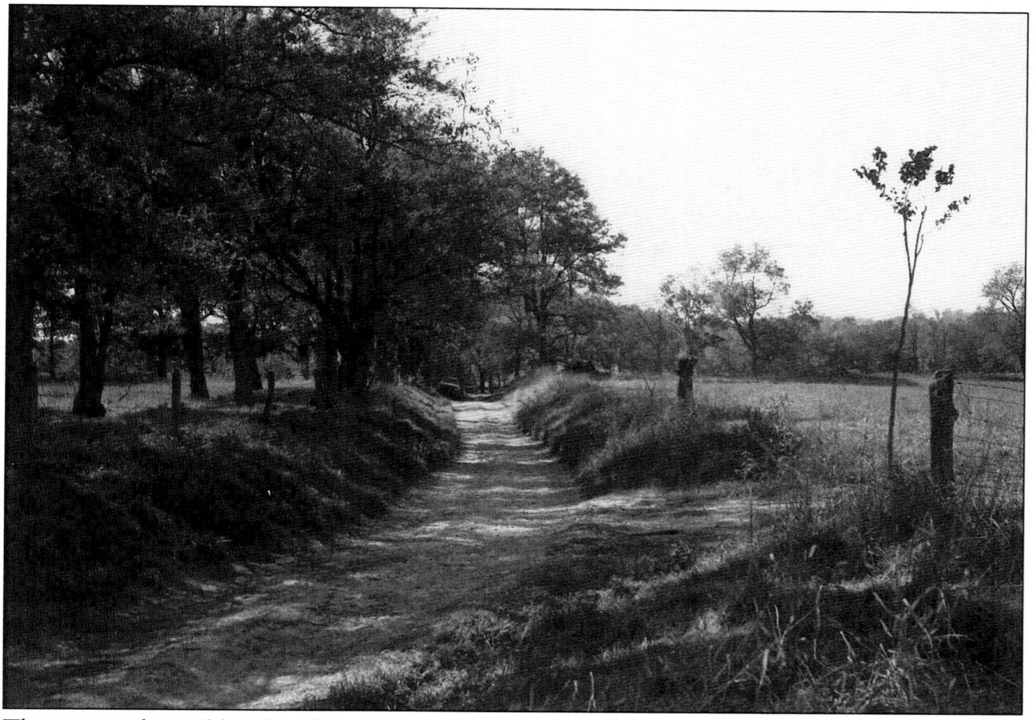

This view of an old railroad bed, located southwest of Georgetown, is a reminder that the heyday of railroading lies in the past. The lane was part of the old Versailles, Midway, and Georgetown line that opened in 1888. Passenger service stopped in 1932, and the track was abandoned in 1941.

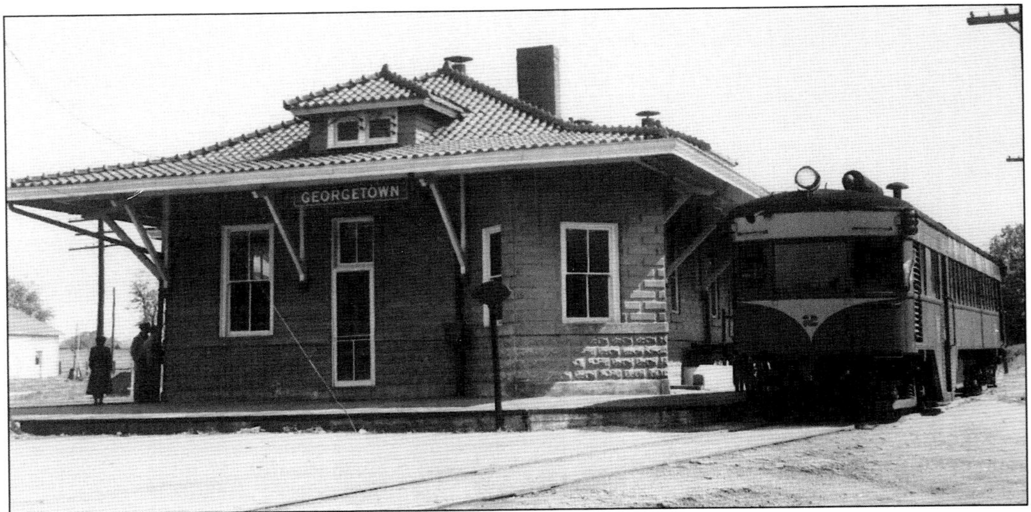

Beginning in the late 1920s, passenger service on the Frankfort and Cincinnati Railroad was provided by a self-powered passenger car which became known as the "Dinky." Shown above at the Georgetown Southern depot, the Dinky made several trips from Frankfort to Paris daily, stopping at Stamping Ground, Duvall, Georgetown, and Newtown, and, sometimes, at smaller flag stations.

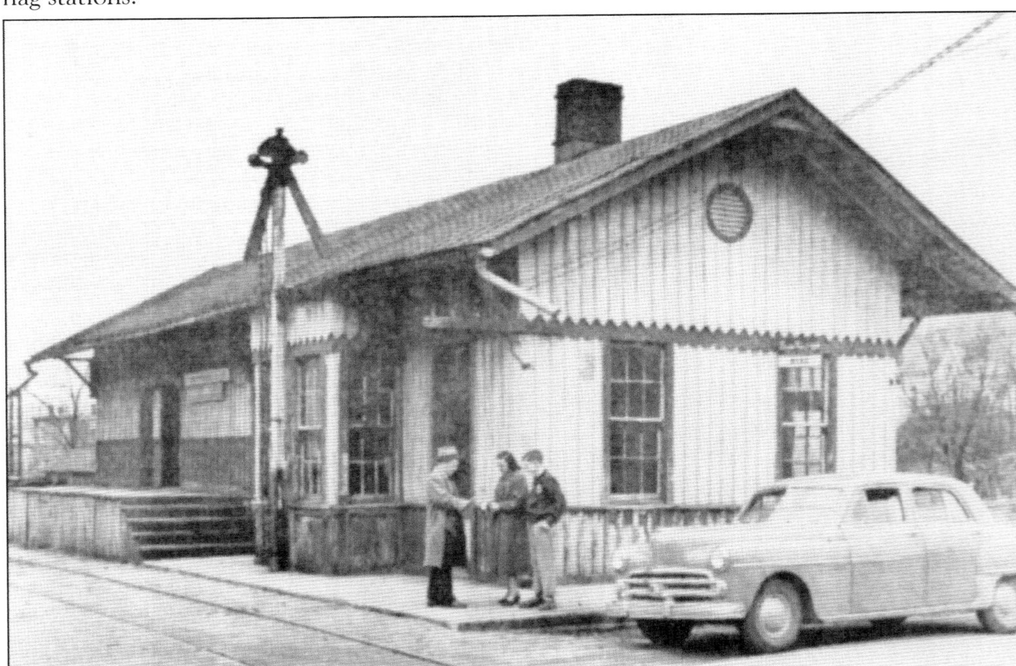

Passenger service on the F&C ended in January 1953. Above, Patsy Martin purchases the last commercial passenger ticket for the Dinky at the Stamping Ground depot. Unfortunately, the Dinky suffered a broken axle, and Ms. Martin's trip to town ended up being made by a railroad official's automobile.

Harry Williams stands near the Georgetown F&C depot on Bourbon Street. Originally called the Kentucky Midland Railroad, the F&C was built through the county in 1888. Known as the "whiskey line" because of its large distillery freight business, the road was significantly hurt by the Prohibition years. By 1971, the railroad was a memory.

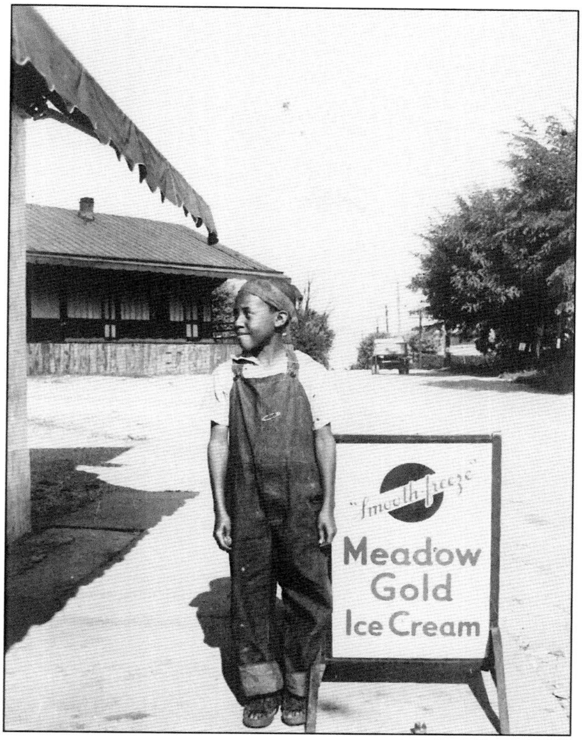

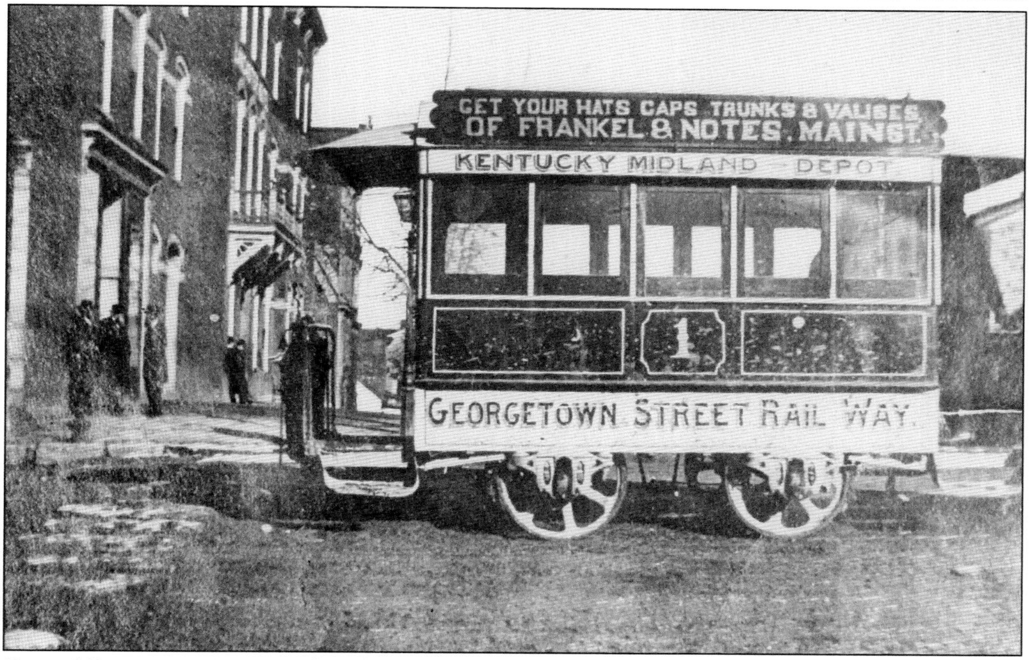

One of Georgetown's original mule-drawn streetcars prepares to leave the Lancaster Hotel. The line was converted to electricity in 1895. Ridership declined as automobiles became popular and, in 1922, the cars stopped running. The interurban connection to Lexington went bankrupt in 1934, and the rails on South Broadway were finally removed in 1941.

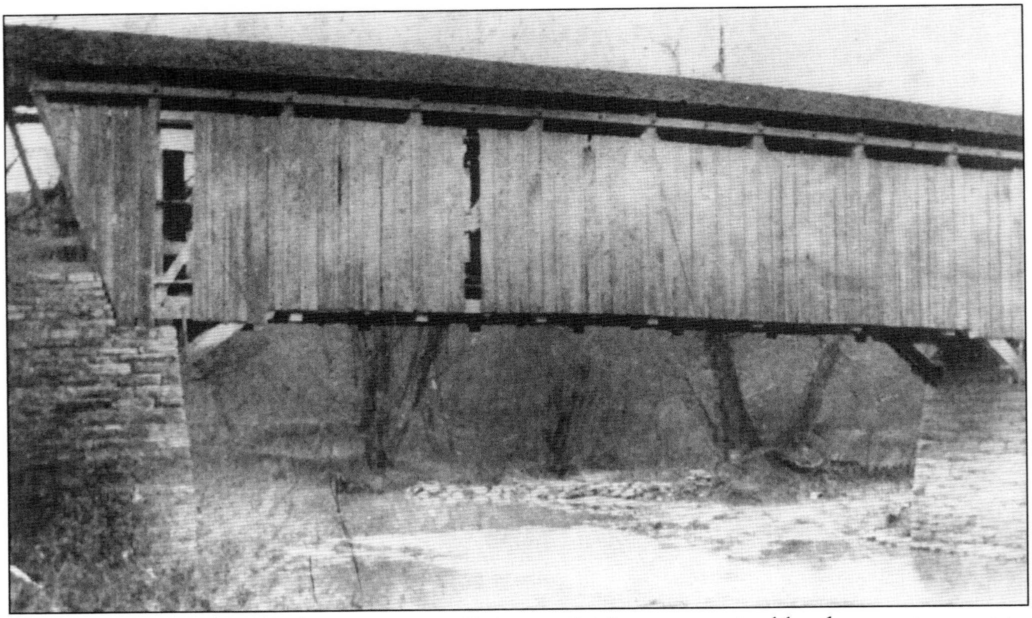

Scott County's earliest bridges were its mill dams, which were required by the county court to be at least 12 feet wide to allow for wagon traffic. As roads improved, the wood-covered bridge with sides and roof to protect its timbers became popular. This example stood in northern Scott County near Sadieville.

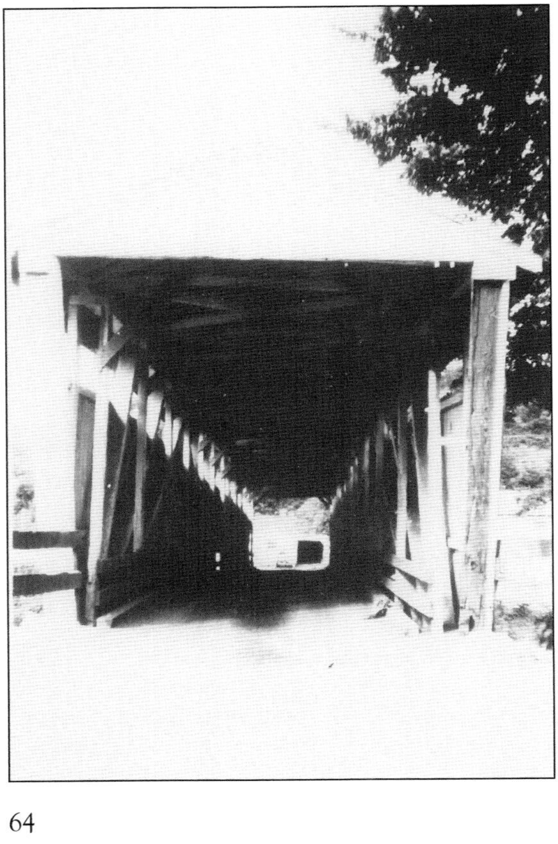

This local bridge is typical of the more than 20 covered bridges that once spanned local streams. Scott County's last covered bridge, over South Elkhorn at Fisher's Mill, collapsed into the creek in 1947.

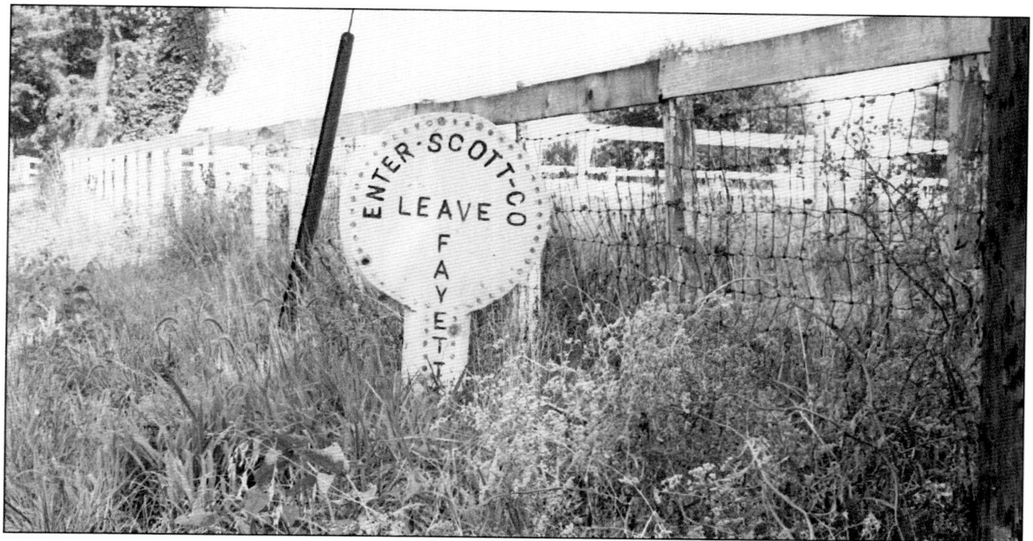

Formerly a common sight on rural roads, few of the old concrete county boundary markers remain. The exact location of the county line on each local road became of major interest to county officials following the takeover of the private toll roads by county government during the 1890s. No county road department wanted to use precious highway funds to inadvertently repair a road lying in another county!

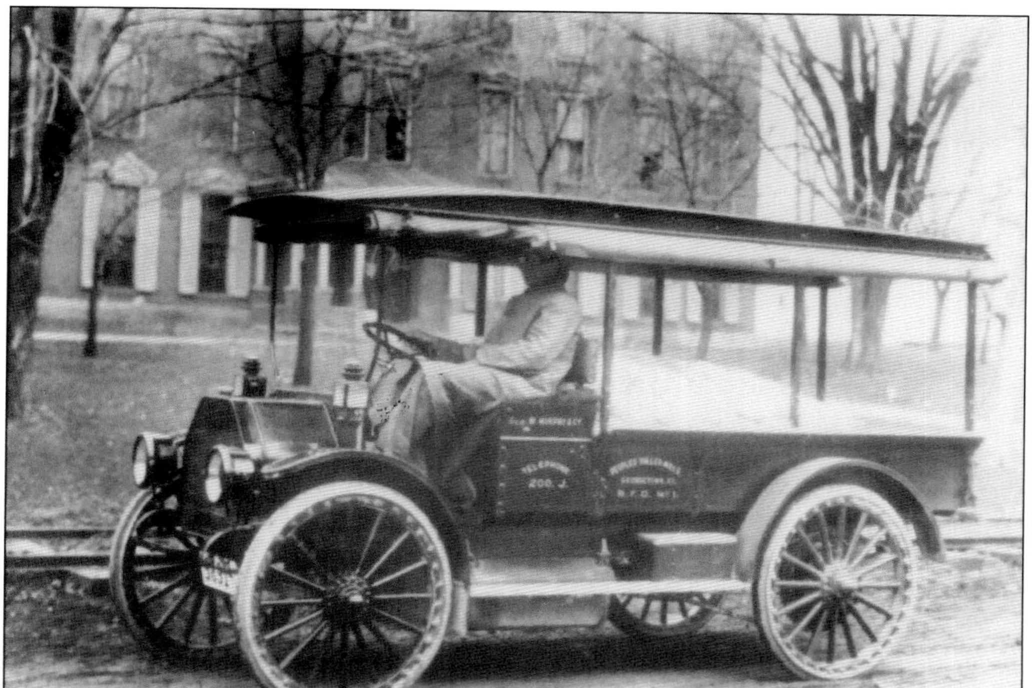

In hopes of increasing their shares of the local market through faster, more efficient, and longer range deliveries of goods and services, progressive local businessmen were among the first to abandon their old, horse-drawn vehicles. In this view, the new delivery truck of the People's Roller Mills (formerly Johnson's Mill) stops on a Georgetown street.

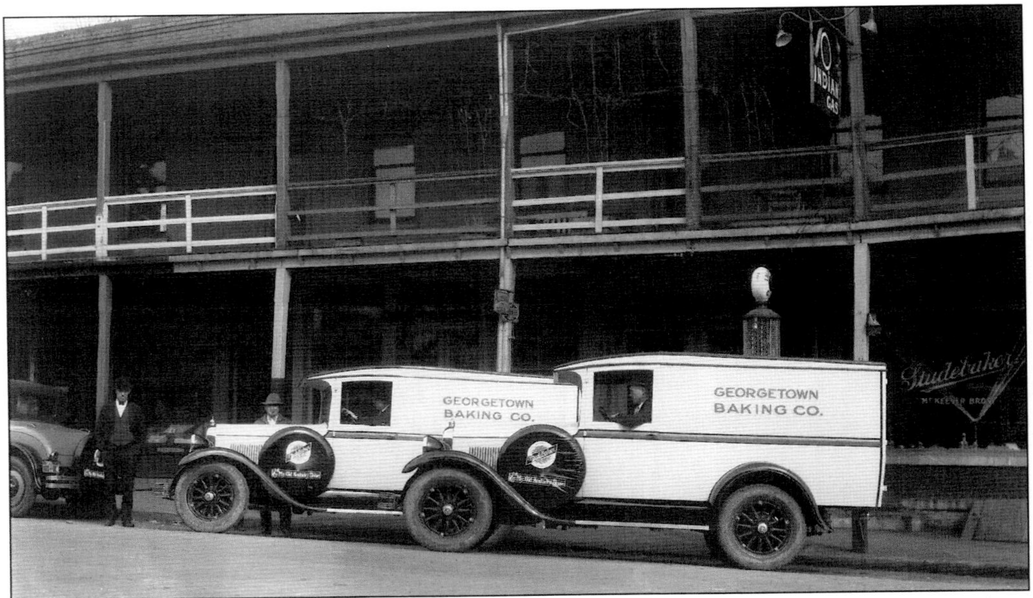

In addition to longtime auto dealers Logan, Haggin, and Cooper Ford and Prather Brothers Chevrolet, many other automobile agents competed for the Georgetown market. Here Willie and George McKeever display the newly arrived Georgetown Baking Company delivery trucks at their Studebaker dealership on North Broadway.

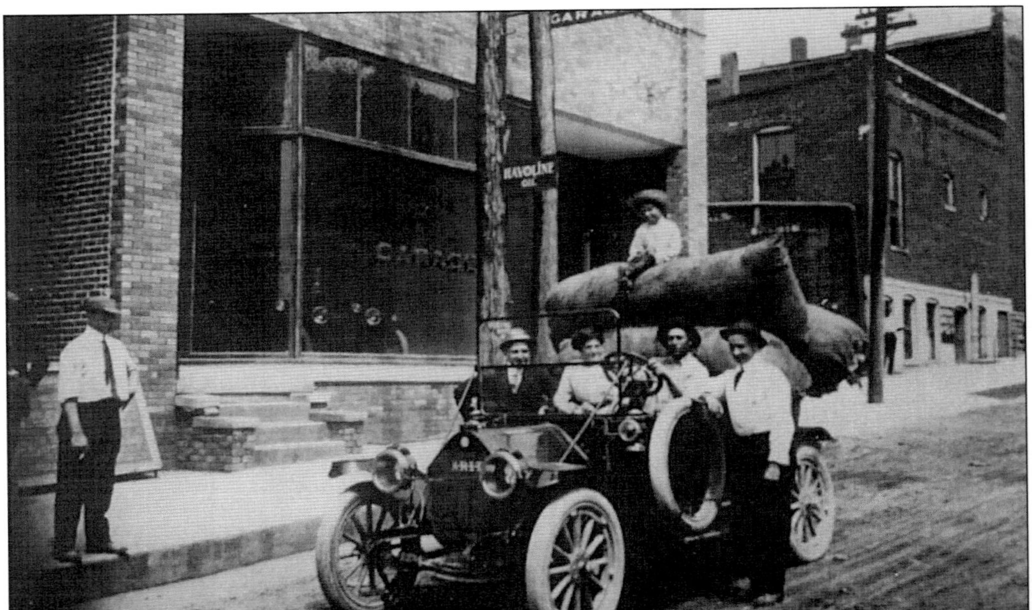

A new KRIT car displays its load-carrying capabilities in front of E. Jack Prather's Mitchell-KRIT dealership on South Broadway, which is now part of the Georgetown Antique Mall. Prather also sold Reos and Whippets, and in 1927, opened Georgetown's first car wash, the Clean Car Auto Laundry, with partner James Lewis.

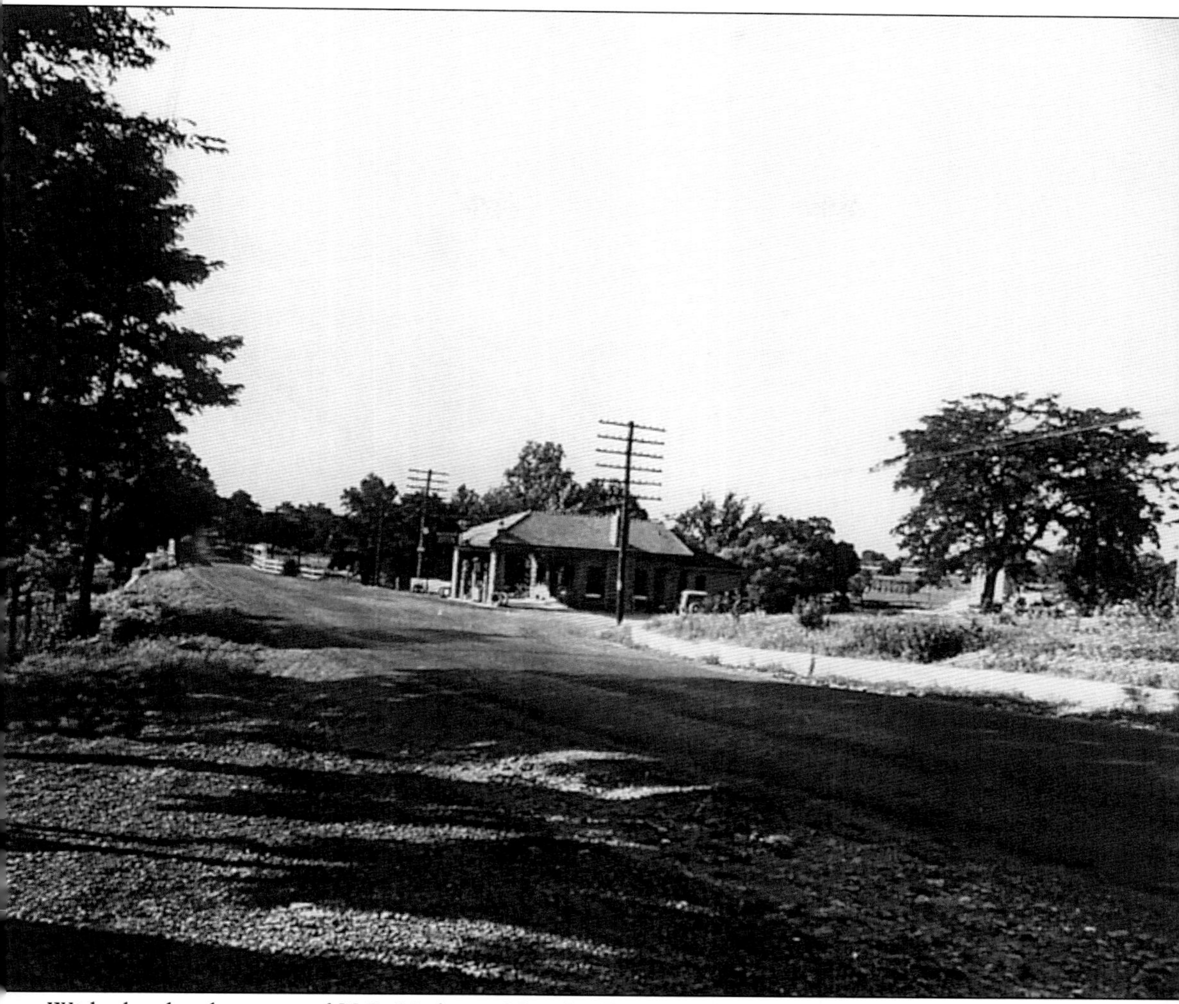

With the development of U.S. Highway 25—the Dixie Highway—Scott County became an important north-south transportation link. The huge increase in traffic brought prosperity to a large number of gas stations, tourist camps, and roadhouses that appeared all along the route. But during the 1960s, the new interstate highway system passed them by and few of the old structures remain. One survivor, shown here, is the Rock House, an arts-and-crafts-style gas station built by Henry Moss on property purchased in 1932, just south of the Elkhorn bridge leading north out of Georgetown. Two tourist cabins stood behind the structure, and fishing was available at the adjacent dam. Behind the business was Moss Park, the scene of many county fairs and events.

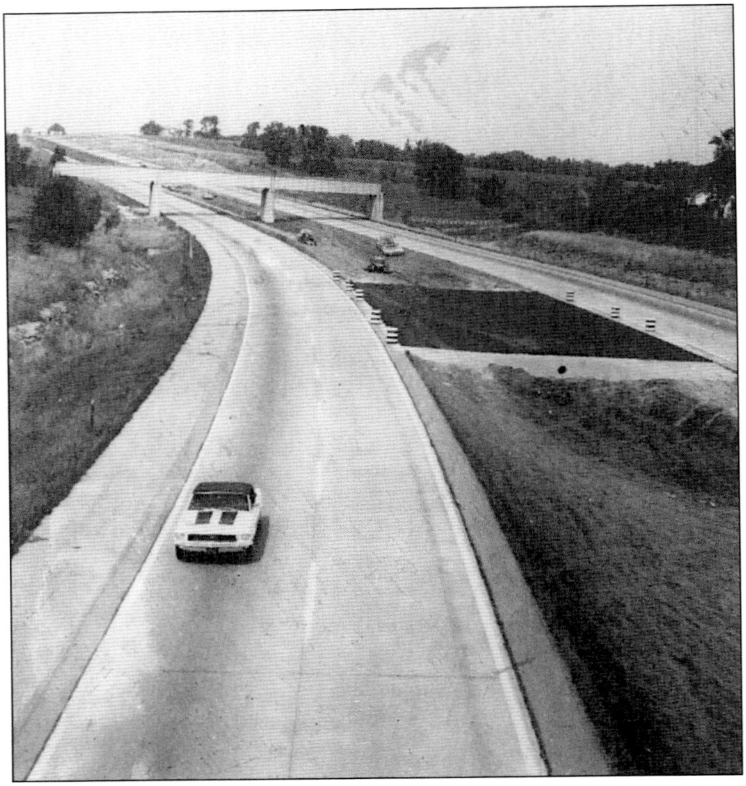

In 1956, Congress provided for the construction of an interstate highway system to provide better access between all areas of the nation. Development-minded local officials breathed a sigh of relief when Scott County was chosen to be a major route of I-75. Construction began at Paris Pike in August 1960. The F&C bridge, removed in 1971, is visible in the above view, which was taken north of Lemon's Mill Road.

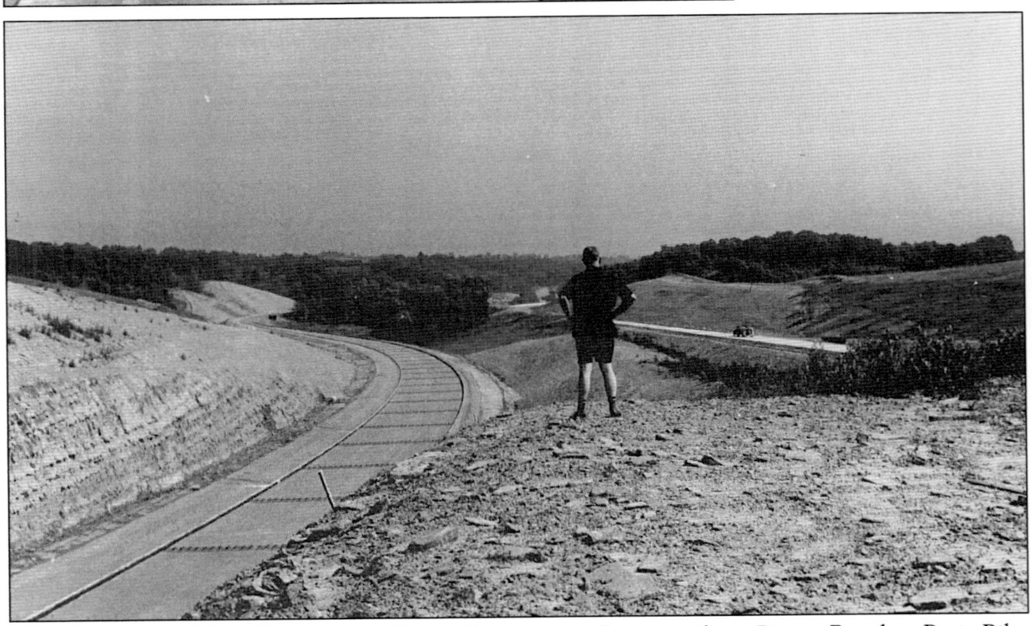

The first section of I-75 to open in Scott County was the route from Porter Road to Paris Pike in August 1963. A portion of the road is pictured in this view. Four months later, the stretch from Georgetown south to the six-mile bridge in Fayette County opened. Completion of I-75 was followed by construction of I-64 through the southern tip of the county.

Six
POLITICS AND WAR

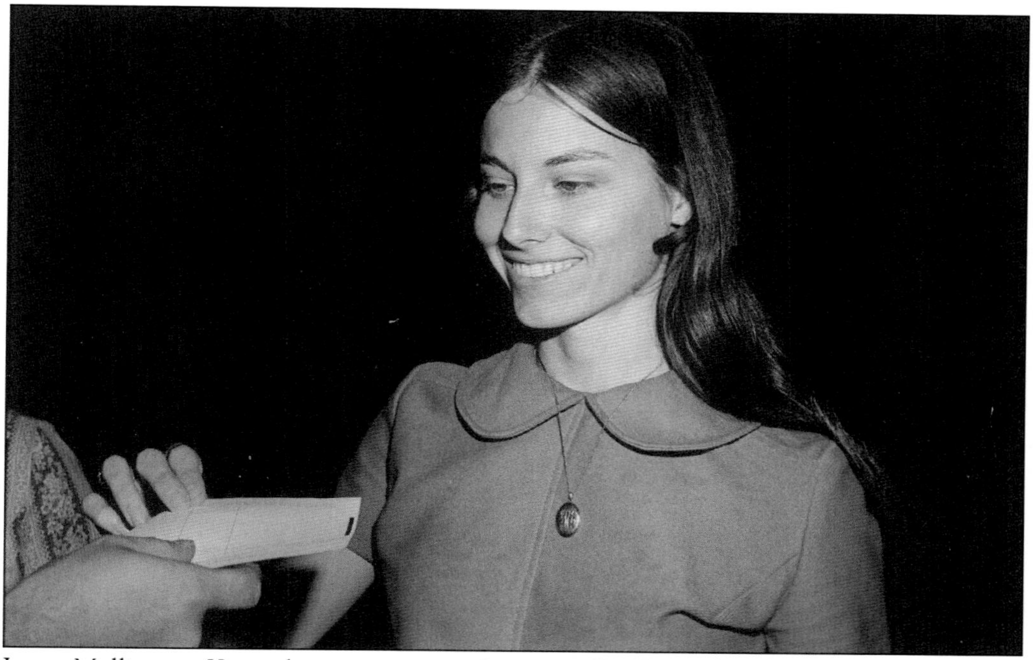

James Mulligan, a Kentucky poet, wrote in his poem "In Kentucky" that politics in the state were "the damnedest!" Certainly politicians have sometimes been at war among themselves, but in Scott County, there is a more positive connection between politics and war. The nation chooses its leaders at the national, state, and local levels. Citizens depend upon those elected officials to protect access to the courts, the freedoms of speech, press, and religion, and the right to participate in the process. When necessary, county residents have joined the nation to defend those rights so sacred and so central to the Republic. The first pages of this section relate to the political process. Throughout our history, those Scott County residents eligible to vote have done so in large numbers. In the nineteenth century, even the cemetery precincts voted upon occasion, and white males voted with such exuberance it was thought fit to close the liquor stores on election day, a practice that remains in effect today. In 1867, African-American men cast the ballot, and women successfully demanded the right in 1920. Pictured above, Earlene Hawkins Arnett receives a voting ticket in the days before machines were used in county voting precincts. The second part of the section celebrates those residents who protected our rights at significant risk to their own lives. As the home of many Revolutionary War veterans, the county has sent its sons to participate in every American war, large or small. As a result, citizens can continue to exercise the rights that the nation claims for all its people.

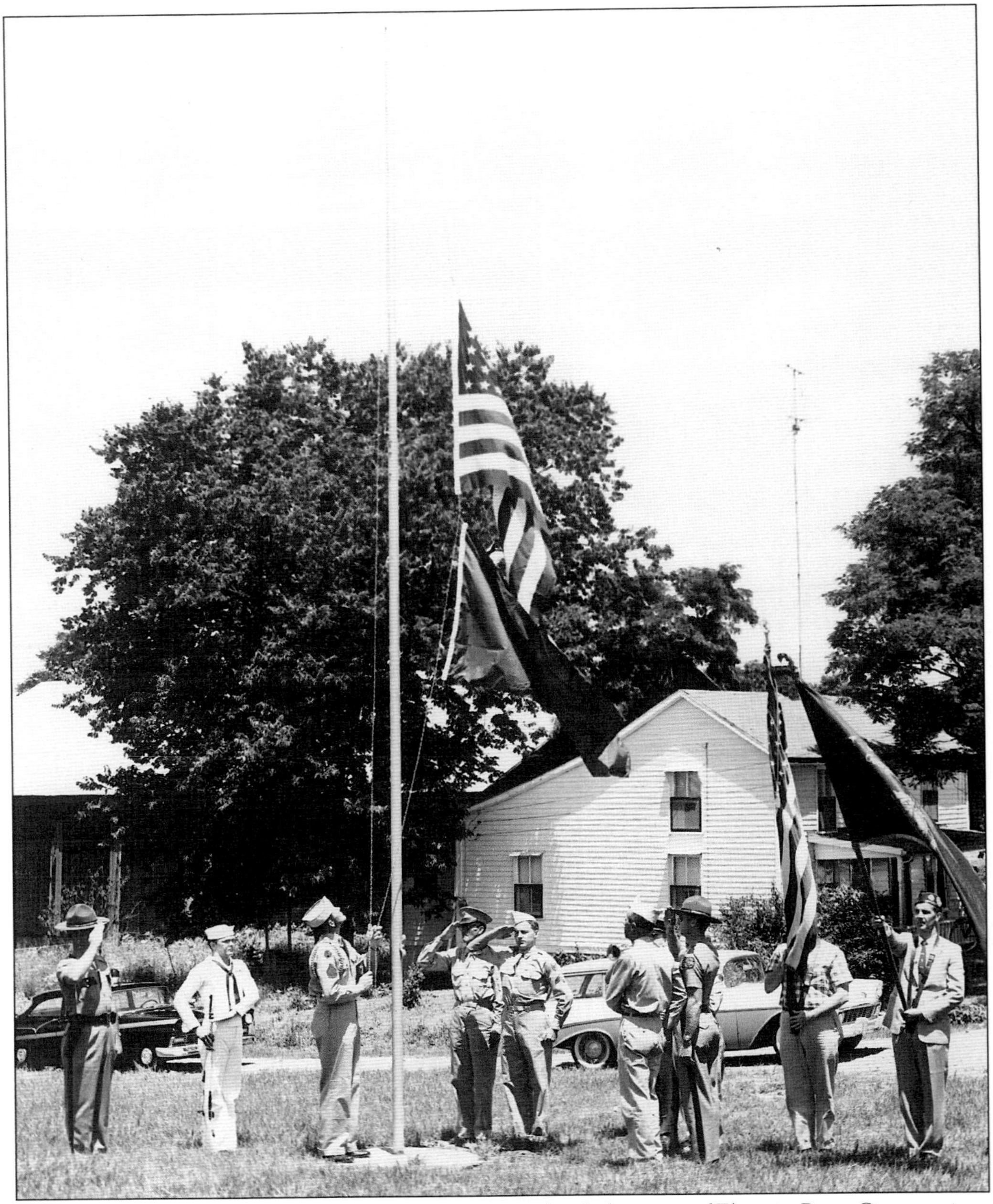

The American Legion raises the stars and stripes at the dedication of Electric Parts Corporation. Veterans with service in several branches participate in a ceremony repeated throughout this century. The automobiles, one perhaps purchased at Logan, Haggin, Cooper (Ford dealership), the other, a General Motors product, purchased at either Prather Brothers or Bevins Motor Company, corroborate that this flag-raising occurred in 1956.

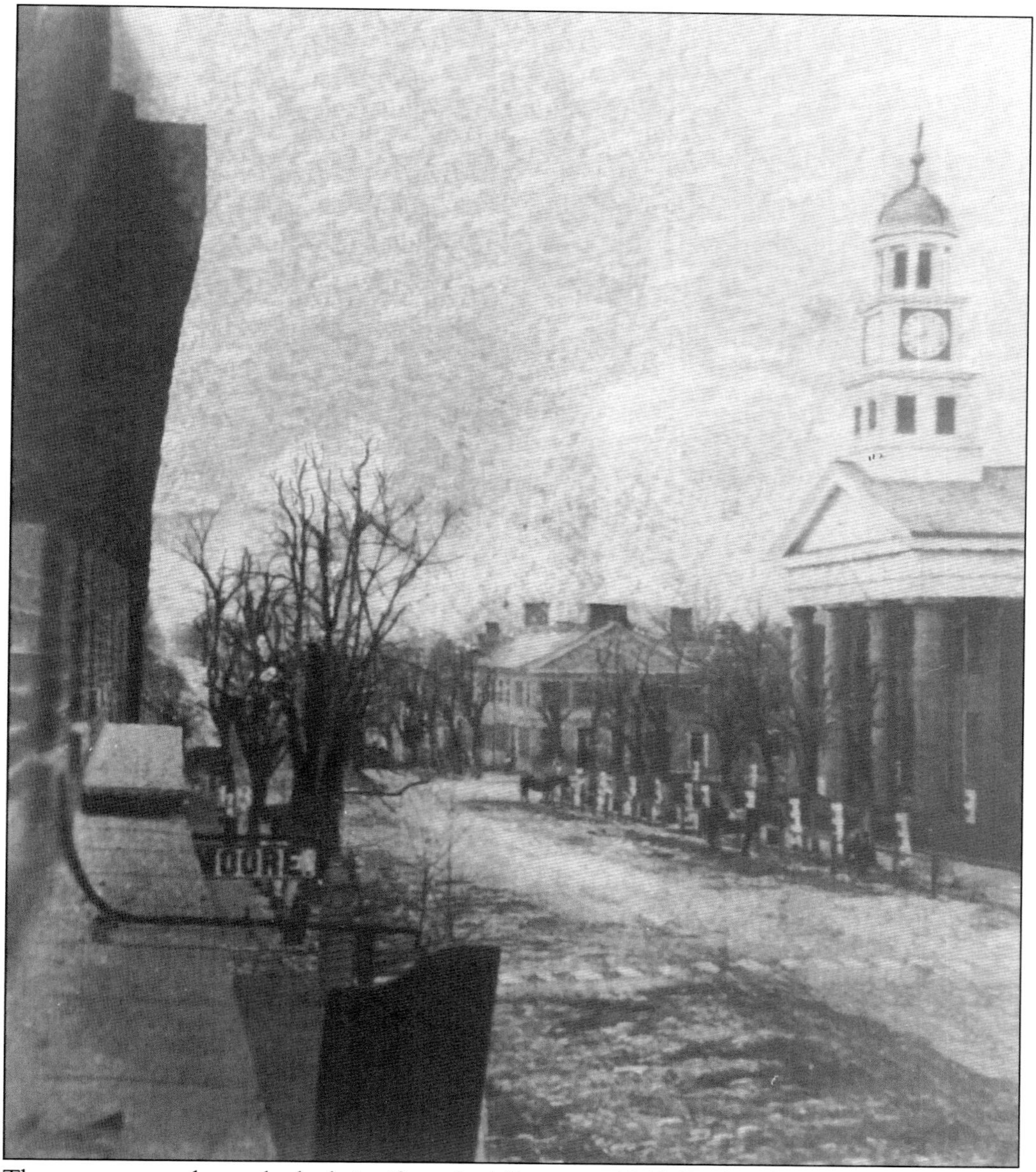

The county courthouse looked significantly different in 1846. Brick columns and a bell tower faced a deserted and muddy Main Street. Court was perhaps in session as the buggies in front of the building awaited their passengers. The building in the background is the Georgetown Hotel on the corner of Main and Broadway. It is the present site of First National Bank. The hotel burned in 1881.

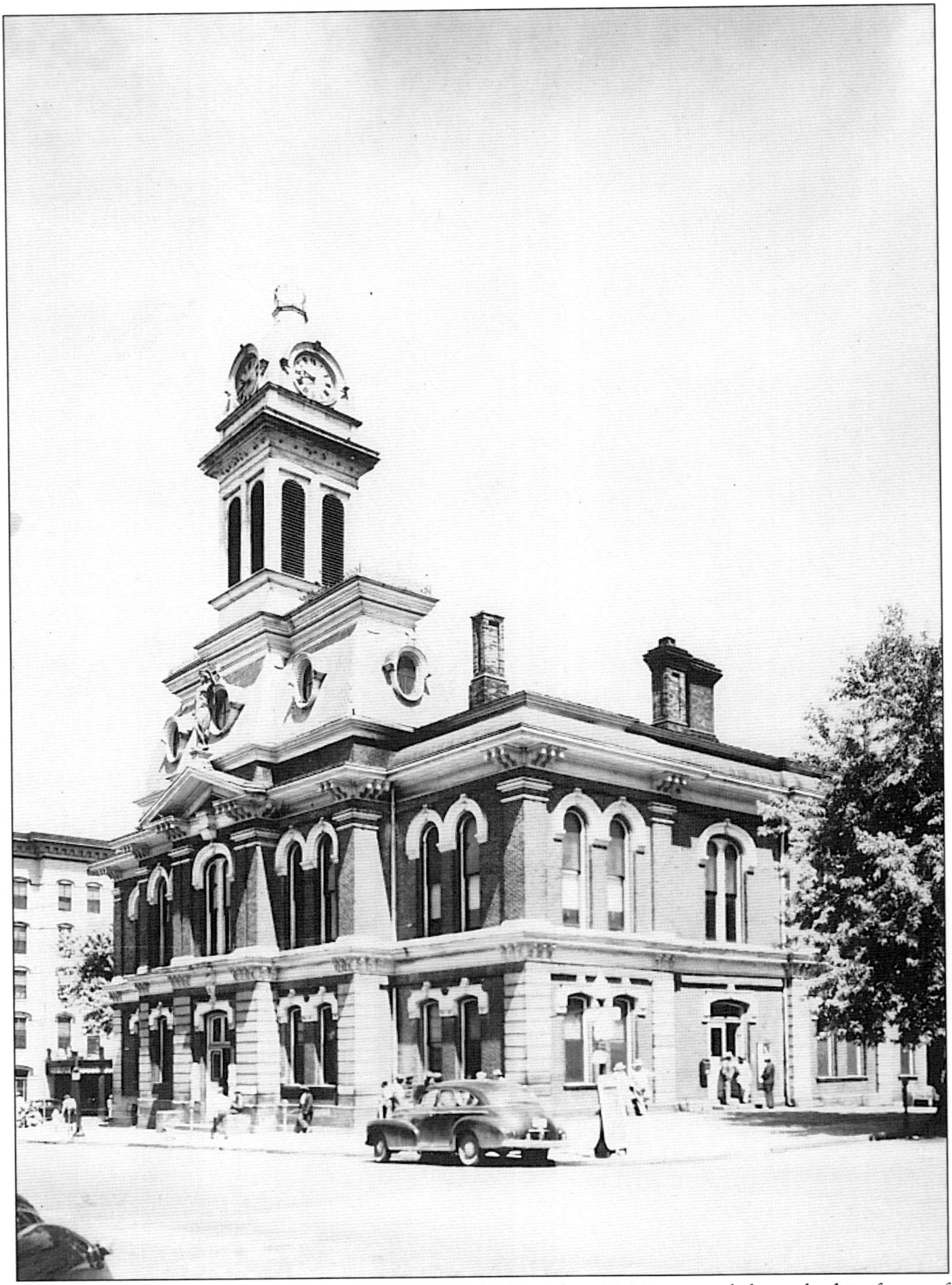

The 1877 courthouse assumes a more modern look with a 1946 automobile parked in front of it. The entrance as well as the window treatment have changed significantly. Some things, however, seem to always remain the same. Local citizens share conversation, perhaps an assessment of an upcoming election, at the courthouse doors.

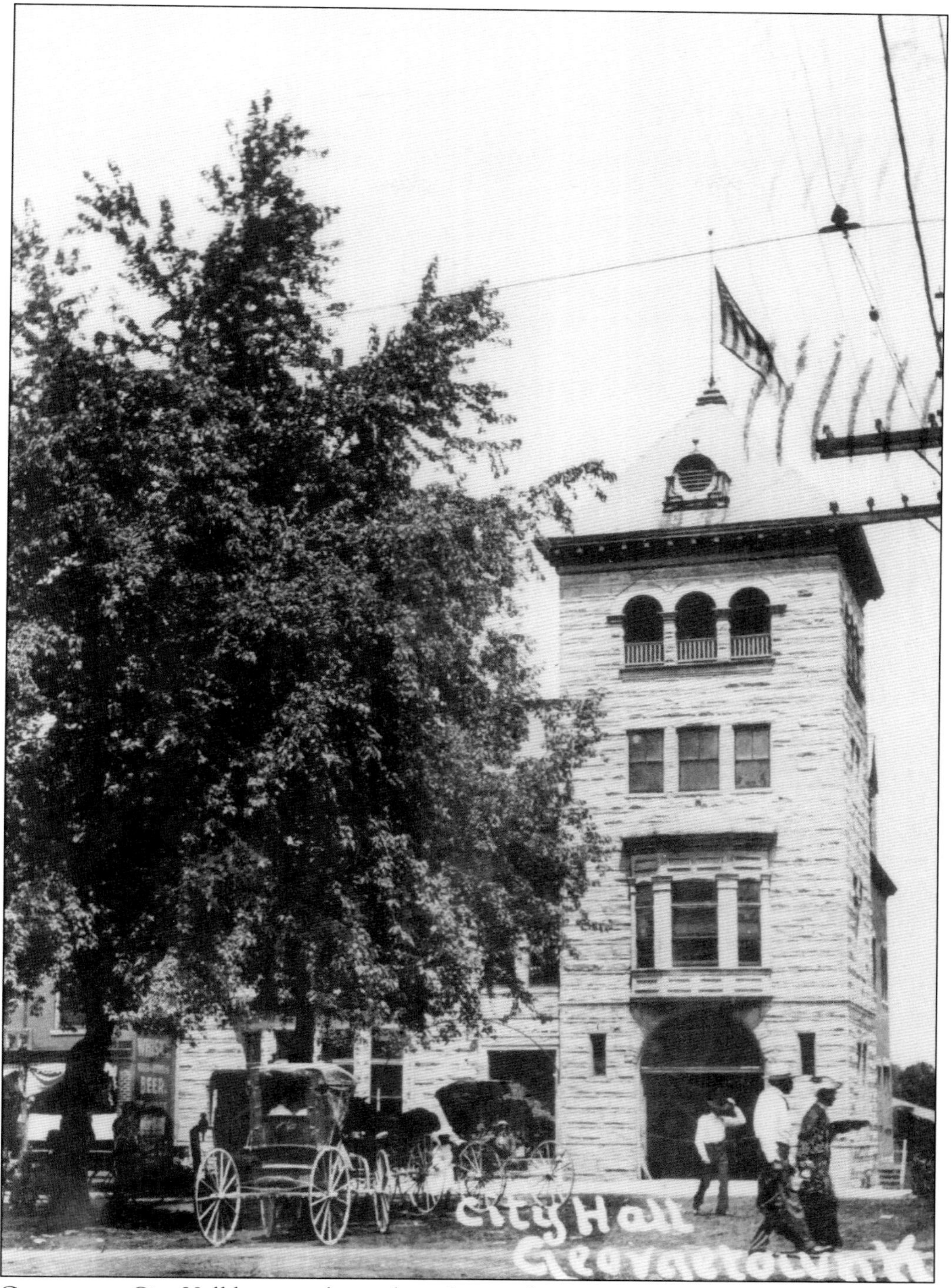

Georgetown City Hall has not changed much over the years. Citizens now park automobiles instead of carriages, and there are no trees for shade. The fire station that occupied a portion of the ground floor has also been removed, but many city services remain in the same building today.

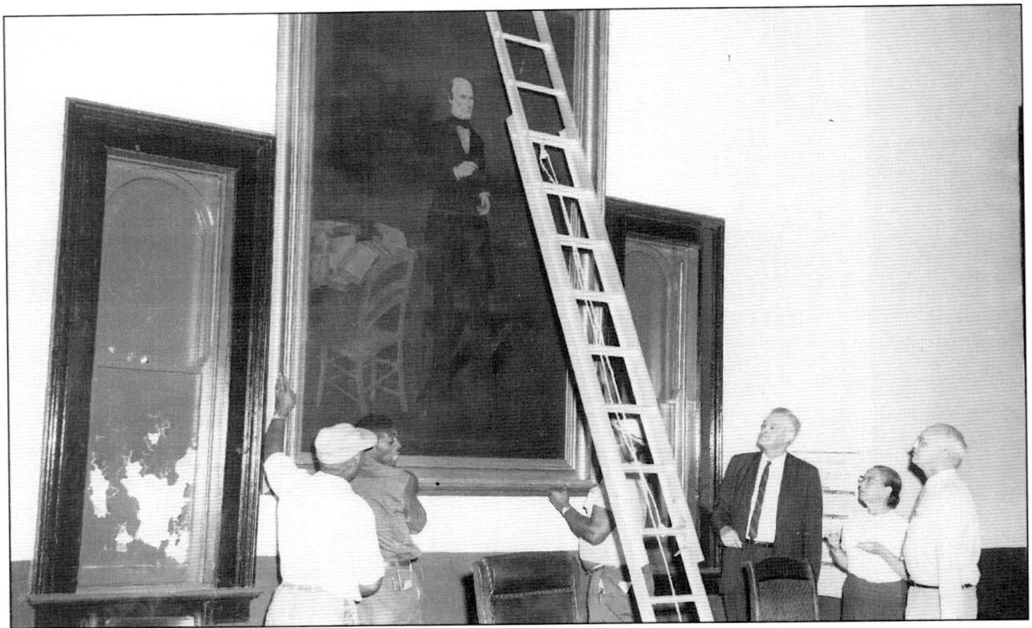

Gov. James F. Robinson gets hanged in the courthouse! Actually, it is only his portrait, but many southern sympathizers may have wanted to hang the Union governor of the state after the Civil War. One of Scott County's most prominent sons, Robinson was governor of the state in 1862–1863 and a member of the state legislature in the difficult years at the end of the Civil War. He was also a community leader and trustee of Georgetown College. Robinson and his family lived at Cardome.

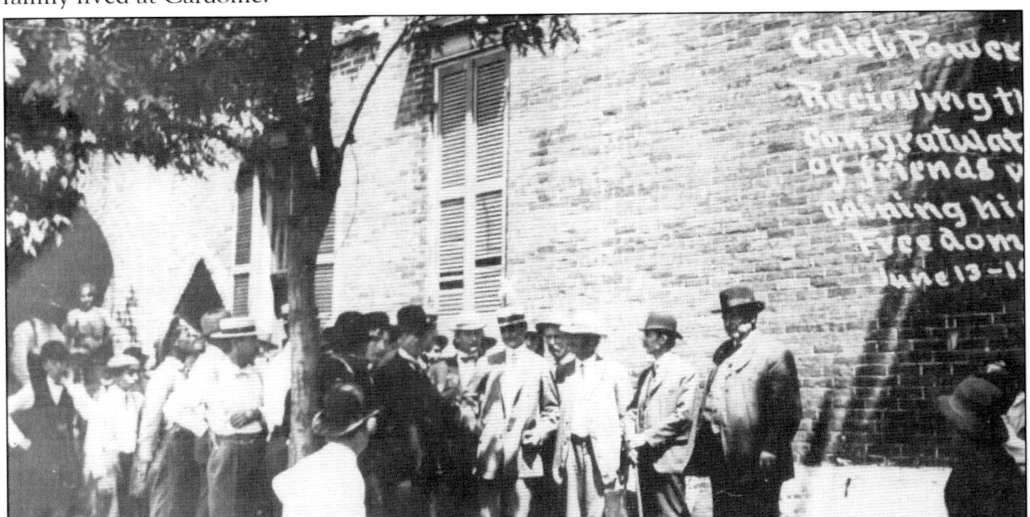

Caleb Powers receives his freedom! Accused of complicity in the murder of William Goebel, Powers was tried before Judge James Cantrill in the Scott County Courthouse. He became a very popular man, particularly among the young ladies of the county, who visited him and took him freshly baked pies during his incarceration. Convicted by Democrats, Powers was pardoned by Republican Gov. Augustus Willson. Kentucky politicians do sometimes go to war with each other.

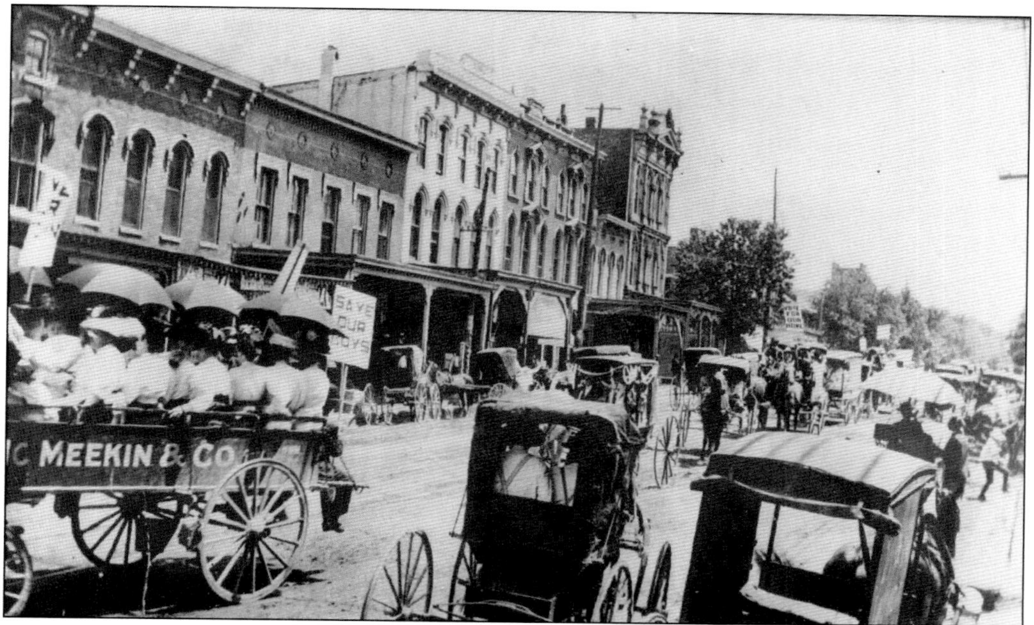

"Gonna be a hot time in the old town tonight." Or maybe not. No political issue was fought in more war-like fashion than Prohibition. A temperance parade through downtown Georgetown drums up support against "demon rum." On this issue, the women of the community, though they had no vote, were quick to express their opinion. Georgetown would be wet, dry, and wet again. WW II veterans complained that the community had a quick election to vote the town dry before they got home.

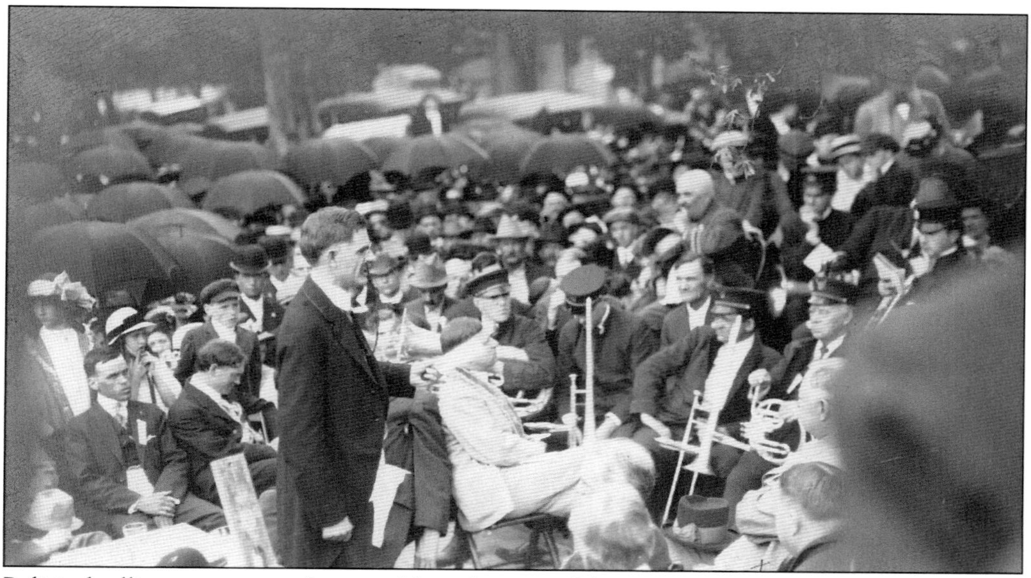

Political rallies were a part of county life at the turn of the century. Bands played and politicians gave rousing speeches. Personal attacks on opponents were as harsh then as they are in modern politics. U.S. Representative J.C. Cantrill, speaking to a Scott County rally, was a masterful campaigner and an able representative. He was a strong advocate of tobacco farmers, but suffragists considered him a bitter enemy.

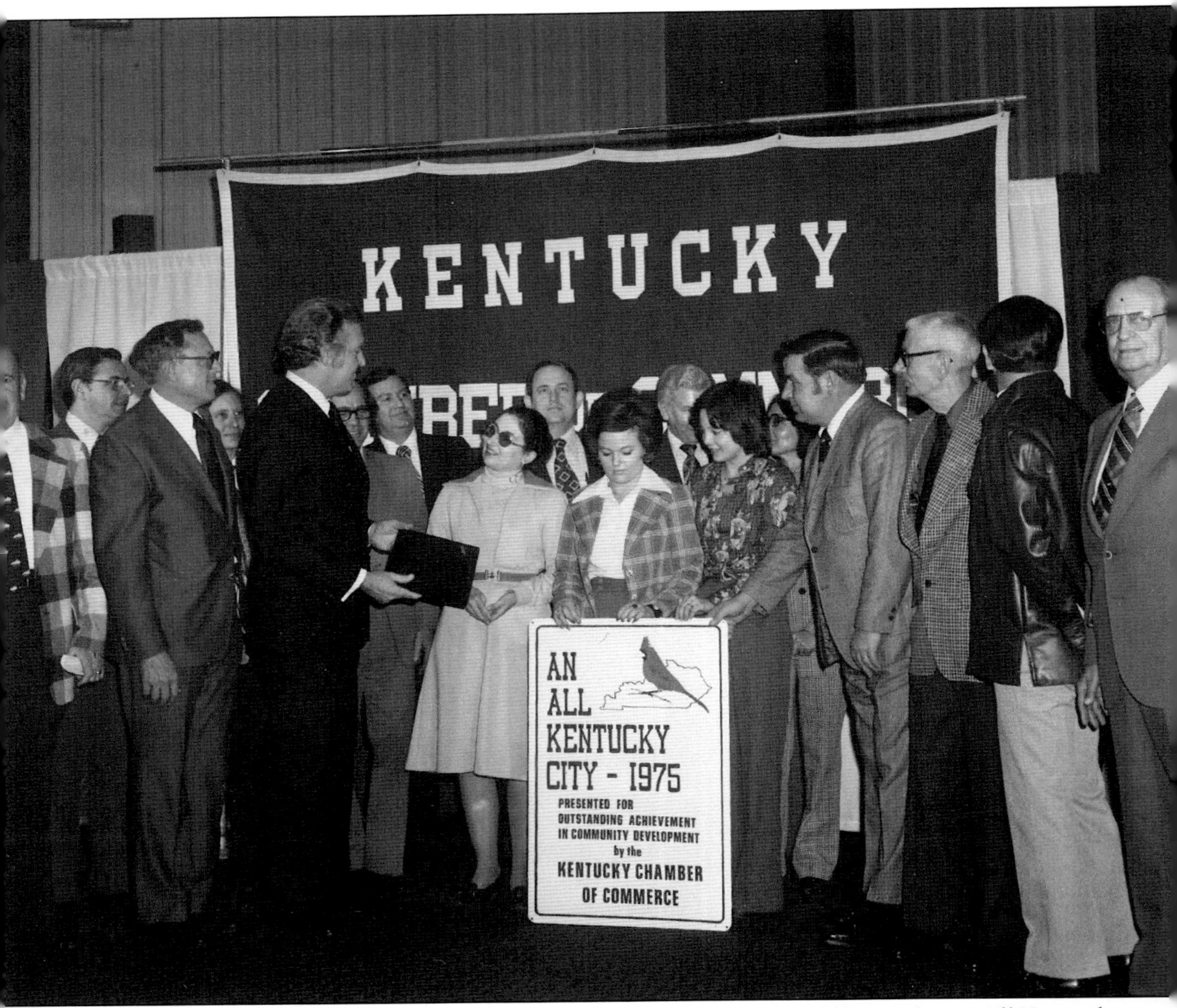

Developing strong civic pride, Georgetown citizens worked successfully to achieve All Kentucky City status in 1975. Mrs. Nancy Brown receives the certificate of commendation. Community leaders such as Warren Powers, Bob Henderson, Bob Snyder, Ralph Burrows, Bobby Vance, and Bill Henry are seen in this photograph.

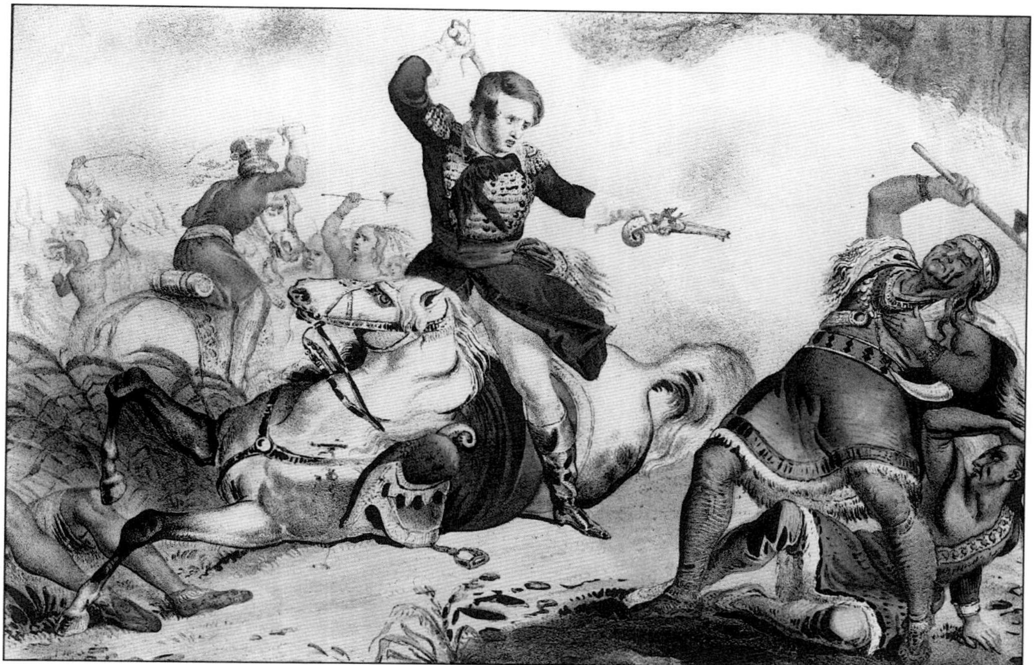

Who shot Tecumseh? Richard M. Johnson was credited by his party, the Jacksonian Democrats, with that feat and given responsibility for victory at the Battle of the Thames in the War of 1812. His political opponents denied the claim. Wounded five times in a suicide mission, Johnson rode military success to political fame as vice president under Martin Van Buren.

Three Confederate veterans, Joseph Fields, Joel Neale, and Will Henry McCabe, represent hundreds who returned from service with Confederacy or Union. Unlike Kentucky as a whole, Scott County sent more men south, but the Grand Army of the Republic and the United Confederate Veterans were active in the county until the early-20th century. In Kentucky, the Civil War was a "Brothers' War," a sad occasion when American politics turned to war.

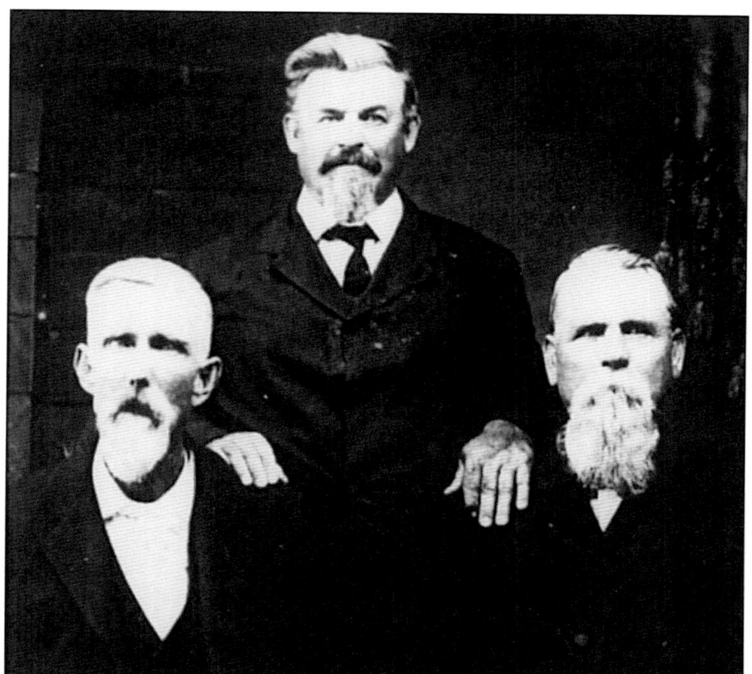

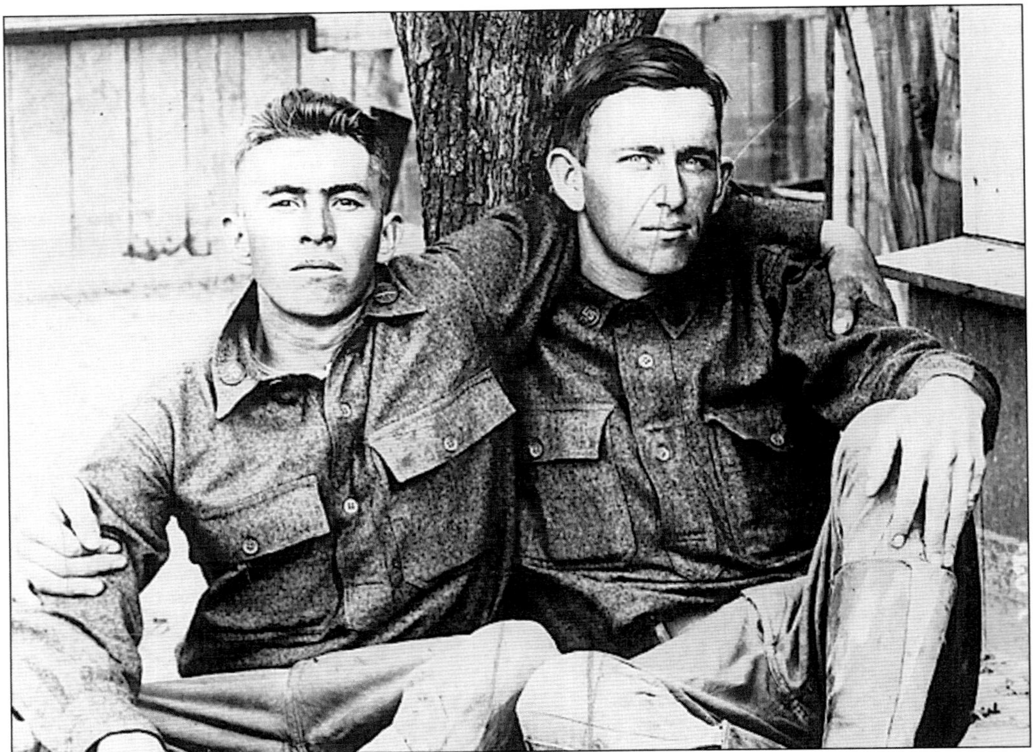

In WW I, Scott County men joined the U.S. Army to fight in Europe. The war to make the world a safe place for democracy did not achieve its goal, though the Germans were defeated. Owen Shelton, seen here with a friend, represents a number of Scott County residents who served. The names of those who did not return from the nation's wars are preserved on a monument at the county court house.

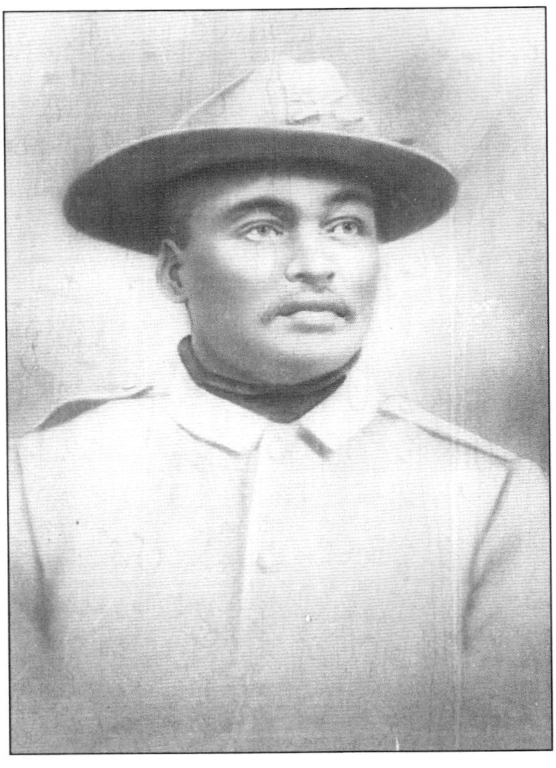

Americans of all races and creeds answered the nation's call. The face of Henry French reflects the commitment and purpose of Scott County men in uniform. French was one of the famous buffalo soldiers. A member of the Tenth Cavalry, he saw service in the Spanish American War and WW I. French is buried in New Zion.

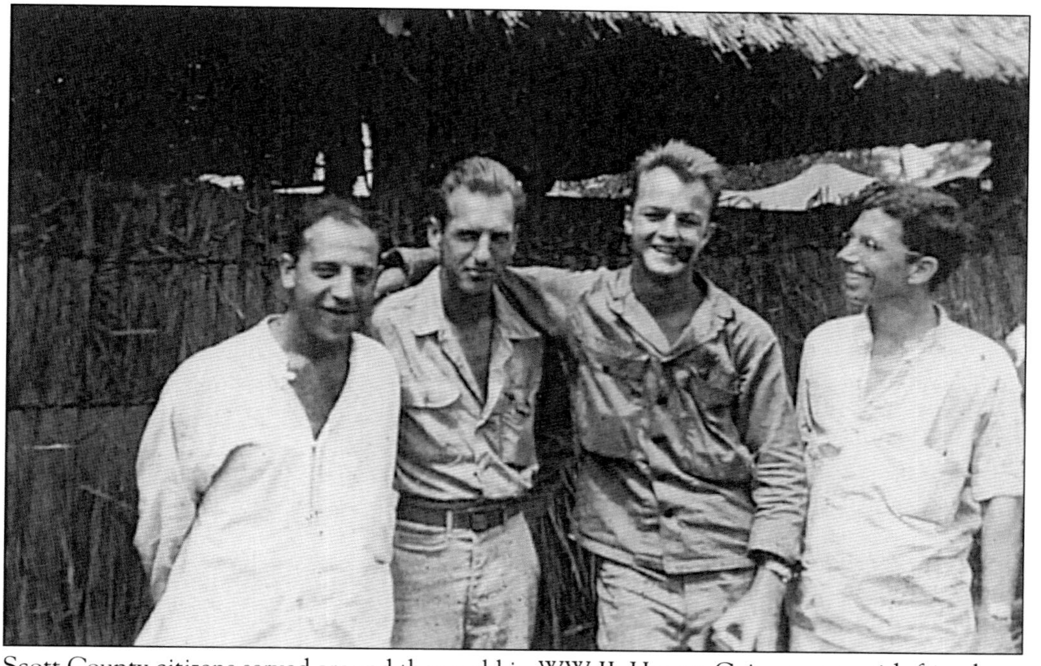

Scott County citizens served around the world in WW II. Horace Gaines poses with friends on duty in New Guinea. At the close of the war, Gaines was a part of the American forces that occupied Japan.

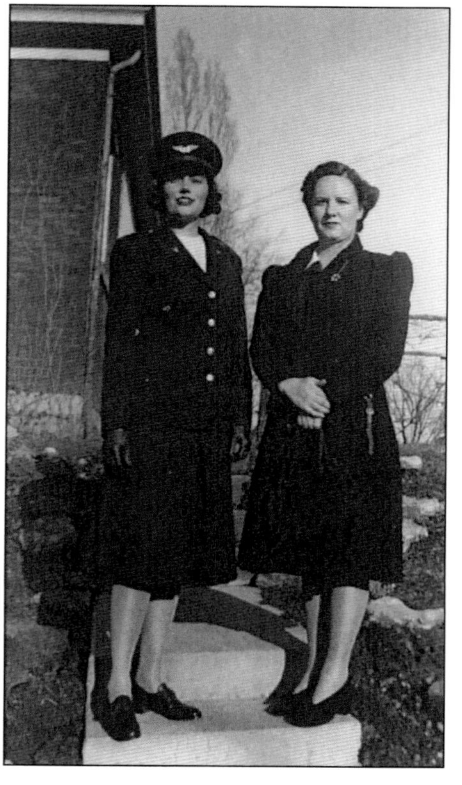

Twentieth-century wars were total wars. All citizens participated. Betsy Herndon, shown here with another WAVE, represented the efforts of women in war time. Hundreds of women joined the women's branches of the military or took jobs in factories to help the war effort. Many women found WW II to be a liberating experience. Great changes would come in the role of women as a result of their sacrifices during the war.

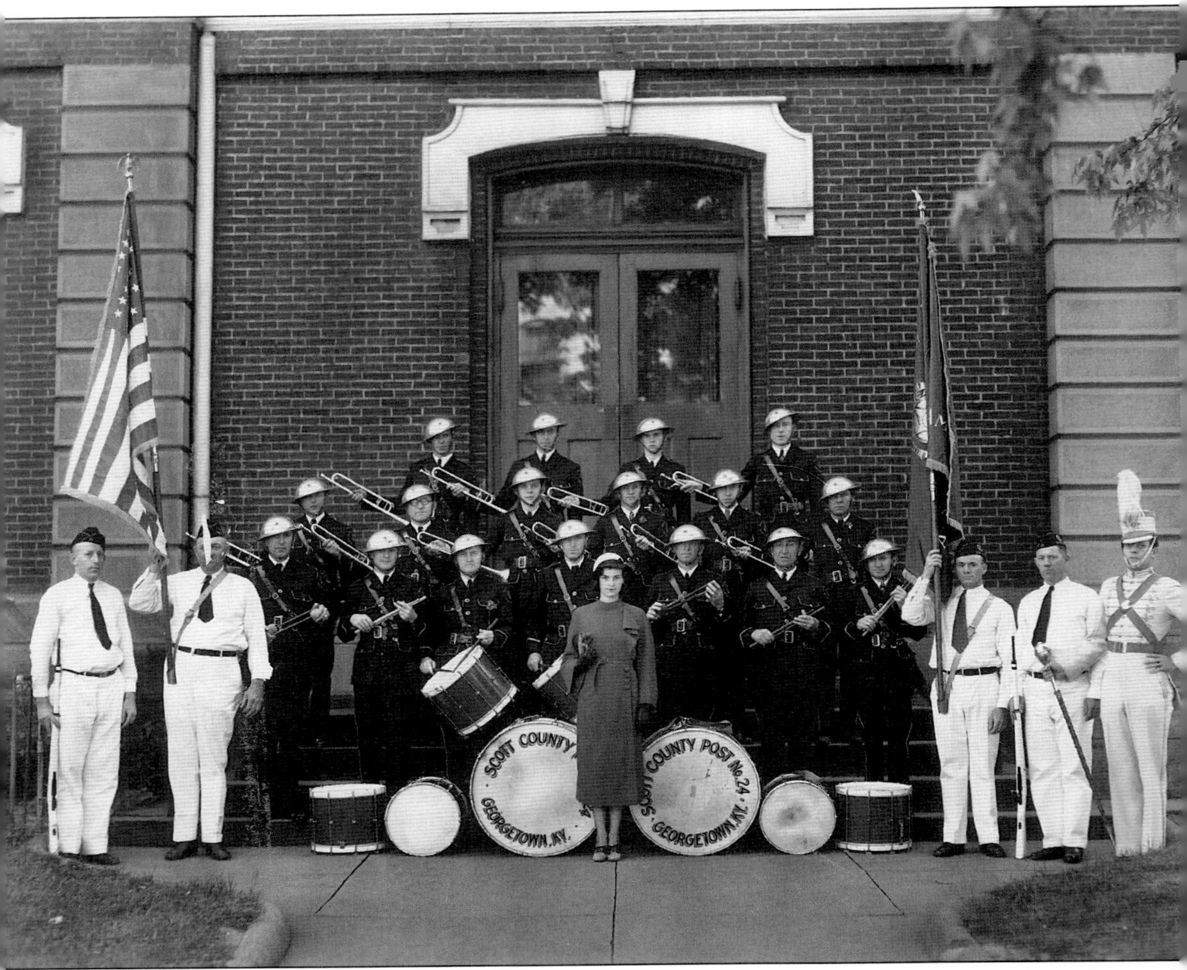

Three Cheers for the Red, White, and Blue! Scott County Post No. 24 shows the colors. Despite wars within and without, the freedoms of Americans to express their views, worship as they see fit, and participate in governmental decision making remain the cherished hallmarks of a vibrant society. Politics in Kentucky may indeed be the damnedest, but our heritage is a proud one.

Seven
School Activities

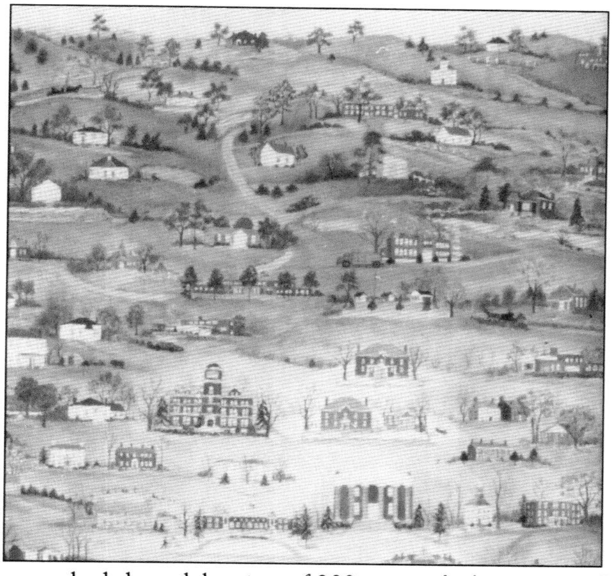

In 1987, Edith Clifton marked the celebration of 200 years of education in Scott County with a painting of historic school buildings. Scott County residents have always sought to provide schools for their children. The Rittenhouse Academy existed in pioneer days, and other private academies and individual instructors advertised for students. The Choctaw Academy was particularly unusual for its time and place. When most Americans were forcing Native Americans into the far west, Richard M. Johnson created a school to educate Native-American youths. The Reverend Thomas Henderson also trained others at the Academy. Some local white youths, some of Johnson's slaves, and his two mulatto daughters were educated by Henderson at the school, making the institution most unusual for its time.

Public education grew slowly in an agrarian region where labor was considered more important than education. African-American education, separate and unequal, depended on the dedication of families, students, and teachers because adequate funding was more dream than reality. Integrated education came when six school children from New Zion filed suit in 1956. Consolidation also proved important to educational opportunity.

Georgetown College has anchored higher education in the county. Created by the community and Kentucky Baptists, the college has provided the opportunity for higher education close to home and cultural opportunities missing from many small towns.

As the 20th century draws to a close, the educational institutions of the county appear more secure than at any time in the county's history.

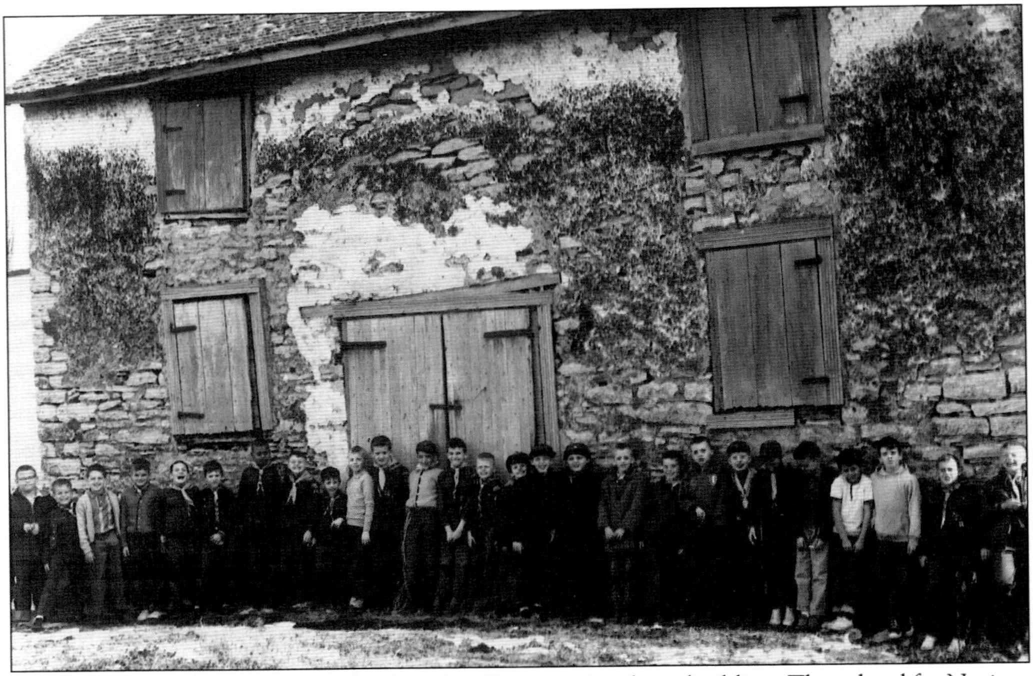

A group of school children stand before the Choctaw Academy building. The school for Native-American youths operated intermittently from 1819 to 1842. In 1835, enrollment reached a high of 188 students but it declined thereafter, due to the creation of mission schools in the Oklahoma Territory. Richard M. Johnson, its guiding spirit, helped found the school that became George Washington University. He urged the creation of military academies across the nation and served for many years as a trustee of Georgetown College.

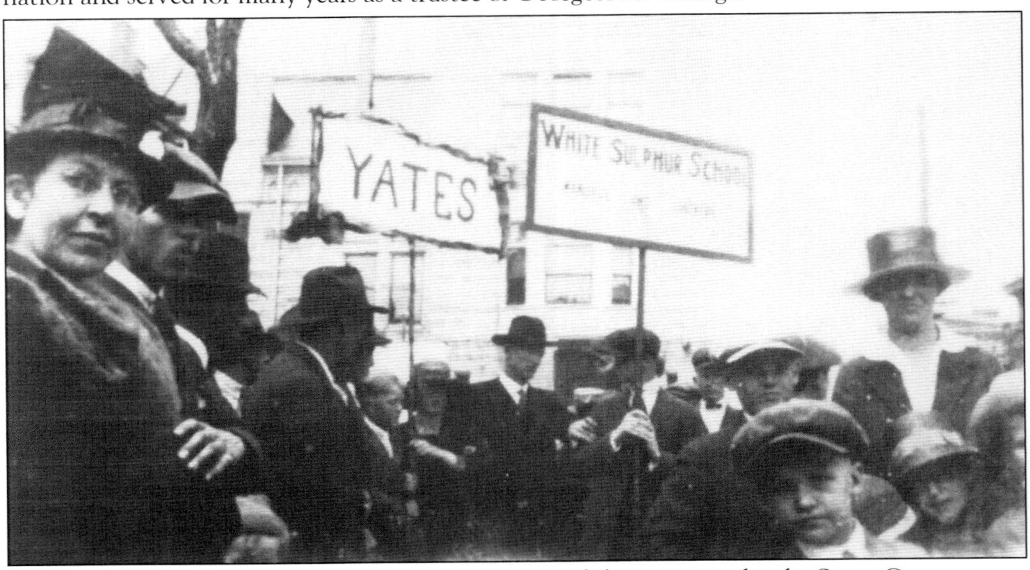

Pictured is a rally near the court house in support of the county schools. Scott County men, women, and children seek improvements for education. The women, led by Mrs. Anna Payne Coffman, played a central role in improving county schools in the Progressive Era, near the turn of the century.

Mary Elizabeth Bradley served as superintendent of Scott County schools from 1913 to 1923. She demanded patriotic teaching during WW I, opposed school consolidation, and promoted health programs in the county schools. She represents the political leadership of women even before they received the vote.

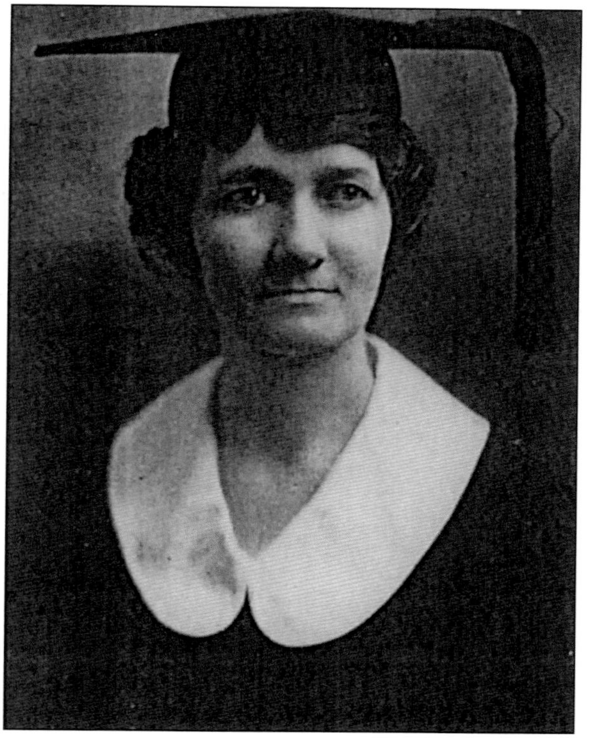

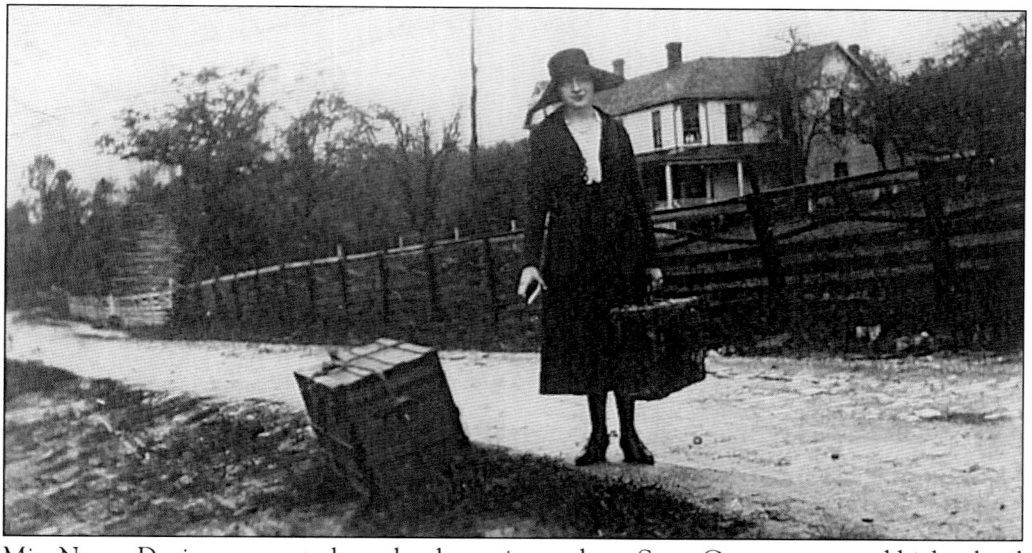

Miss Nancy Davis prepares to leave her home in northern Scott County to attend high school in Berea. In order to acquire an education, young women and their families had to make significant sacrifices. Miss Davis went to Berea in 1919.

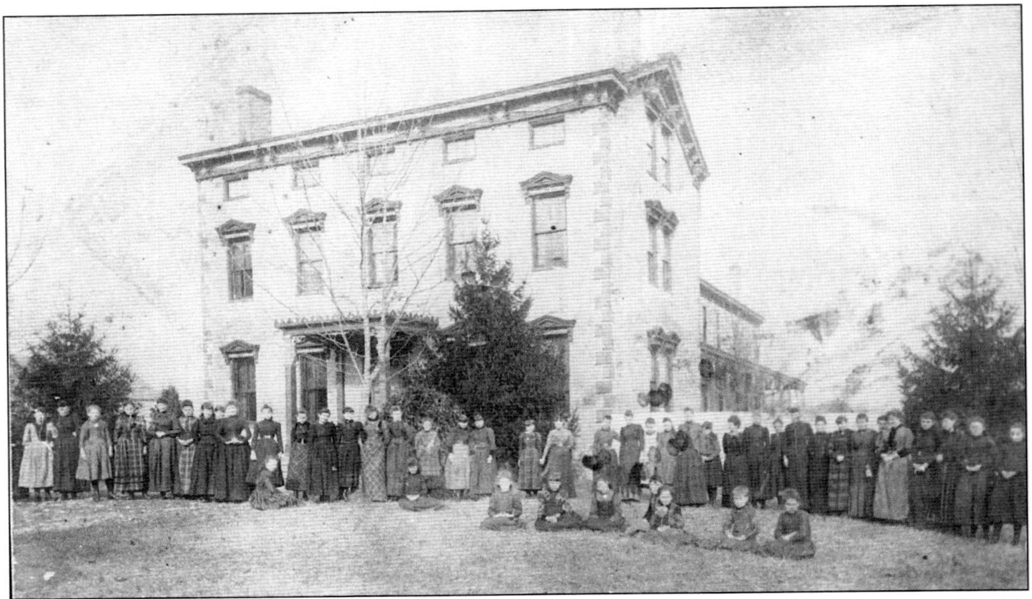

Mt. Admirabilis, a Catholic school for women, was established in 1875 by the Maysville Convent of the Sisters of the Visitation of Holy Mary. It operated at the former seminary at White Sulphur until 1896, when the nuns moved to Cardome.

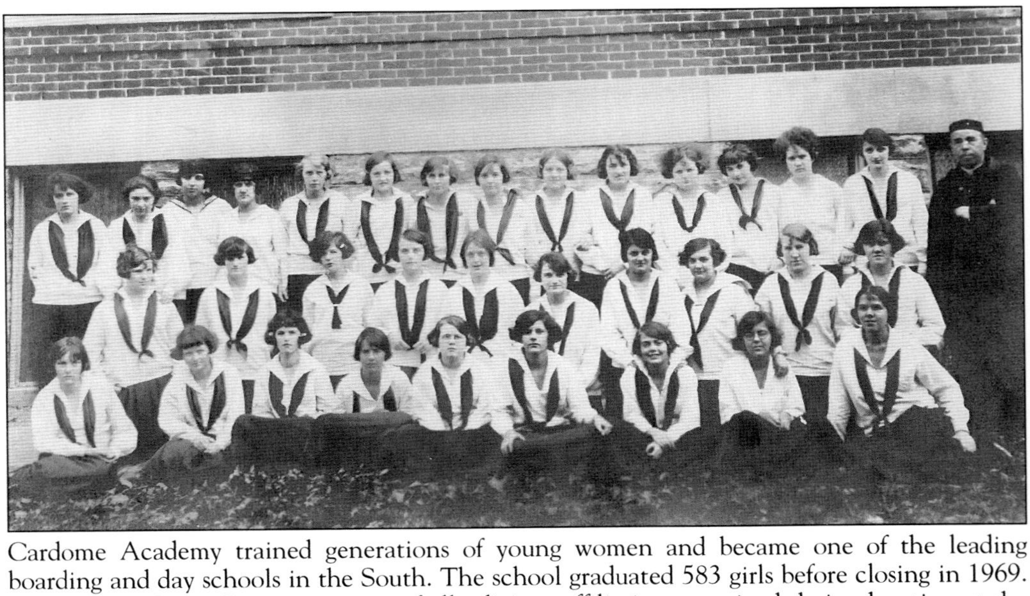

Cardome Academy trained generations of young women and became one of the leading boarding and day schools in the South. The school graduated 583 girls before closing in 1969. Many young Scott County women, of all religious affiliations, received their education at the private school.

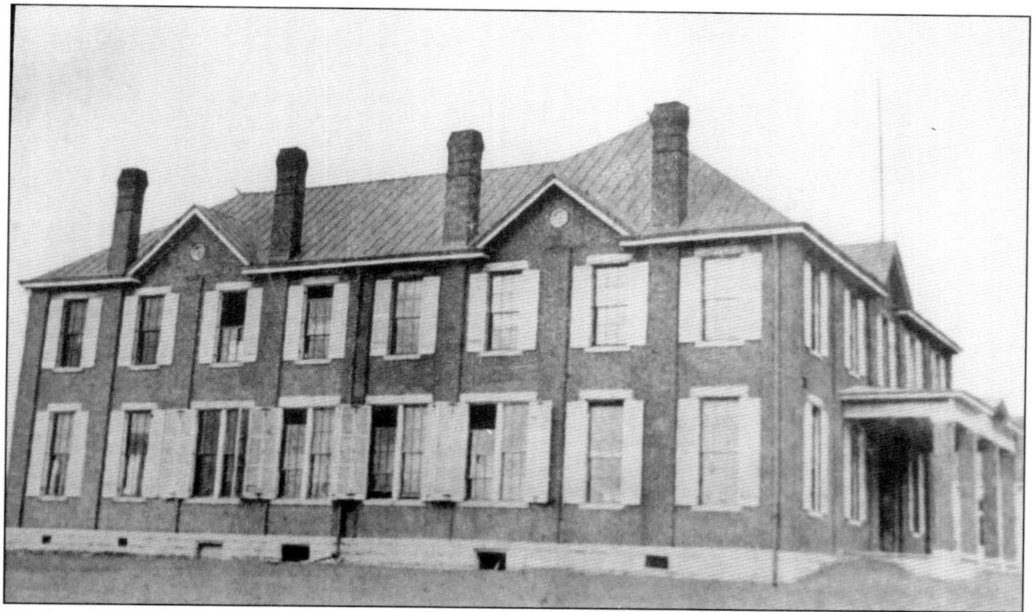

Under the leadership of its principal, Ed Davis, Chambers Avenue School became one of only 19 accredited black high schools in the state in 1924. Its faculty were leaders in the Black community. The school became a symbol of African-American identity and pride in a segregated community. The school was later named in honor of Ed Davis.

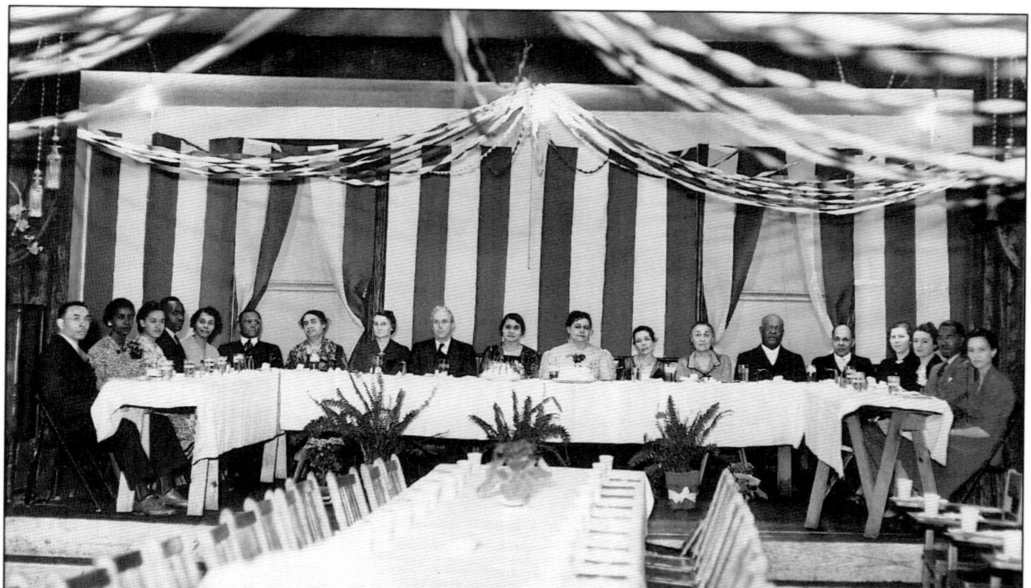

The faculty at Ed Davis High School awaits the students in a banquet setting. Faculty members included B.G. Patterson, Fannie Spotts, Sallie Tilford, John H. Clayborn, Mrs. J.P. Wilson, Mrs. Ed Davis, Katie C. Jones, Katy White, and Ida Embry. Several local ministers and their wives attended the banquet as well.

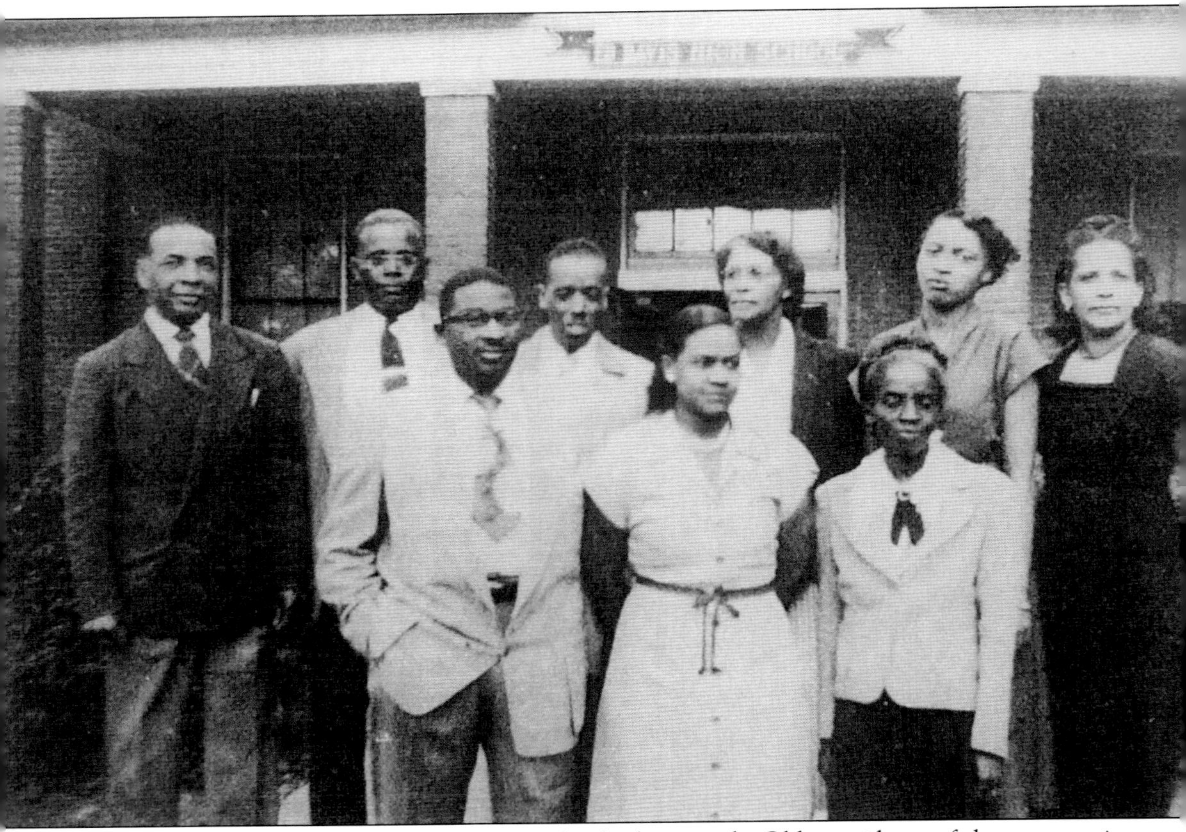

Ed Davis faculty members pose for a yearbook photograph. Older residents of the community remember the teachers as strict disciplinarians who expected their students to be prepared. They command a high degree of respect from those who sat in their classes.

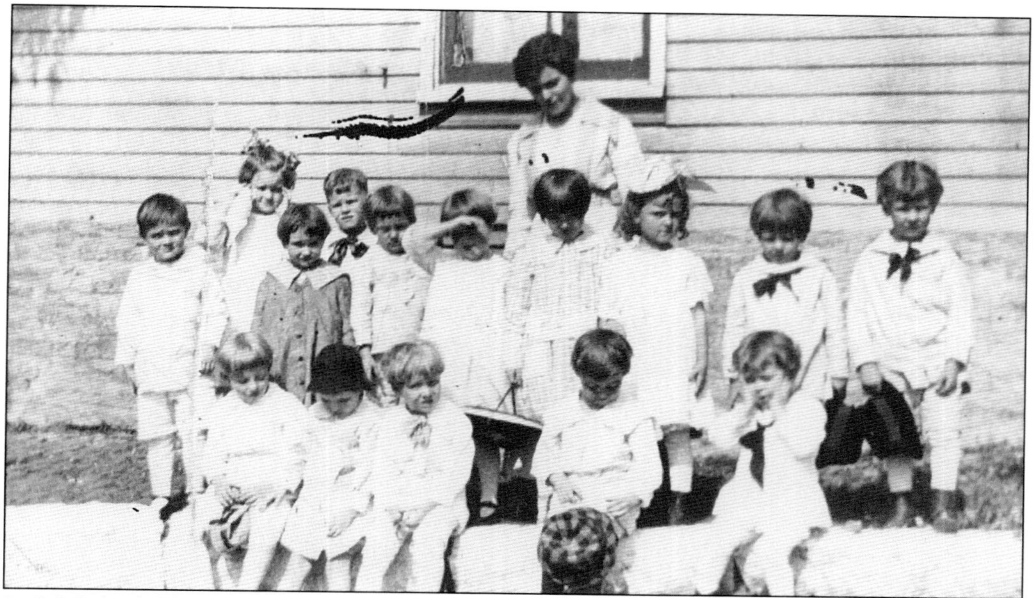

It didn't look like much but it was where the white children of Georgetown attended school. These students, photographed *c.* 1918, pose in front of the old city school on the corner of Washington and Mulberry Streets. Vic Bradley is pictured on the front row and Emily Askew (Rawdon) is in the second row.

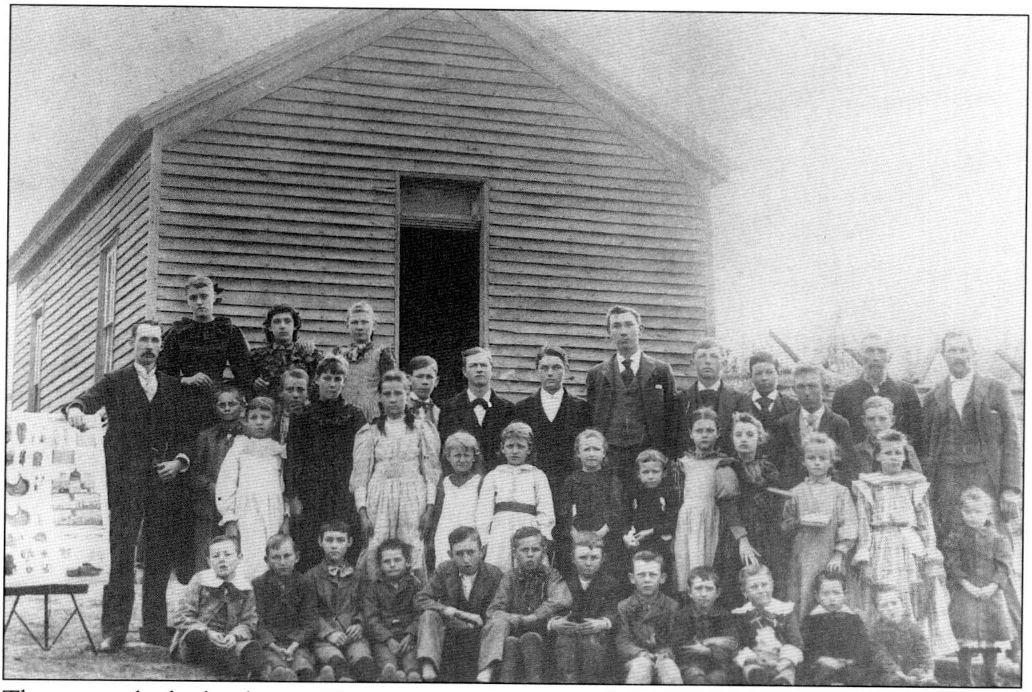

The county had schools, too. Transportation was more difficult in the county than in the city, but dedicated parents dreamed of obtaining an education for their children and were willing to sacrifice to achieve the dream. Students and teachers pose in front of the old Salem School on Burton Road.

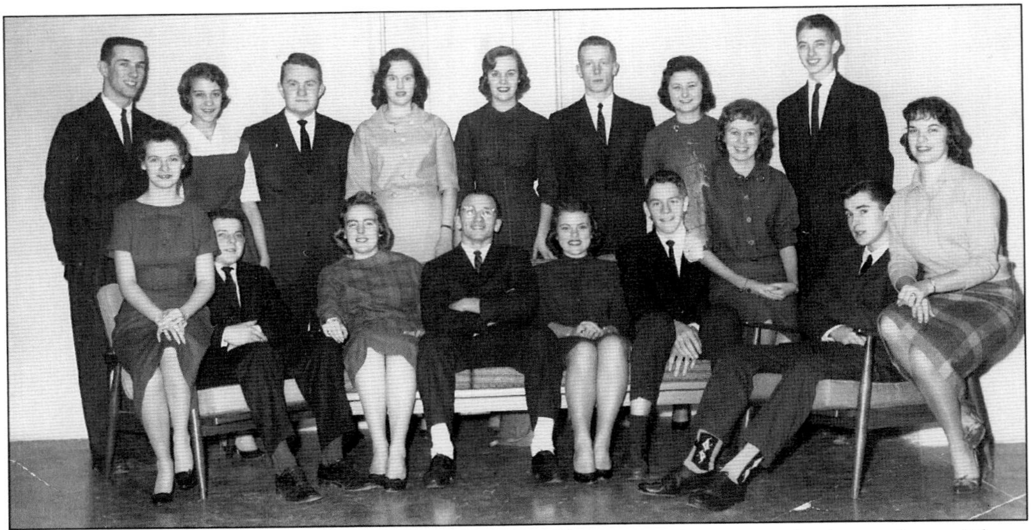

The school system sought to provide many types of learning experiences for its students. These students were cast members in the annual school play at the high school in 1960. Some of the budding actors and actresses continue to perform as local businessmen and women and as citizens of the community.

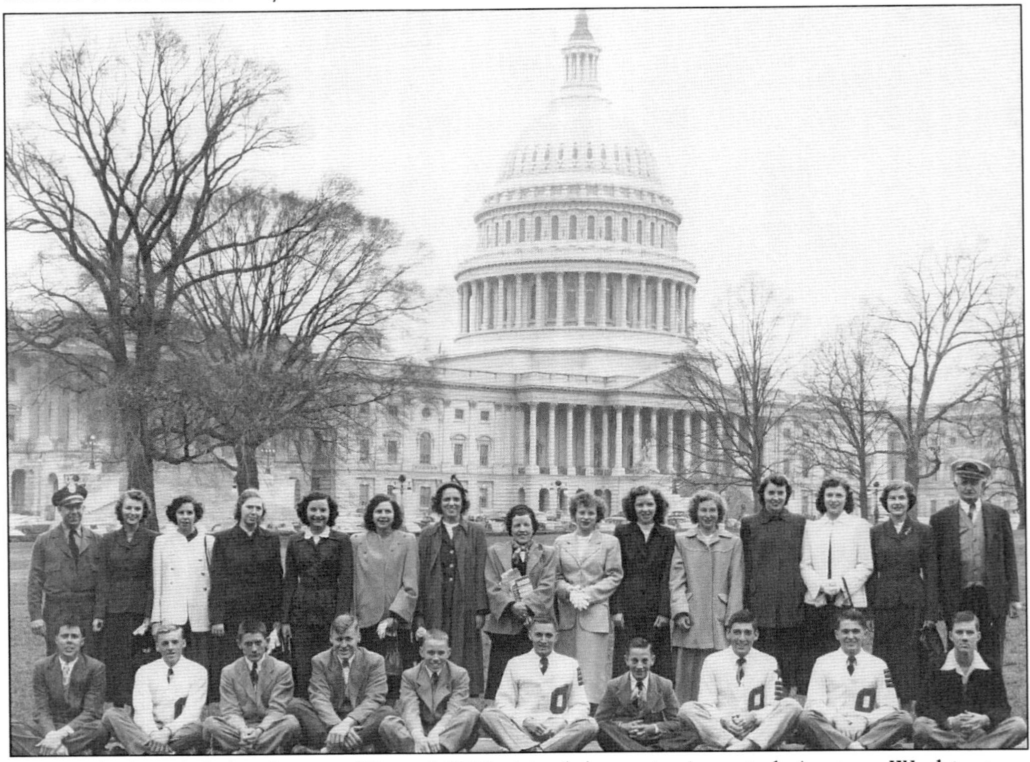

The Oxford High School senior Class of 1950 visited the nation's capital. A trip to Washington, D.C. was a traditional year-ending and career-ending capstone for many high school seniors across Kentucky and the nation. In this case, a few underclassmen were allowed to go along to fill up the bus. The trip was led by Miss Willye Amerson.

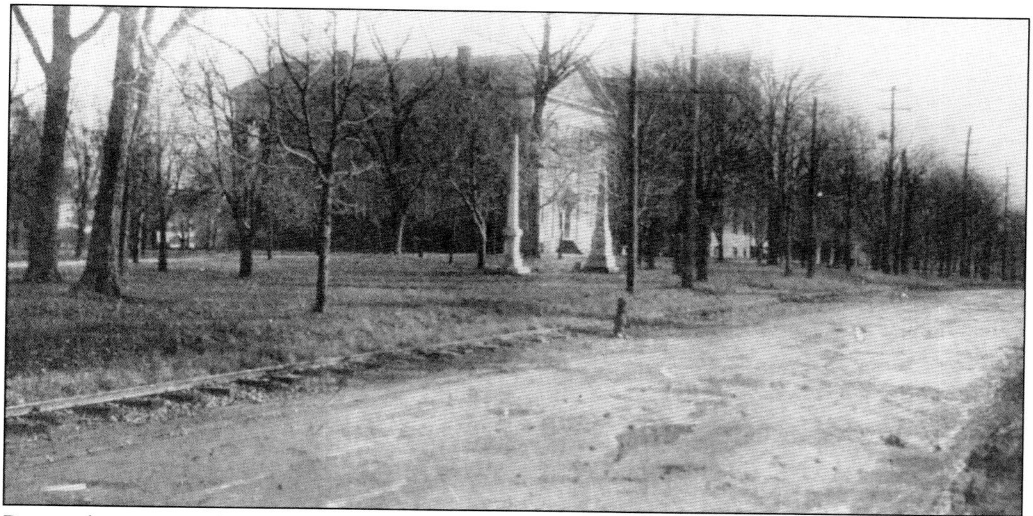

Pictured is a view of Giddings Hall at Georgetown College when Jackson Street was more mud than asphalt. Along the edge of the street are the tracks of the Georgetown Street Railway loop. In later years, it was used to carry ice from the ice plant to the railroad depot. The chapel/library/gymnasium east of Giddings burned in 1930.

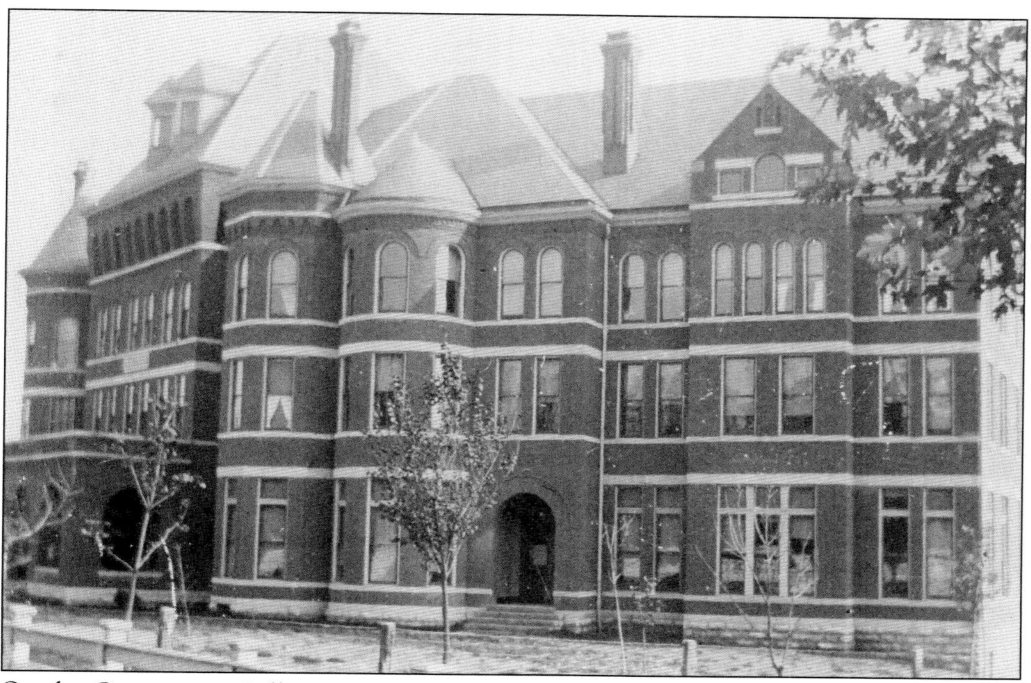

On the Georgetown College campus, Rucker Hall, named for Professor J.J. Rucker, housed many generations of young women. The imposing old structure was also the source of many a story passed to each new entering class. Old Rucker was demolished in 1971 in order to build the Robert L. Mills Residence Park.

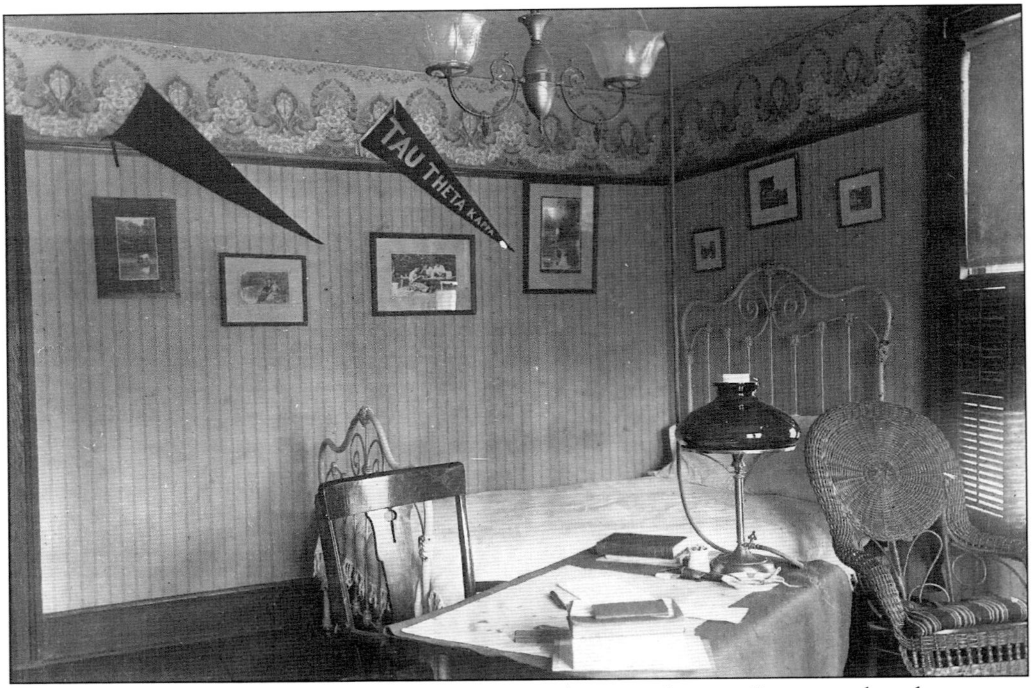

This is a view of a modern dormitory room (*c.* 1910). House "parents" inspected student rooms each day to make sure beds were made and floors were swept. The cleanliness of this room was probably the rule in 1910 rather than the exception.

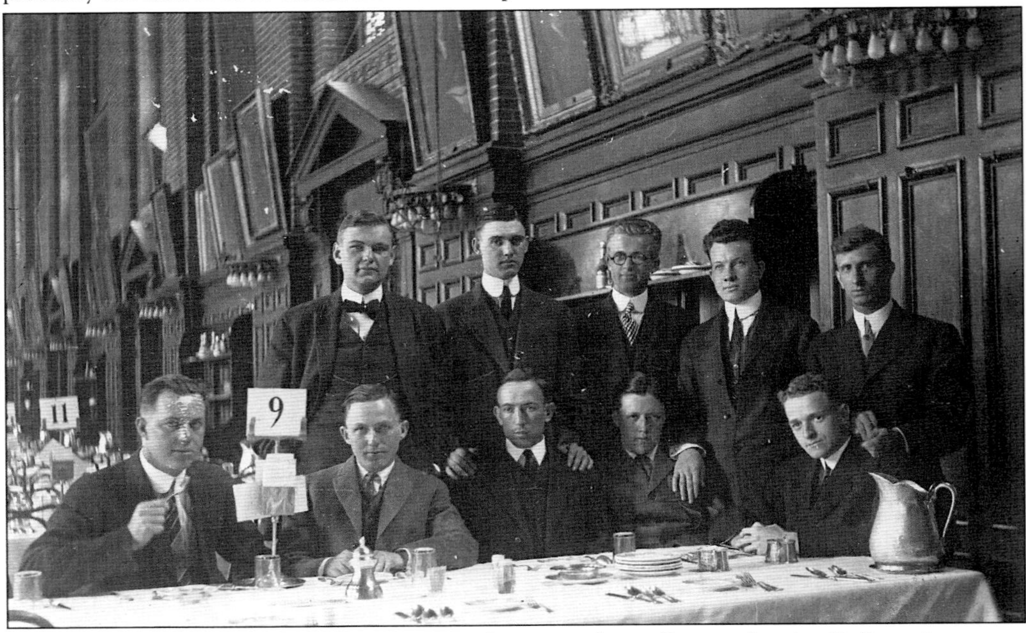

Male students came to dinner in coats and ties in the college cafeteria. Believe it or not, meal time was still an opportunity to socialize with old friends or to make new ones. The dining rooms were located in the chapel/library/gymnasium, which was literally the center of campus activities.

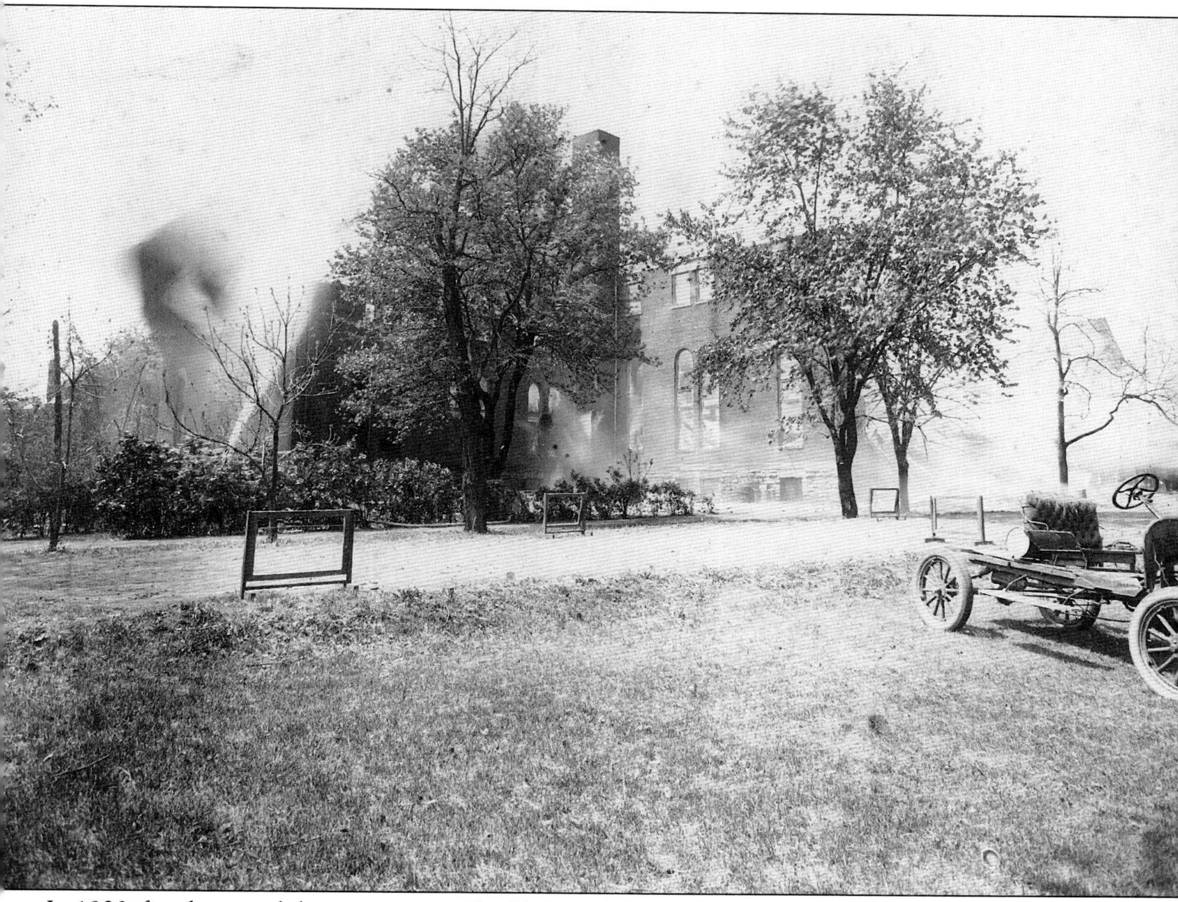

In 1930, fire destroyed the main campus building. A fine classical library was one of the treasures consumed by the blaze. The loss was a bad omen of the Depression years ahead.

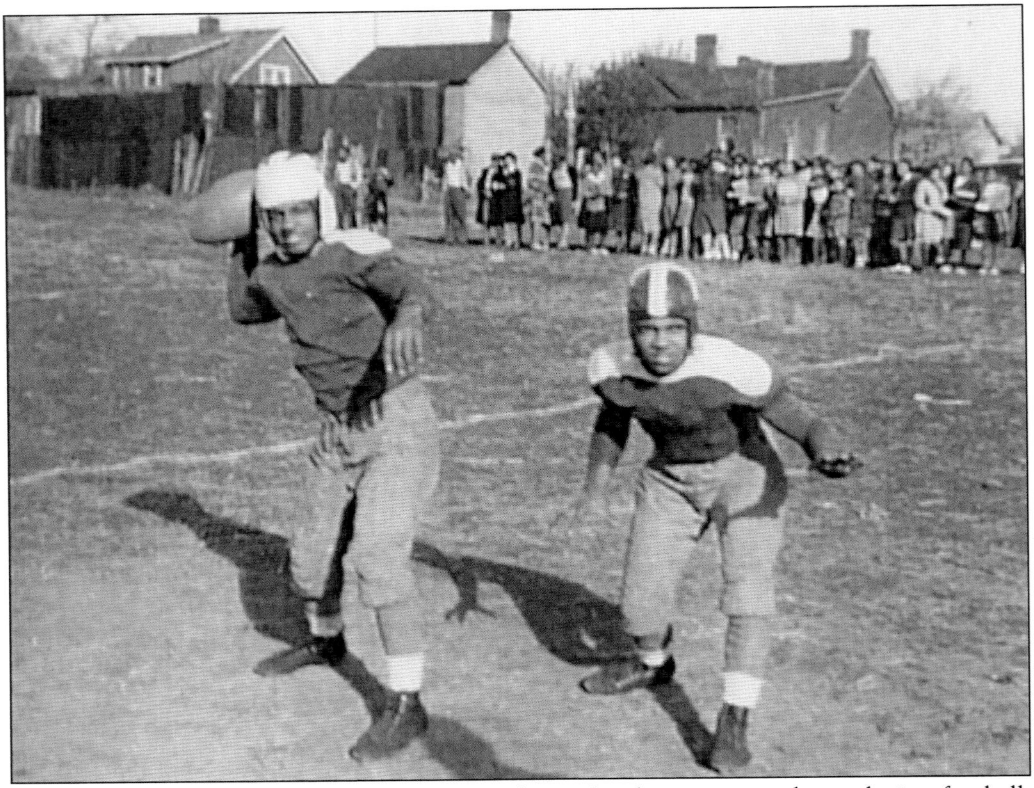

Where would we be without sports? The Dishman brothers are seen here playing football. Oscar Dishman Jr. would go on to excel in another sport. Horses trained by Dishman won the Hawthorne, Ohio, and American derbies in the 1970s.

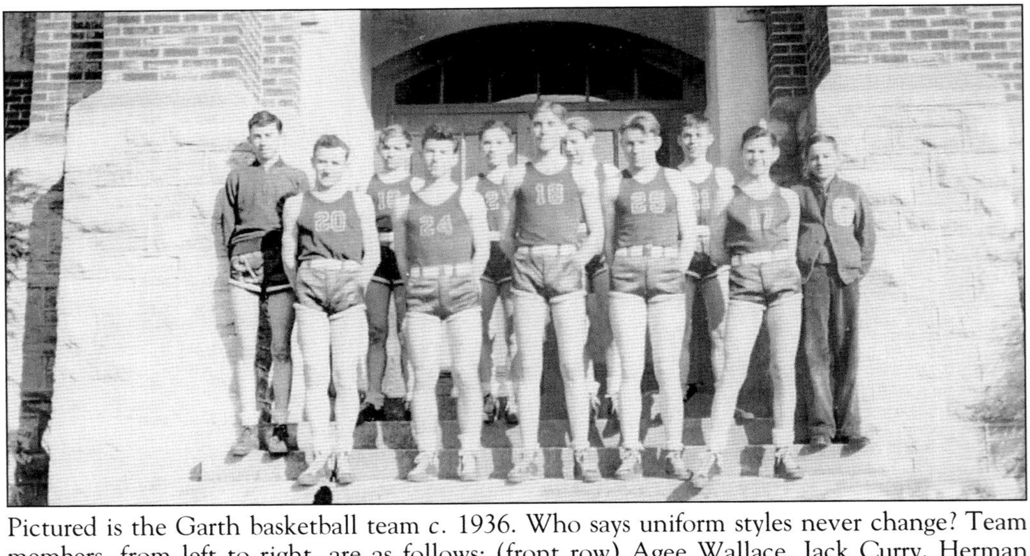

Pictured is the Garth basketball team *c.* 1936. Who says uniform styles never change? Team members, from left to right, are as follows: (front row) Agee Wallace, Jack Curry, Herman Glass, Junior Hostetter, and Witt Honaker; (second row) Holly Covington, Millard Hambrick, Harold Davidson, Jack Osborne, Elwood Cortez, and Tom Porter.

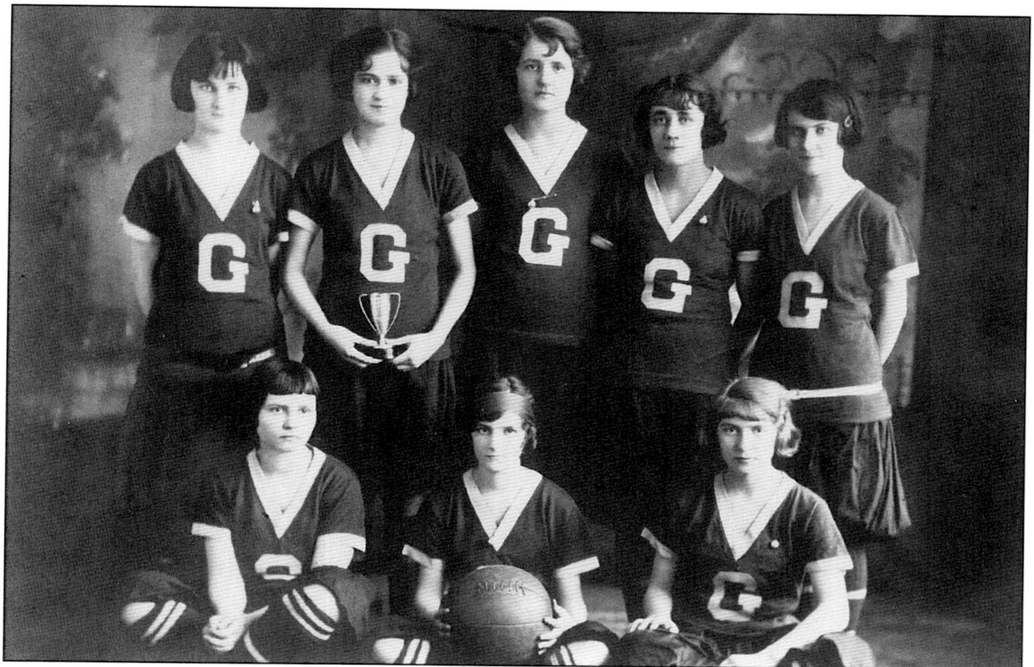

The Georgetown girls' basketball team was known as the "wonder team." They won the state championship in 1925. Some of the members, from left to right, are as follows: (front row) Elizabeth Cook, Frances Ware, Ruby Stigers; (second row) Lillie Biddle, Beulah Wallace, Elizabeth Sharp, Margaret Sabel, and Nettie Biddle. In 1929, the school board decided women's basketball was "too strenuous" and abolished the sport.

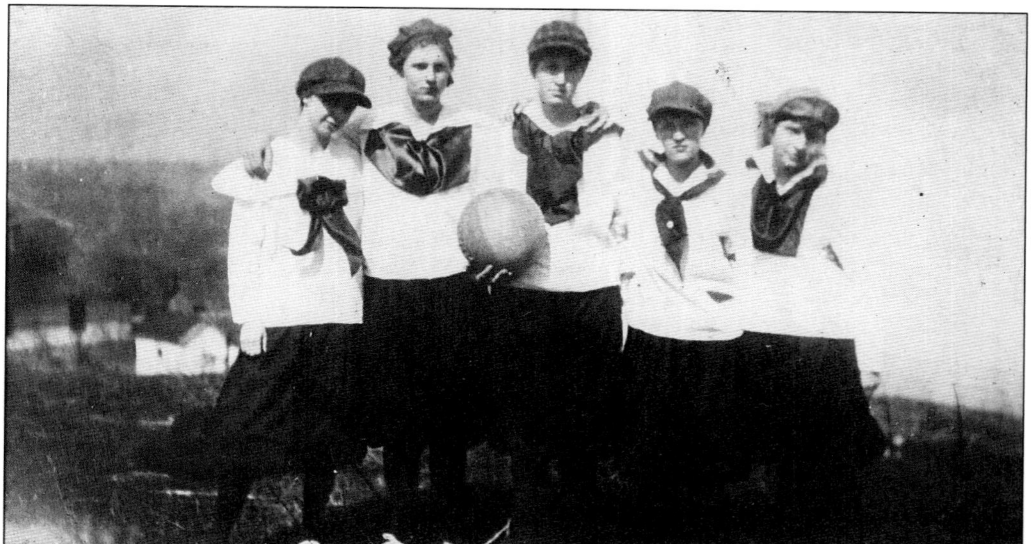

Five iron women! Pictured is the Sadieville girls' basketball team of 1918. When one of the five was sick or got into foul trouble, they borrowed a player from the opposing team. Whatever happened to sportsmanship? Team members, from left to right, are as follows: Hazel Sherritt, Nell Marshall, Sarah Penn, Ophelia Faulconer, and Nancy Davis. Allie Shelton coached the team that played on an outdoor court near the old frame school building.

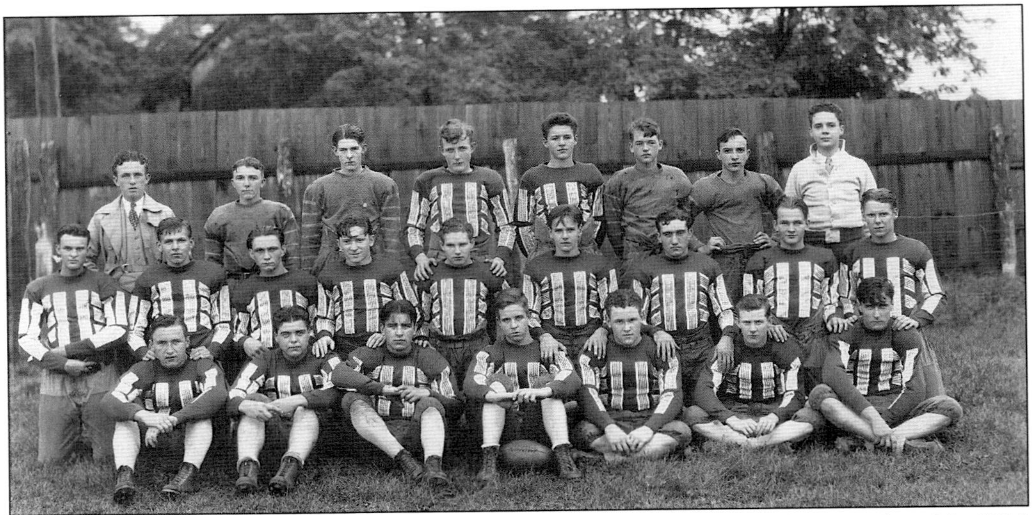

Pictured is the Garth football team in 1929. The *Courier Journal* of September 22, 1929 headlined the article accompanying this photograph "This Husky Bunch to Play Male Friday." Team members, from left to right, are as follows: (first row) Russell Alsop, Dakery Abbott, William Balof, Syd Hawkins, Brute Amerson, John Ireland, and Turk Hughes; (second row) Richard Scudder, Jake Finley, Bill Collins, Monk Cummins, Sharon Williams, Lewis Finley, Abe Shannon, Ralph Wesley, and James Ewing; (third row)Victor Bradley (manager), William Pugh, Chuck Woodruff, John Magoffin, Lewis Robinson, Ed Robinson, Carl Marshall, and Harold Stockdell.

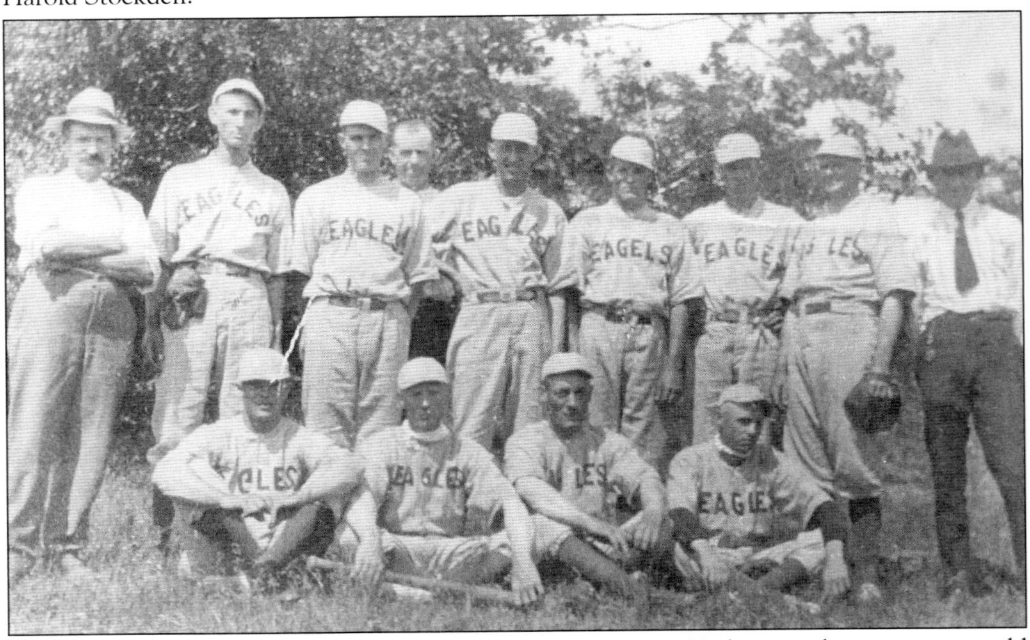

The Sadieville Eagles baseball team poses for the camera. Unfortunately, someone could not spell! Hometown teams were extremely popular in the early part of the century. Their popularity declined as radio then television and interstate highways brought big league teams closer to home. Among the Eagle players are Edgar Marshall, J.K. Marshall, Bailey Rose, and Charlie Holdcraft.

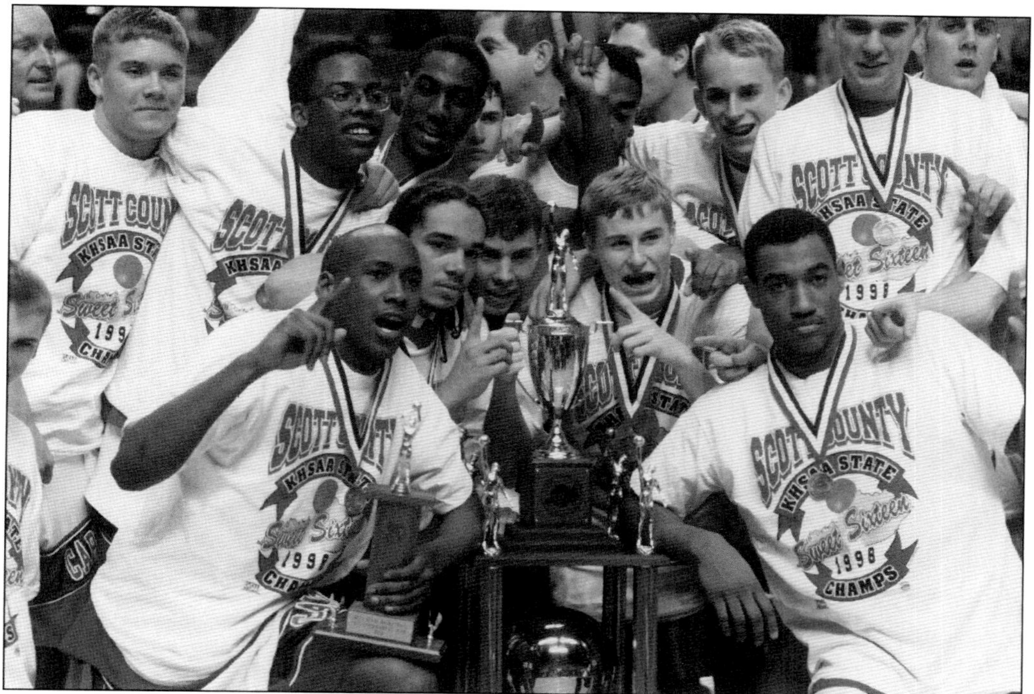

The Scott County men's basketball team wins the sweet 16 in 1998! Led by Coach Billy Hicks, the Scott County men were giant killers, beating three of the best teams in the state to prove they were the very best.

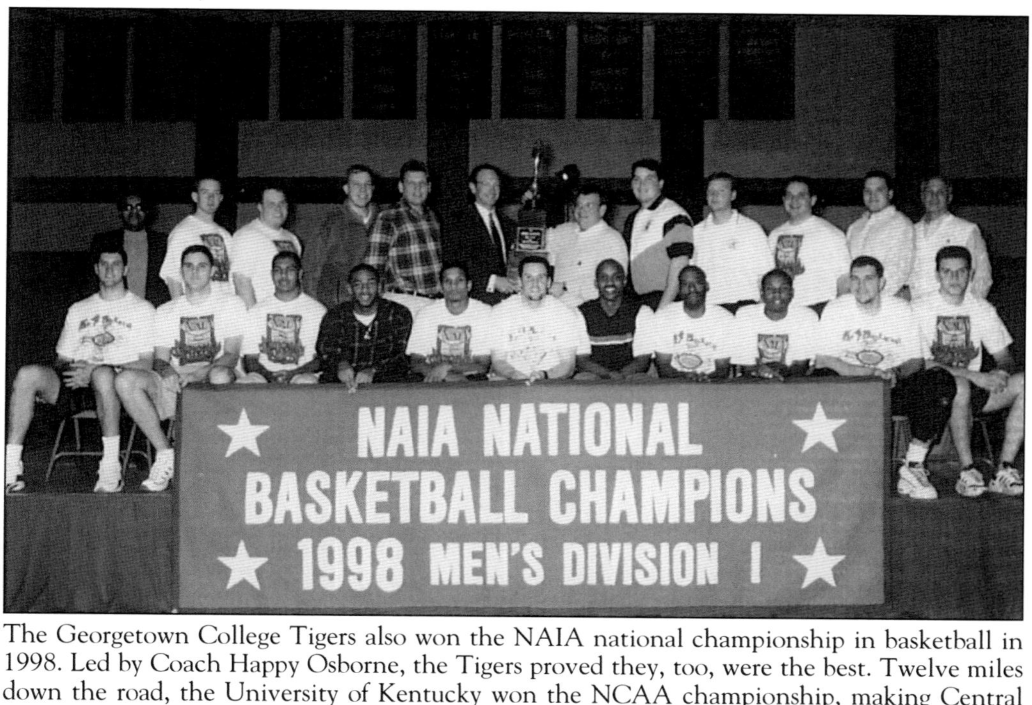

The Georgetown College Tigers also won the NAIA national championship in basketball in 1998. Led by Coach Happy Osborne, the Tigers proved they, too, were the best. Twelve miles down the road, the University of Kentucky won the NCAA championship, making Central Kentucky the basketball capital of the USA, at least for 1998.

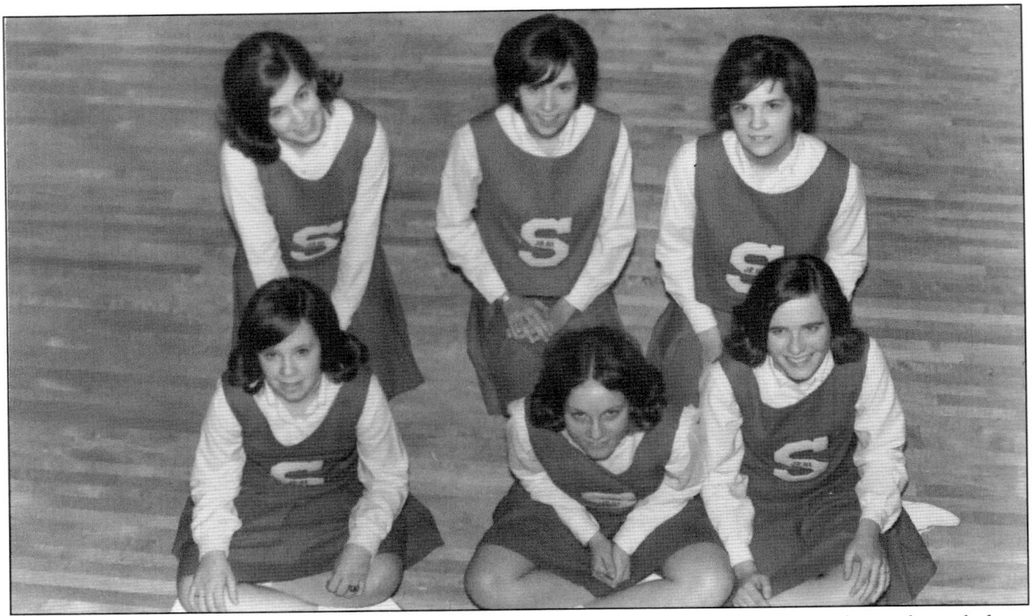

Pictured is the cheerleading squad at Scott County in the late 1960s. Members, from left to right, are as follows: (front row) Sharon Ritchie, Angie McFarland, and Ginger Glass; (second row) Ann Zartman, Mauricia Oakley, and Gini Marshall.

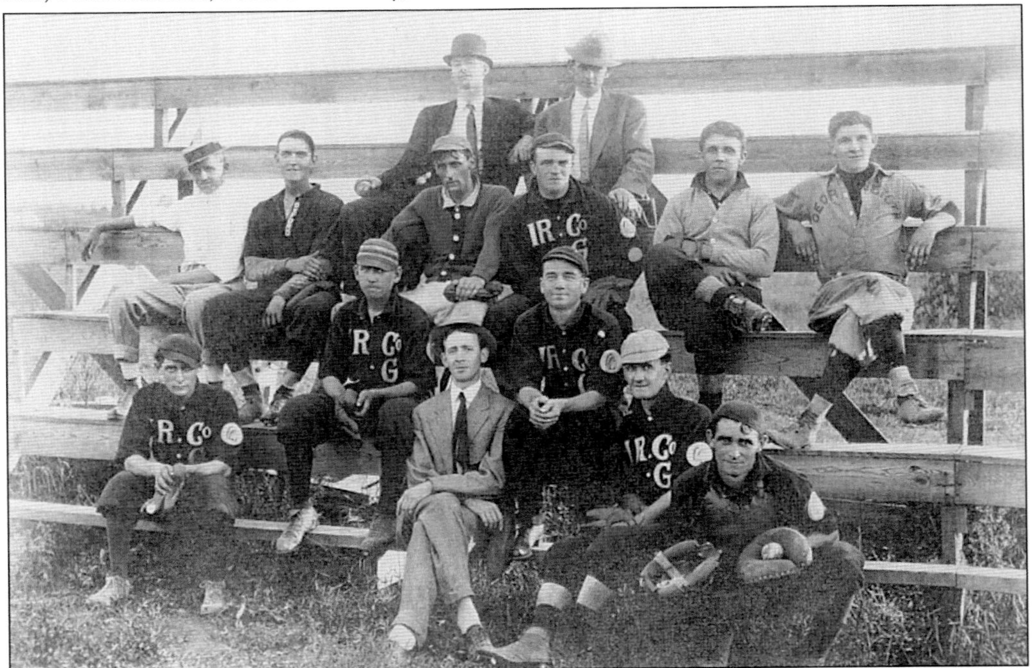

Pictured in this *c.* 1910 view is the Georgetown Athletics department. Members, from left to right, are as follows: (first row) Elmer Craycraft, A.B. Barkley, George Barkley, and Otis Craycraft; (second row) Ethel Hambrick and Alfred Moore (third row) Luke Abbet, Ward Carrick, Joe Sal, Ross Creeklimore, Kelly Linn, and Kay Rossell; (fourth row) Bernard Hines and Bill Forwood.

Eight
Community

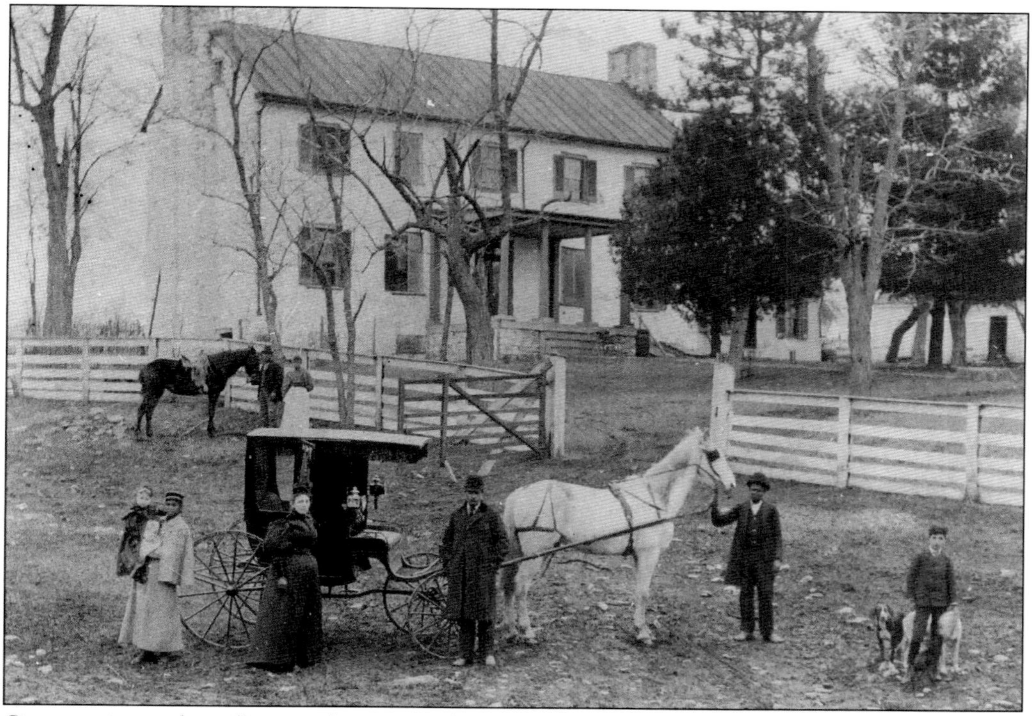

Community is the adhesive that unites humans and the resources that are either necessary or incidental to them. Community takes many forms—one's family or friends, or a town or county. Churches have long provided community to members, and a variety of organizations have conveyed personal and corporate meaning.

There was a time when family units, characteristically much larger than today's families, got together to have a photograph made in the foreground of their dwellings. Many of these photographs included family servants, neighbors, pets, horses, and vehicles.

Next to home in importance for many persons, are church and school. Many of Central Kentucky's first settlements consisted of groups of families sharing a religious affiliation. Lodges, schools, civic organizations, commercial clubs, patriotic and political groups, social outreach programs, organizations, sports, and festivals play important roles in forming community.

The family of George and Ruth Carrick Ware and their servants are shown at their historic stone house on Millers Run, along with favorite horses and carriage. The boy on the right is William, and Robert is carried by a servant. Perhaps the first person to call the center passage stone house "home" was Charles Whitacre, settlement period explorer.

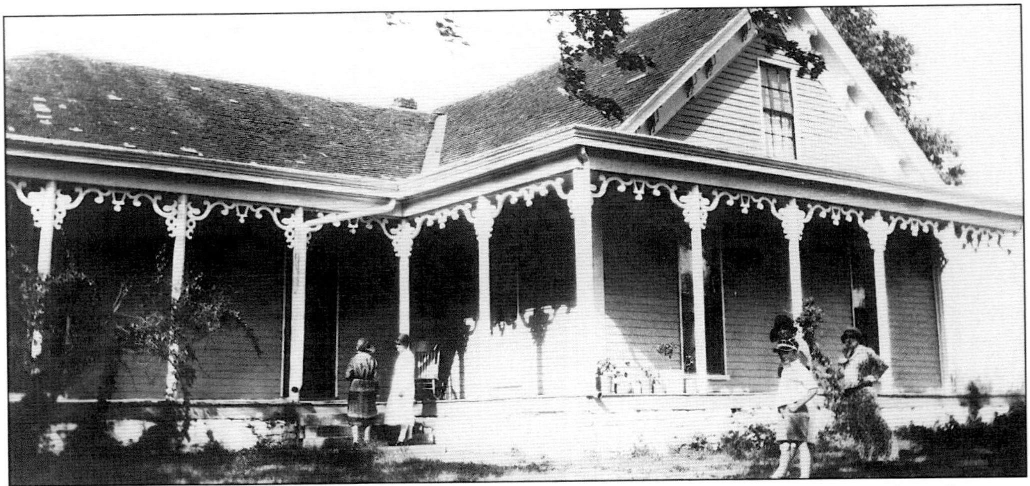

Descendants of Robert and Jemima Suggett Johnson view the Johnson home that dates to the late 1790s. The house occupies the site of Johnson Station, the county's first permanent settlement. It was established in 1783 at a large buffalo ford on Elkhorn, and gave the resulting community the name "Big Crossings" and later, "Great Crossings." Victor Kenney Glass is credited with the Italianate remodeling of the timber frame house after he acquired the farm in 1875.

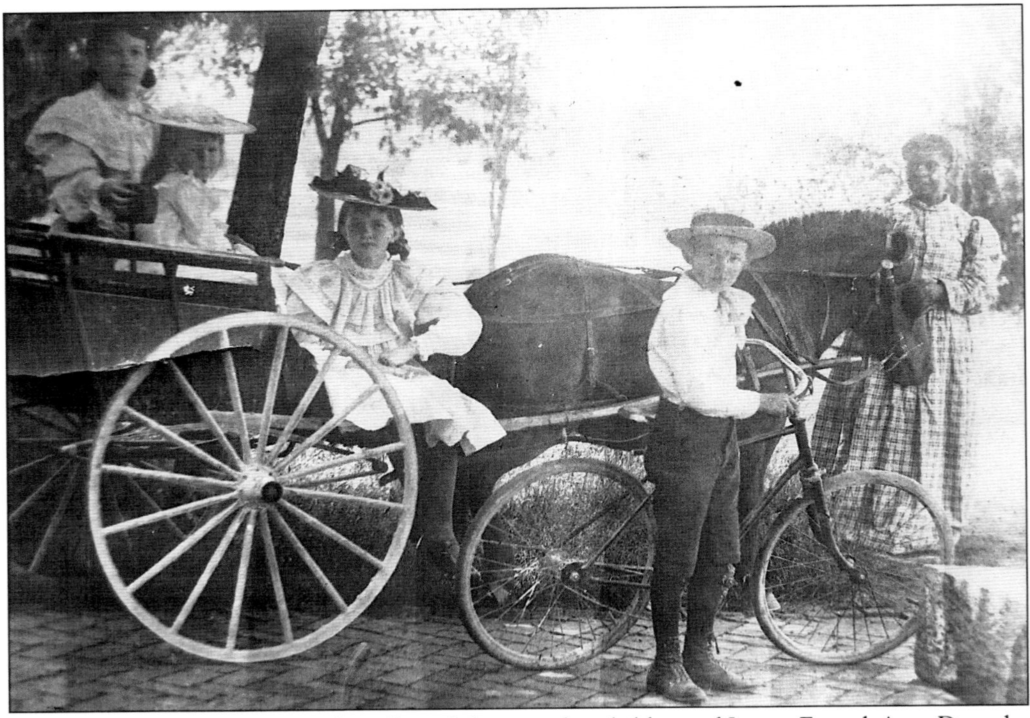

Louise, James F. Jr., Ann, and William Johnson, the children of James F. and Ann Darnaby Askew, pose with a horse and buggy and bicycle in their Sunday finery with Aunt Emily Horner, a firm hand and friend in their upbringing. Aunt Emily, who in slavery times was a part of the Bradford household, thrilled the children with stories of her grandmother's adventures with bears and Indians. Her husband, John, was a servant of Governor Horner of Virginia.

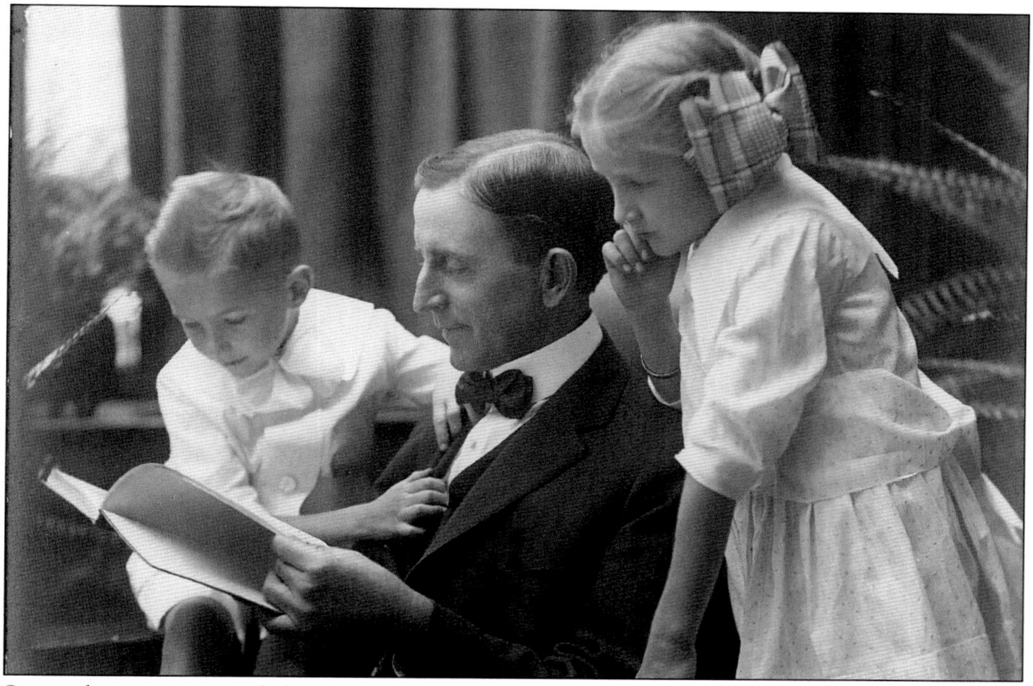

Since the invention of the printing press, which encouraged the ownership of books and mandated development of reading and writing skills, adults have enjoyed reading to children and children have cherished the memories of being "read to." Edward Gaines Graves (1872–1949) is shown reading to his grandchildren Susan Frances Graves (1909–1990) and Wilford Hambrick Graves (1911–1987). Edward was a son of William Hayes Graves.

Margaret "Puggie" Daviess Samuell, shown c. 1880 with her aging mother, Mary Ann Patterson Patterson Offutt (a Patterson who married a Patterson) was recalled in her obituary in 1935 as "one of Georgetown's most dearly beloved women." At the right is one of Mrs. Offutt's grandchildren. In the background are J.W. Samuell and an unidentified gentleman. The setting is the lawn of the present Millspring, located at 353 North Broadway in Georgetown.

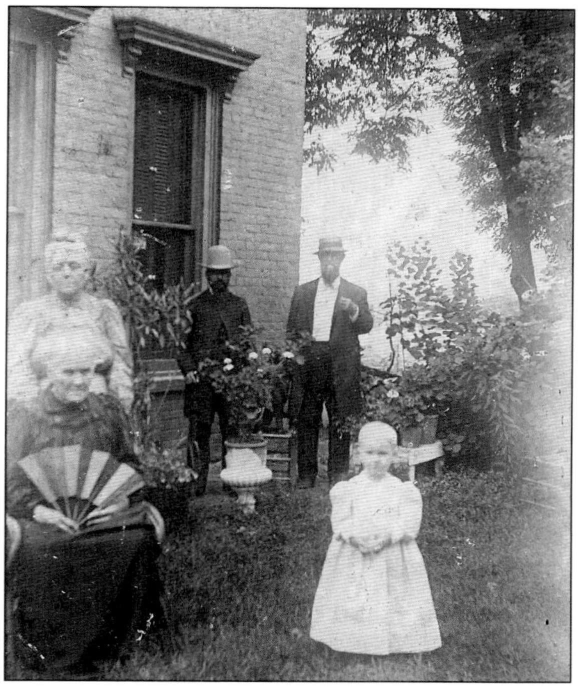

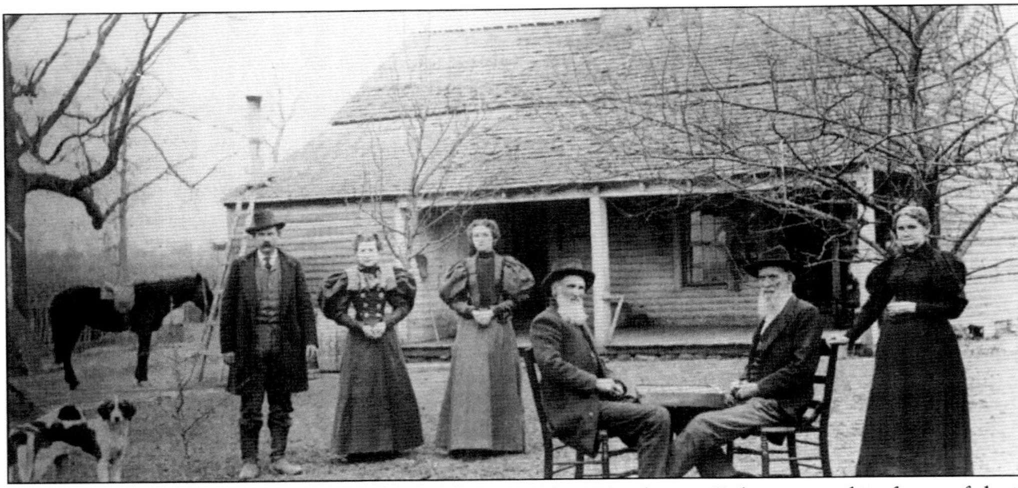

The family and pets of William Henry and Nancy Ann Anderson Salyers posed in front of their home between Oxford and Muddy Ford in the 1890s. Pictured, from left to right, are as follows: (noted with birth years) Arthur Payne Salyers (1864), Hester Salyers (1874), and Minnie Ross Salyers (1876), children of William and Nancy; John Barkley (father of Bud and Jenks, not shown), William Henry Salyers (1822), and Nancy Ann Anderson Salyers (1838).

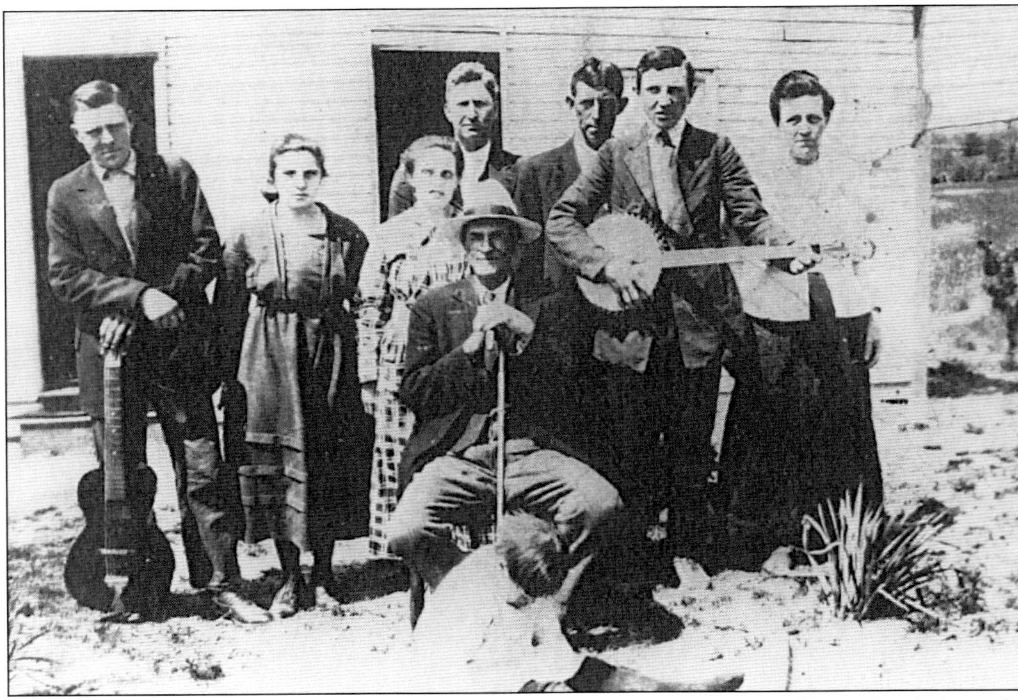

Family really became community when members of the Jimmie Sum Mulberry family brought along their musical instruments for an evening of song and fellowship. Mulberry occupies the central position on the front row with a granddaughter, Aletha Jane Green. Pictured in the second row, from left to right, are as follows: Arthur Green Mulberry, Minnie Mulberry Brewer, Della Mulberry Hiles, Ed Martin, Luther Hiles, J.W. "Willie" Mulberry, and Sarah Ellen Hiles Green.

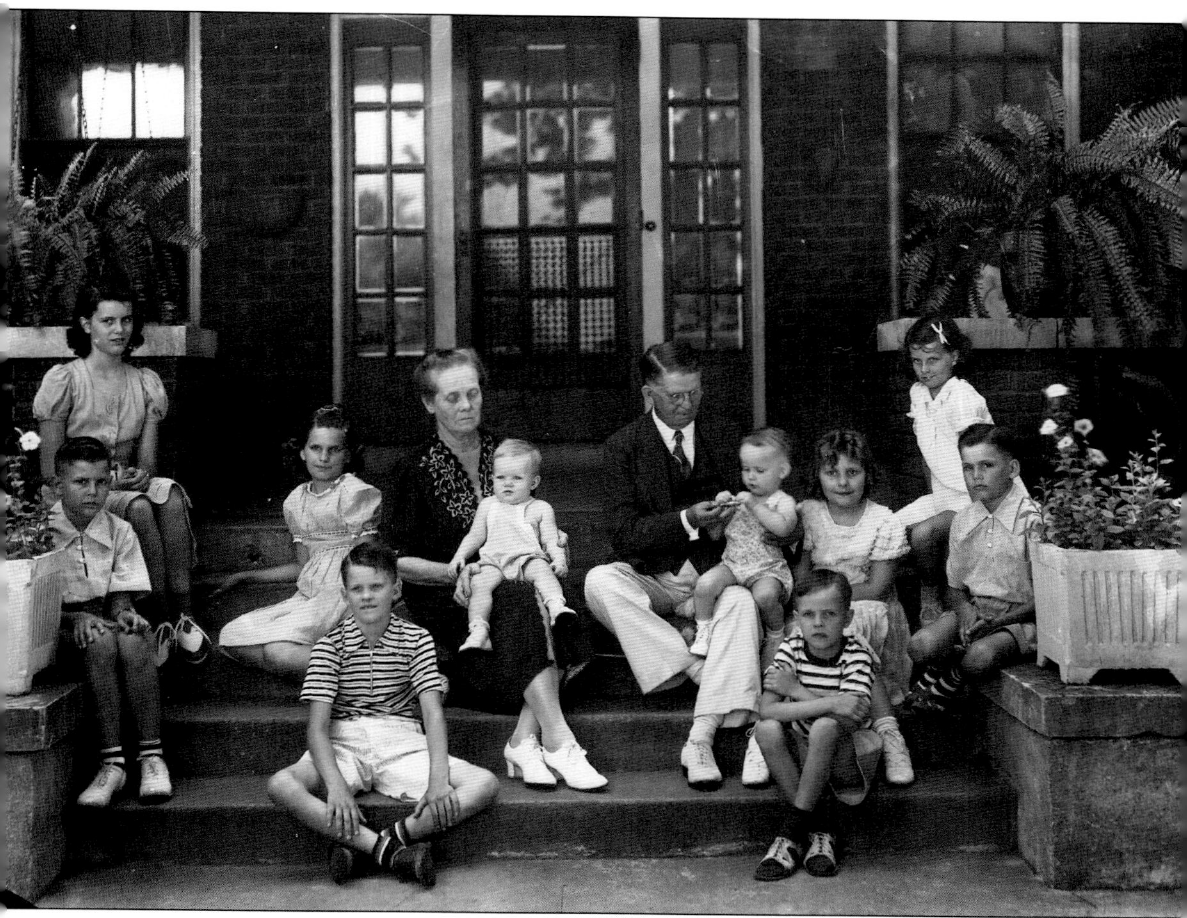

In 1914, James P. (1869–1942) and Maria Caudill Lewis (1872–1950) moved from Whitesburg to Georgetown to be near Georgetown College. The Lewis's commitment to family inspired them to establish three dwellings on their farm on the outskirts of Georgetown in order to be close to their children and grandchildren. Lewis, a former Letcher County judge, banker, and Kentucky secretary of state, became Kentucky's banking commissioner in 1924. He also chaired the Georgetown College board of trustees. The Lewises are shown with the earliest of their 33 grandchildren. On the left antepodium are Jim Maturo and Maria Lewis, and on the right, Frank Maturo and Joy Lewis. Also pictured, from left to right, are the following: (front row) Ted and Howell Lewis (second row, seated) Mary Caudill Lewis, Maria Lewis (holding Bobby Lewis), Judge J.P. Lewis with Billy Lewis, and Margaret Lewis. The first eight grandchildren, all born within four years, were a closely knit group, always referring to themselves as "the first eight."

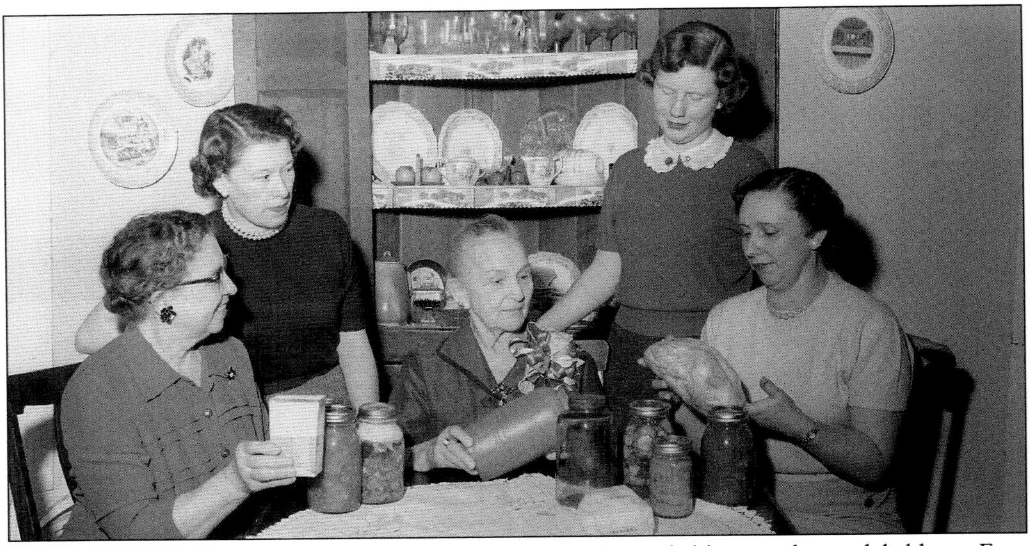

Homemakers continue to pass on culinary skills to their children and grandchildren. Four generations of Great Crossings homemakers joined Nell Baston, home demonstration agent, to admire their collective expertise and share pride in the results of their efforts at foods preservation. Pictured, from left to right are as follows: Mrs. Charlie Kettenring (grandmother), Mrs. Baston, Annie Owens (great-grandmother), Barbara Earl Friedly (granddaughter), and Annie Barbara Friedly (mother).

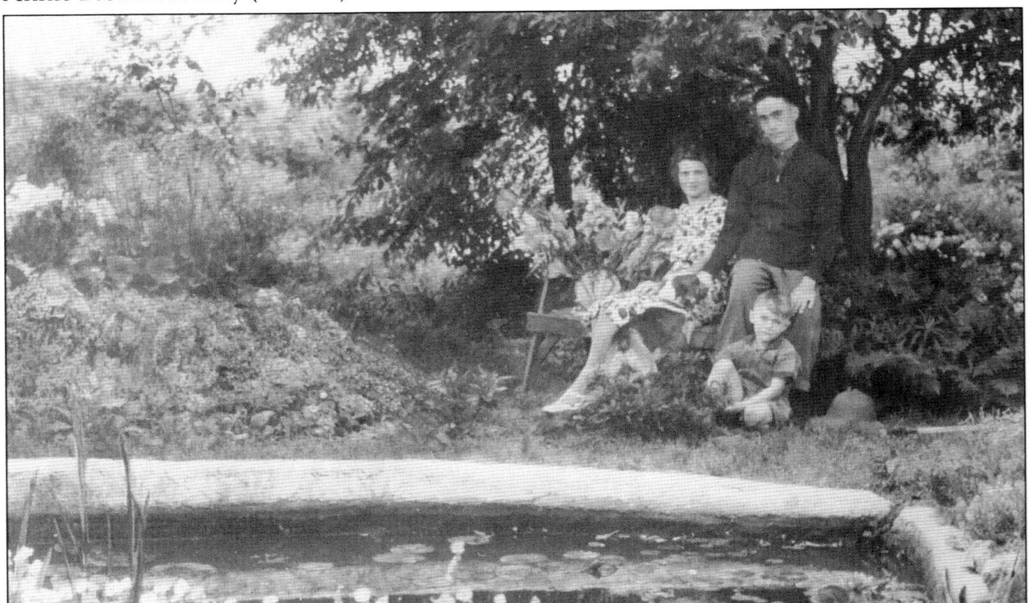

J.W. Singer, commended as "the most brilliant man who had ever graduated from the University of Kentucky in the Classical Languages," in 1929 chose instead a vocation in farming. An avocational naturalist since youth, Singer also marked the beginning of Singer Gardens, an extended nursery and landscaping service. Pictured is a Eugene Bradley photograph of J.W. and Hetty Singer with their son, Jim. Daughter Mary Linnie "Mae" was not present for the photograph.

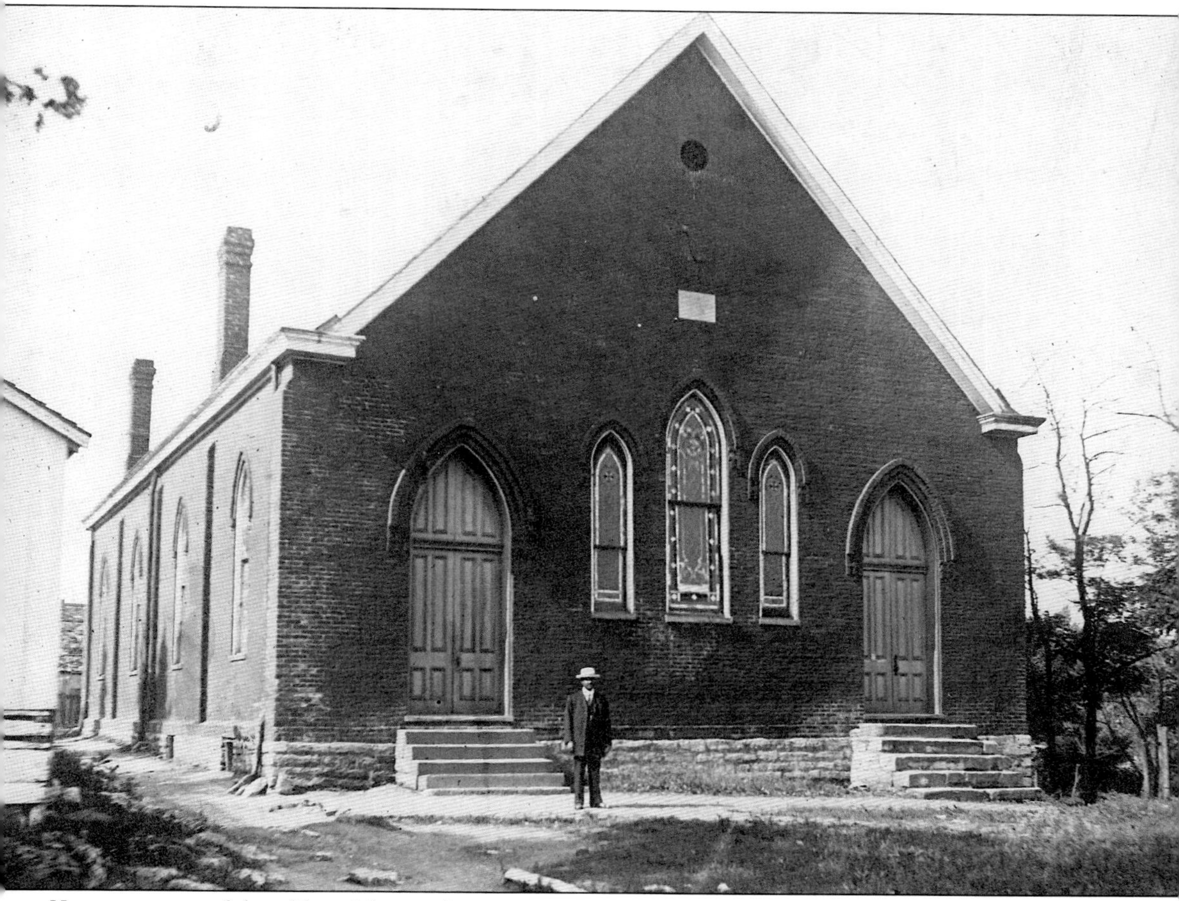

Known as one of the oldest African-American congregations in Kentucky, First Baptist Church had its beginnings when Georgetown College president Howard Malcom convinced the parent church to move to a site near the college campus. By 1842, the relocated portion of the congregation, housed in a new Greek Revival meetinghouse on the corner of South Hamilton and East College Streets, turned the older building over to the African-American members. The first pastor, George Washington Dupee, made history when the Reverend W.M. Pratt of Lexington's First Baptist Church bought Dupee at a slave auction in 1856 for the purpose of setting him free. Afterwards, Black Christians reimbursed Pratt. In 1870, the congregation replaced the original meetinghouse with the present late Gothic Revival brick structure. Like many evangelical churches of its era, it had separate entrances for male and female worshippers, who, once inside, sat on separate sides with members of the same sex. Later, the separate entrances were enclosed and a central one was established.

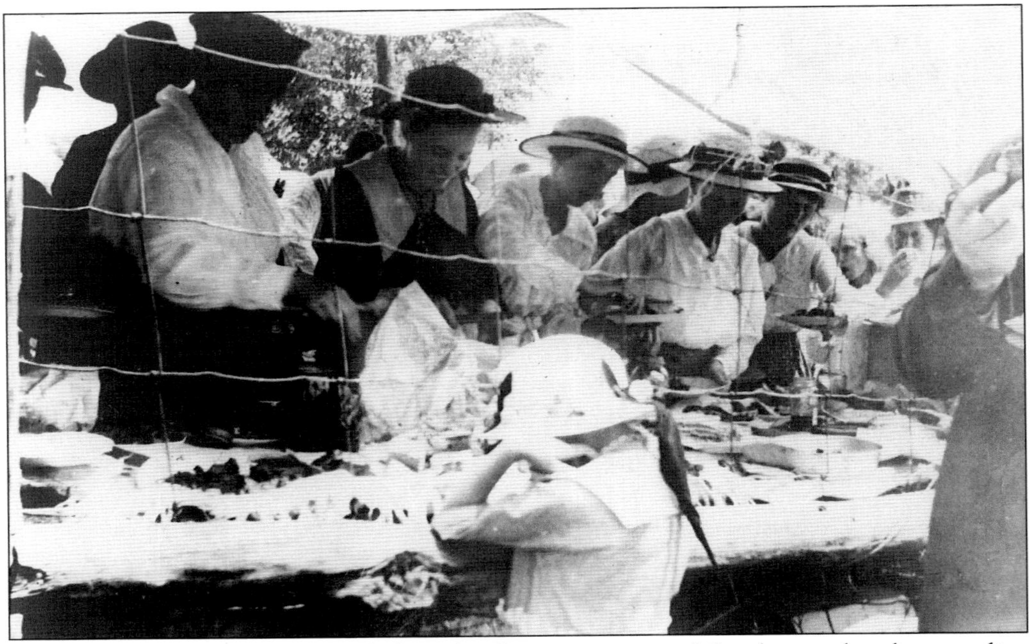

Frequently, church members and their families spent most of Sunday at church, attending worship and staying for "dinner on the grounds," followed by more preaching and singing. Porter Christian Church is shown during such an event on August 11, 1918. The church has served the village of Porter since 1889, when Ben F. Wright donated land for the meetinghouse on a high ridge north of the junction of Mountain Island and Josephine Roads.

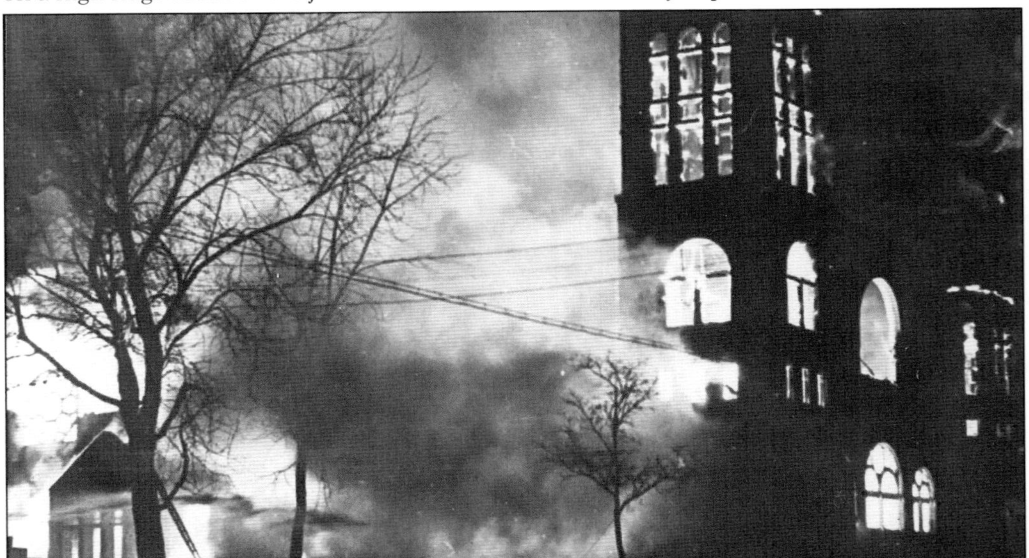

Fire, an ever present danger for churches, seems to present new challenges to members who, in the process of rebuilding, discover a more basic meaning of church—the content of its worship and mission and the fellowship of its members. Georgetown's 1892 Romanesque Revival Christian Church burned on February 11, 1947 after George Jacobs, a candidate for the church's pastorate, preached a sermon on the need for more "fire in the church."

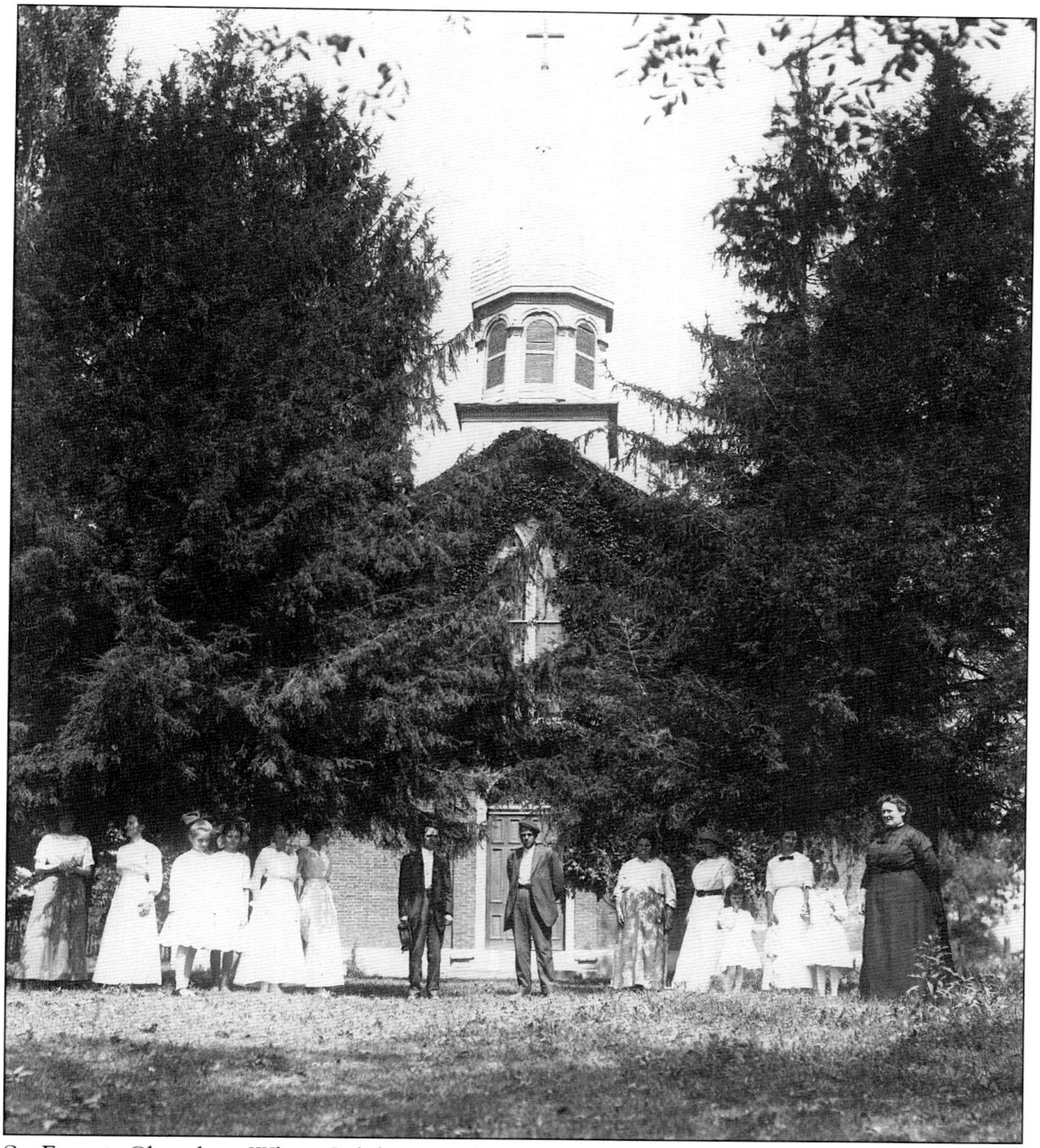

St. Francis Church at White Sulphur, mother church of the Catholic dioceses of Covington and Lexington, worships in Scott County's oldest church building. The parish was established in 1794 with Father Stephen Theodore Badin, the first priest ordained in the United States, as its first pastor. In 1808, the Dominican fathers from Springfield, under the leadership of Father Edward Dominic Fenwick, took over the parish and presided over construction of the 1820 building. It cost $3,600, paid with "one-tenth currency and nine-tenths pork." Four St. Francis pastors became bishops, and one, the Most Reverend George Aloysius Carrell, was pastor between 1854–1856 while he superintended the construction of and presided over the administration of the diocese's first seminary. The seminary closed during the Civil War. In 1875, the Visitation nuns established Mount Admirabilis, a convent and academy for girls, which they moved to Cardome, north of Georgetown, in 1896. Pictured (right of center) are Wiley and Dolly Relaford, members of the parish and important persons in the conduct of the school.

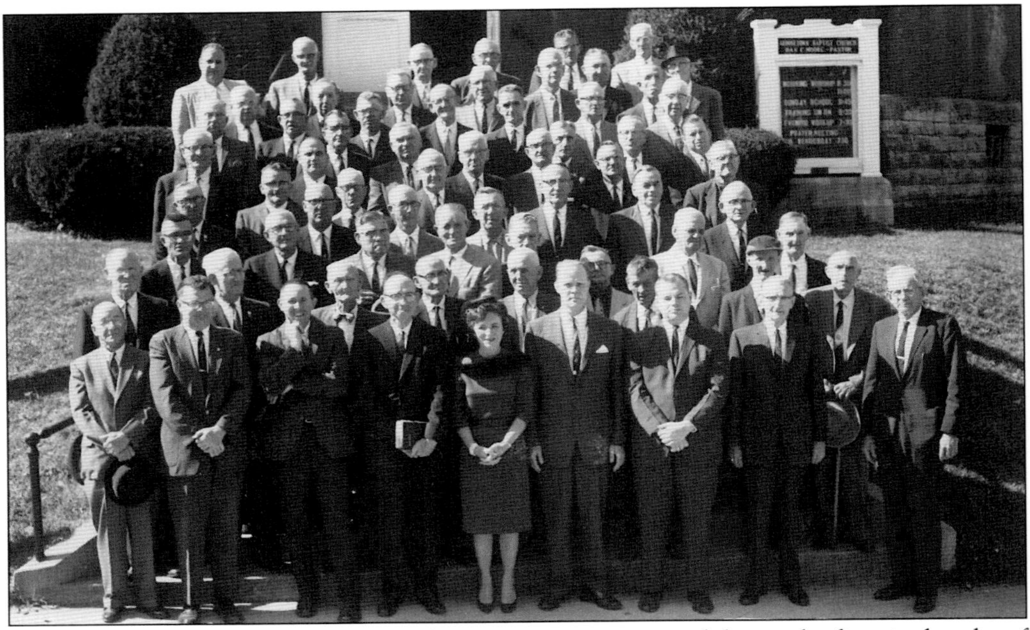

Huge church school classes for men and women were not unusual during the first six decades of the 20th century. At Georgetown Baptist Church, Dr. J. Elmer Weldon, pictured on the front row with the Bible, taught the Baraca Class with Lydia McDonald (center) leading vocal music. V.A. Bradley and Fred Lisanby taught a class of similar size next door at the Christian church. The photograph of Dr. Weldon's class was made in the 1950s.

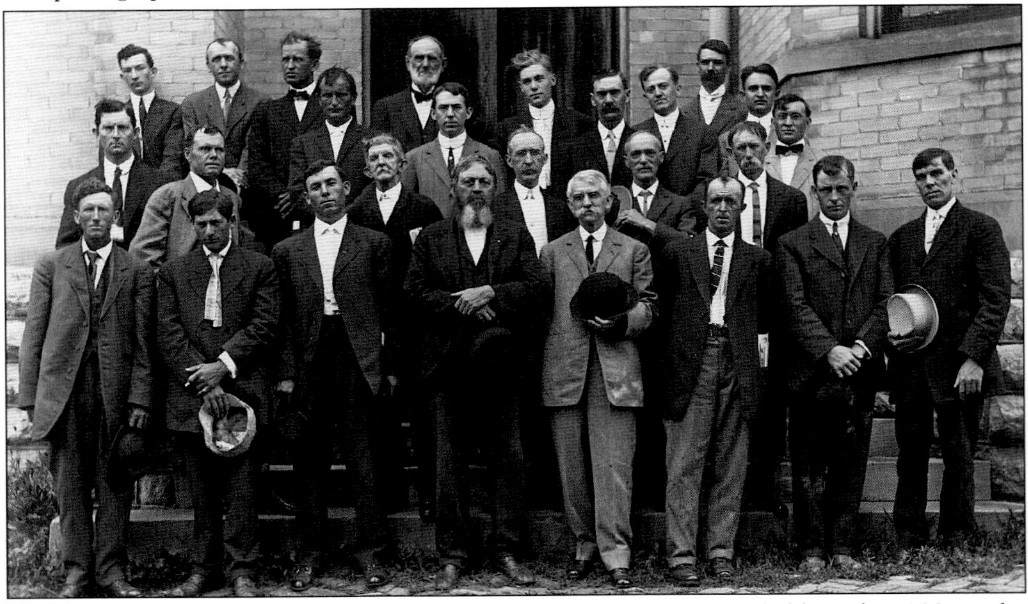

A Sunday school class of the Georgetown Methodist Church posed, probably in the 1920s, at the entrance of their third church house, a buff brick Romanesque Revival building. Among those shown in the photograph, from left to right, are the following: (first row) M.F. Martin, Clarence G. Marshall (second man), and T.J. Jenkins (fifth); (second row) Robert Acke (second); (third row) E.C. Barlow (second), John Nichols (sixth), and Fred Nichols (ninth).

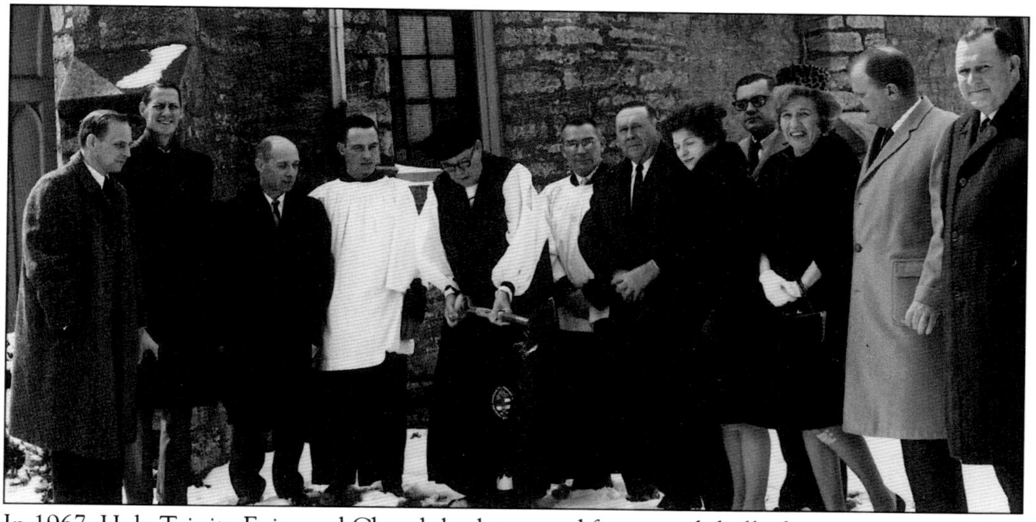

In 1967, Holy Trinity Episcopal Church broke ground for a parish hall of contemporary design, compatible with that of its Gothic Revival (1865–1870) church. Pictured at the groundbreaking, from left to right, are as follows: George Gilbertson, Jim Corbett, Virgil Pryor, unidentified, Bishop William A. Moody, Robert Wohn, Clint Harbison of the Christ Church cathedral parish, Ann Rawdon Lewis, Dr. J. Campbell Cantrill, Emmette Corder, Ben M. "Kelley" Osborne, and Arch W. Hamilton.

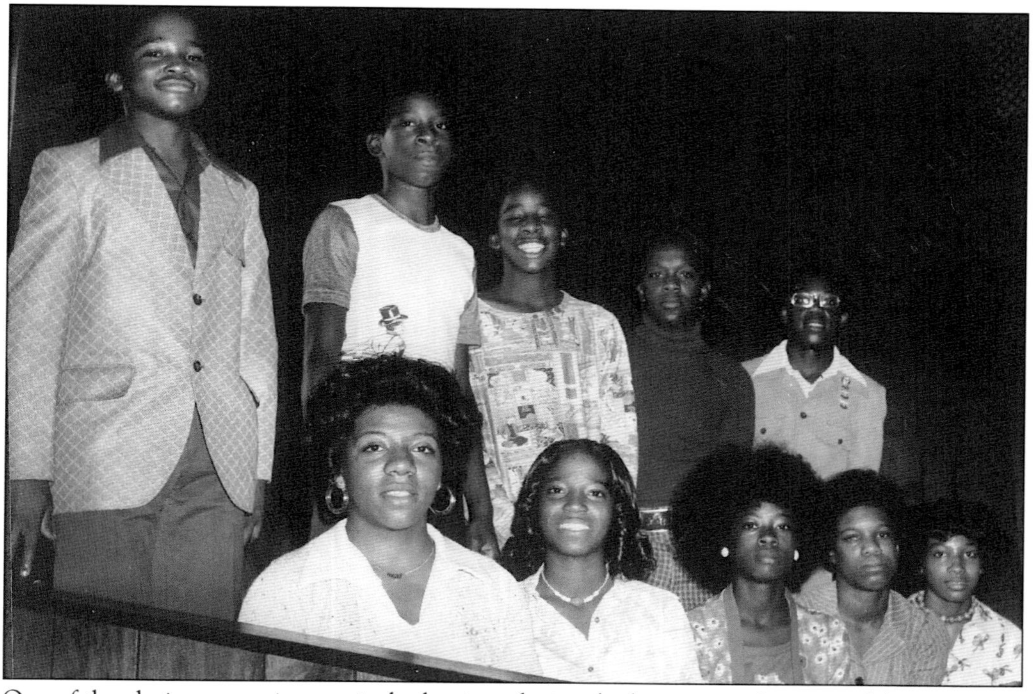

One of the choirs presenting musical selections during the bicentennial events of the 1970s was the youth choir of Zion Baptist Church. Pictured, from left to right, are as follows: (front row) Augusta Washington, Stephanie Dalton, Tondra Tribble, Kathy Boyd, and Cheryl Sidney; (second row) Anthony McIntyre, Charles S. Washington, Othella Washington, Stephon Thompson, and Ralph Pearson.

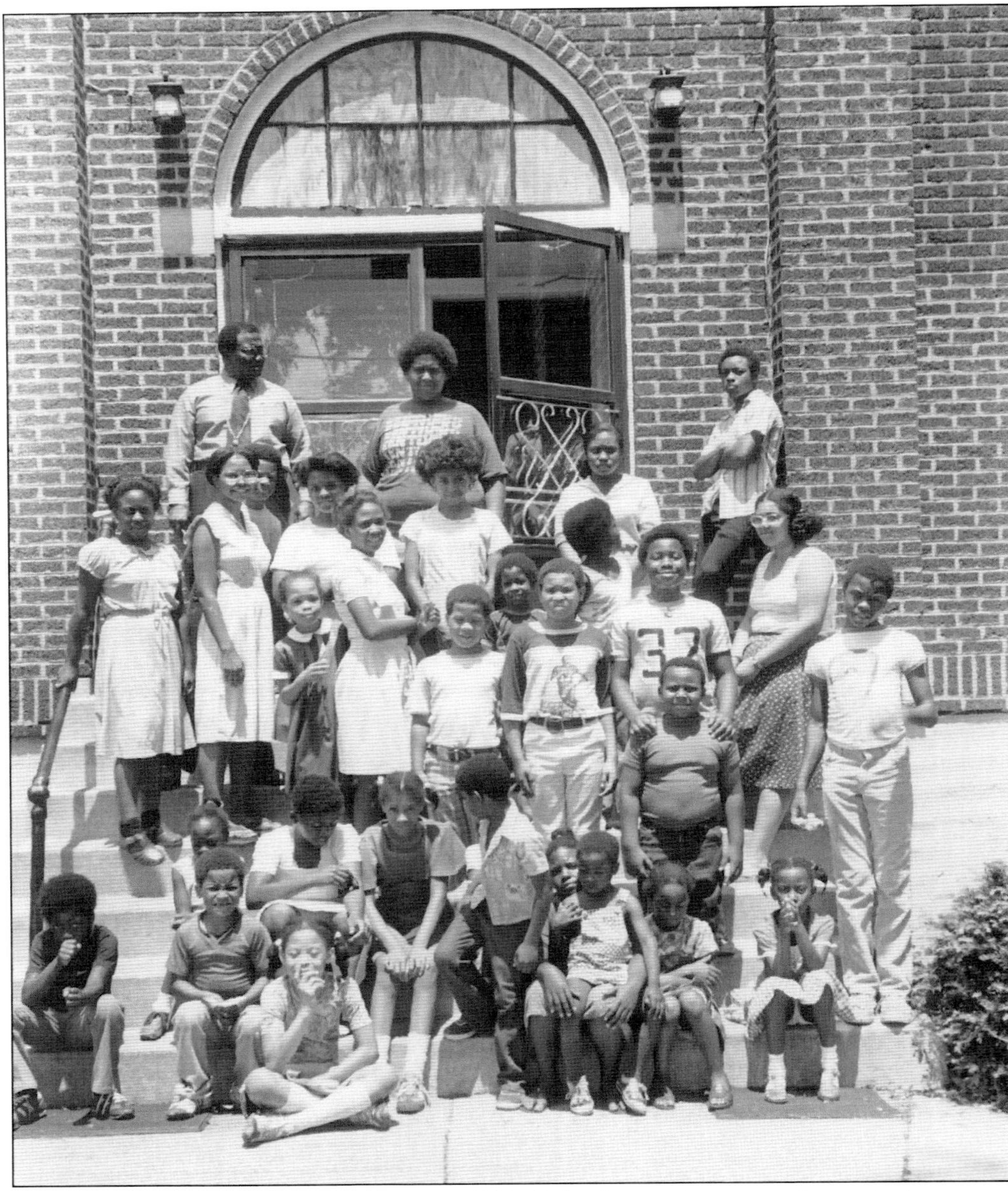

Zion Hill Baptist Church's 1979 Vacation Bible School participants are shown during a recess break. Pictured, from left to right, are as follows: (seated) Anton and Michelle Reed, Octavia Cruse, Erica Mulder, and Lekeetha Banks; (standing) Keith and David Raglin, Henry, Brian, and Jeff Blair; (third row) Carrie Salter, Tammy Hamilton, Lisa Harris, Chandra Scruggs, Gayle Devine, and Carla Lawson; (top) the Reverend Grant Coleman, Tim Bolton, and Spence Hughes. African-American freedmen established the village of Zion Hill during the period following the conclusion of the Civil War and adoption of the Thirteenth Amendment to the U.S. Constitution. Zion Hill's more famous citizens include Whitney M. Young Sr., who, born at Paynes Depot in 1892, was one of the first students to enter Lincoln Institute after its establishment in 1912 as a high school and center for teacher and industrial training. He later guided his alma mater in its role as the leading Black college preparatory school in Kentucky.

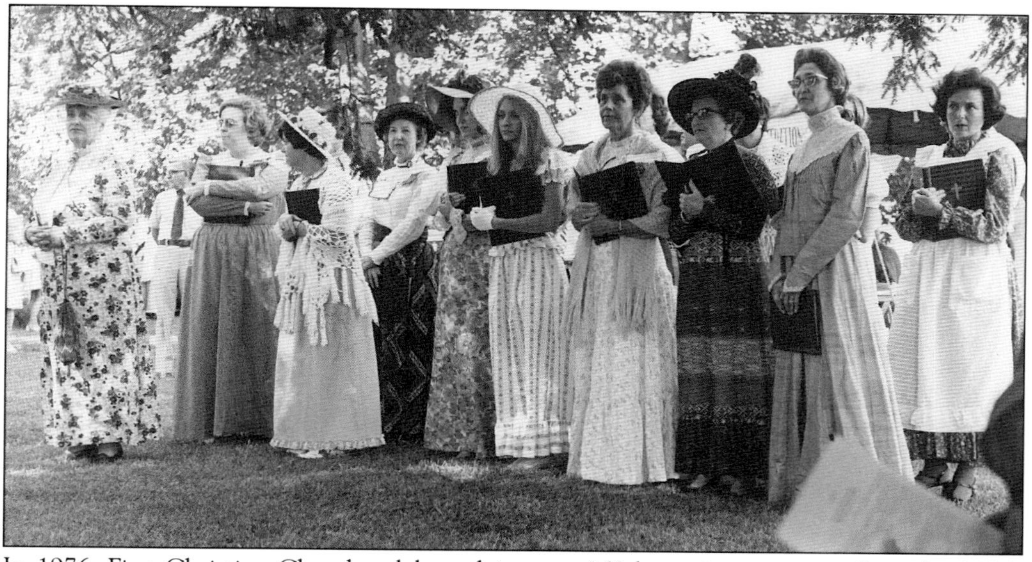

In 1976, First Christian Church celebrated its own 160th anniversary as well as the 200th birthday of the U.S. Constitution. The choir joined the afternoon program at St. Francis Church following the congregation's Sunday morning service. Pictured from left to right are as follows: Sallie Brooking Gibson (director), Anne Tucker Hall, Louise Lewis, Juanita Hutchison, unidentified, Janet Cummins Marcum, Alene Glass, Elizabeth "Teby" Bradley, Margaret Thomson, and Betty Lou Lowery Graves.

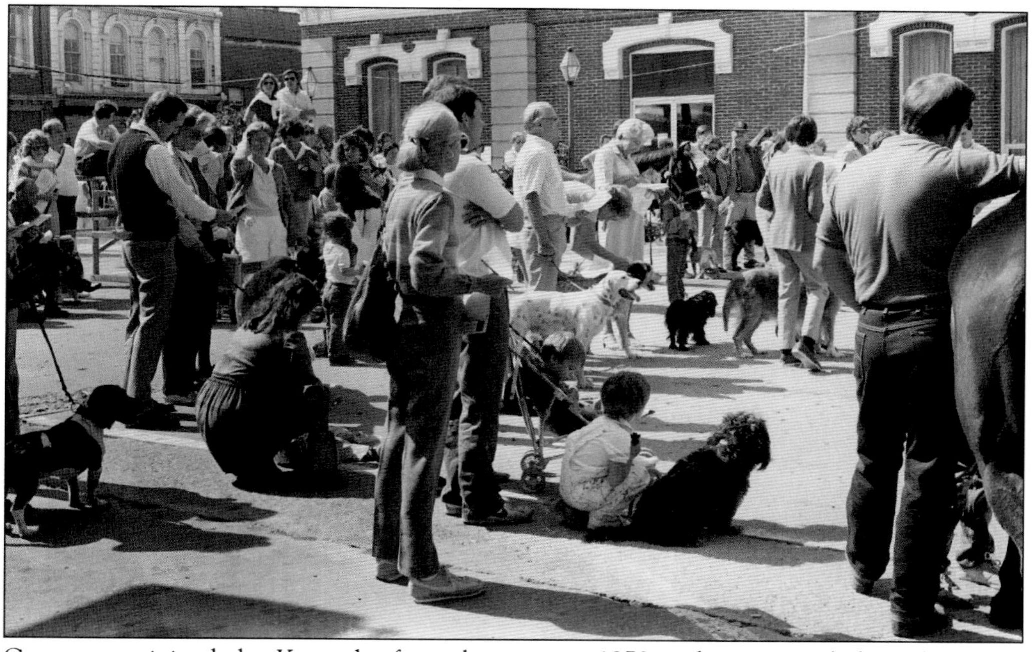

Georgetown joined the Kentucky festival season in 1979 with an annual three-day event dedicated to the horse. On Sunday afternoon, Scott Countians flocked to town with their pets to share in a ceremony based on the ancient English custom of blessing the hounds prior to fox hunts. The rector of Holy Trinity Episcopal Church conducts the blessing of the animals during a service that also includes choral music by the congregation's choirs.

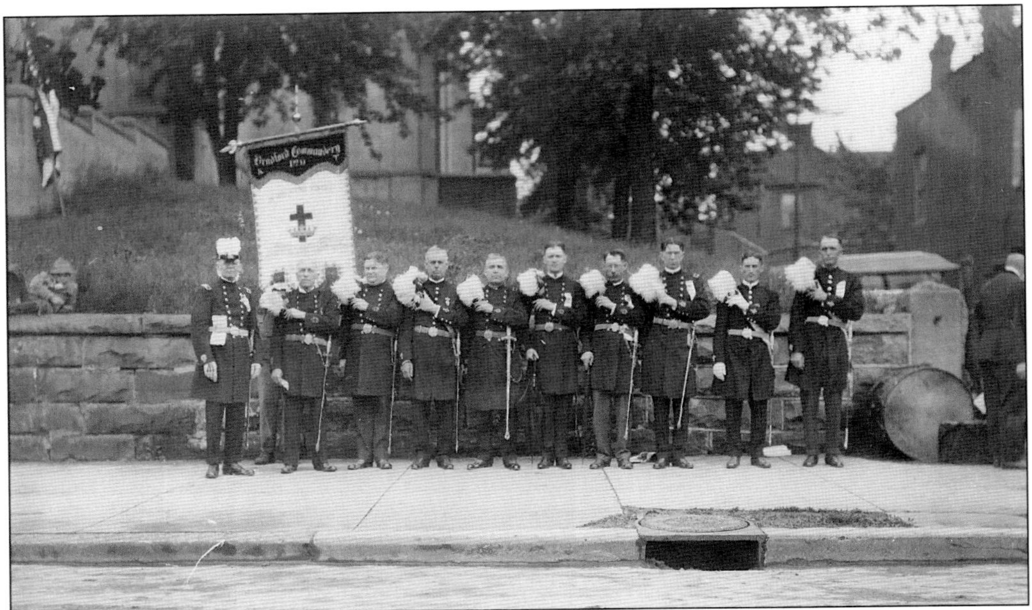

In 1907, members of the Masonic Lodge's Bradford Commandery gathered in full regalia in front of Lexington's Main Street Baptist Church. Pictured are James Irven Daviess (third from left) and and John C. Porter (fifth from left). Other members of the Commandery in 1907 included J.C. Cantrill, J.P. Jackson, W.S. Kissinger, J.E. Warren, B.M. Herndon, C.O. Hook, C.T. Jenkins, Campbell Marshall, H.A. Bourne, William Flaig, Samuel Godey, and J.W. Keller.

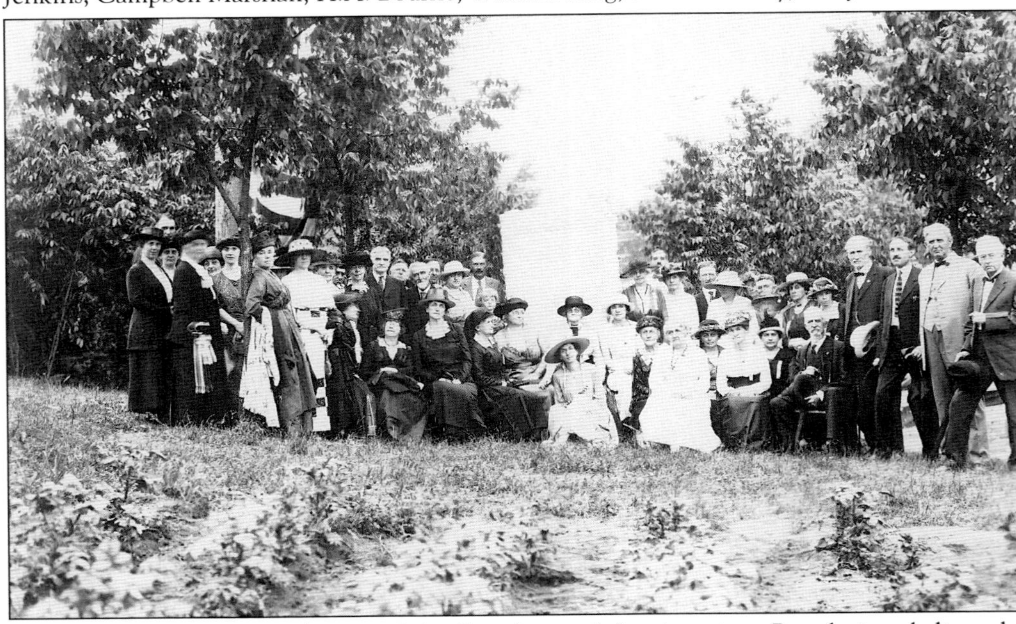

In 1921, the Big Spring Chapter of the Daughters of the American Revolution dedicated a monument to the men and women who had defended McClelland's Fort in 1776–1777 and the county's Revolutionary War veterans. The monument marks the site of the fort. Participants included Judge Samuel Wilson (second from right), Katherine Bradley (center, seated on grass), and Anna Payne Coffman (ninth from right).

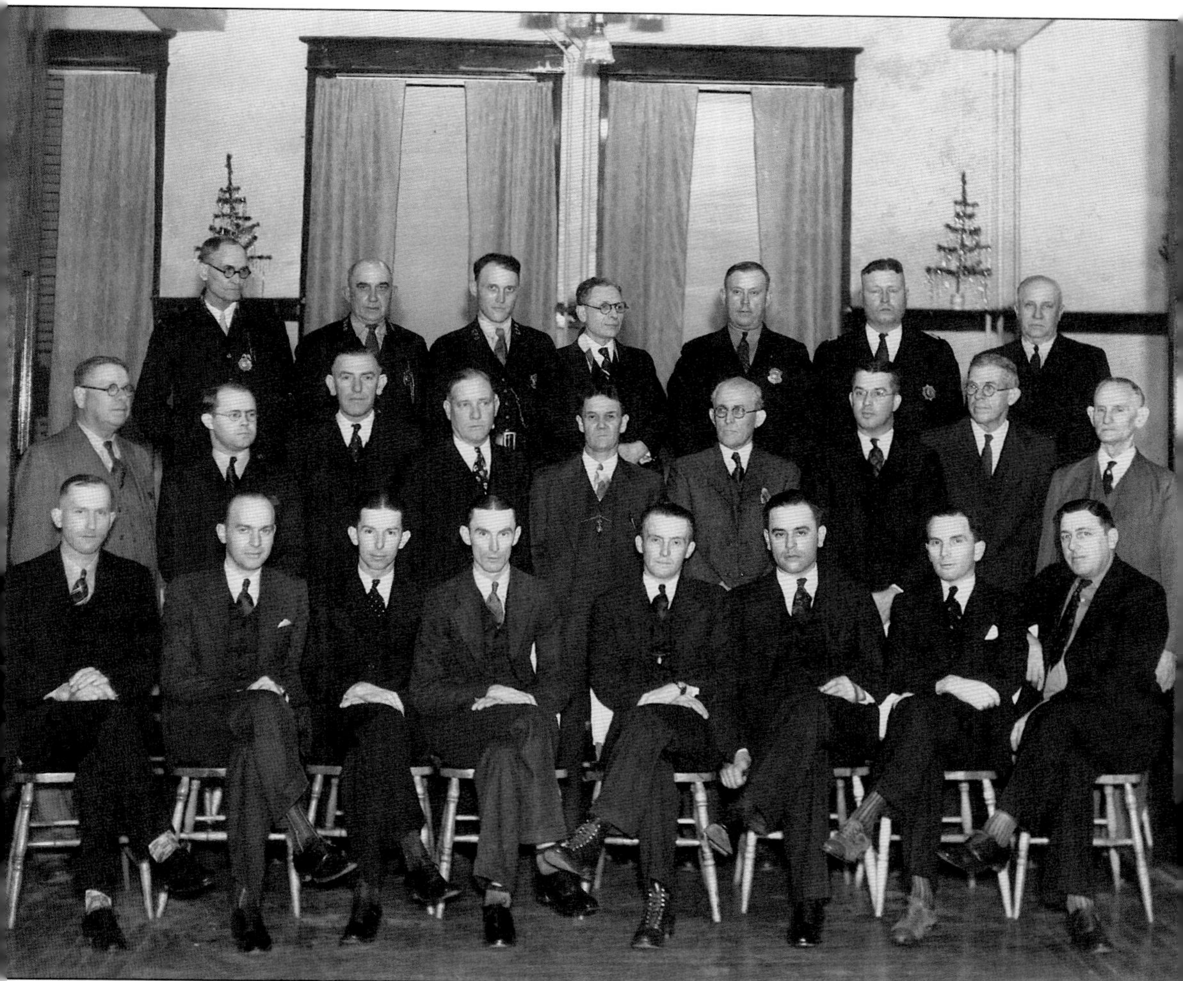

An annual holiday season banquet in the old Lancaster Hotel in the 1930s honored members of the Georgetown police and fire departments and government officials. Pictured from left to right are as follows: (first row) John True, John Ennis, Mike Milner, Tice Calvert, Jack Tucker, Roy Clark, and Oder Milner (firemen), Cecil Bridges (fire chief); (second row) Milligan "Mig" Fleming (city clerk), Fred Lisanby (city attorney), L.S. "Barney" Odell (councilman), A.P. Prather (mayor), Walter Medley, Oscar Jameson, William Luttrell, Will Abbett, and William Beatty; (third row) Al Marshall and William Estes (policemen), Francis Bramlett (patrolman and fire truck driver), Walter Powell and Durand Hamilton (policemen), Buford "Blue Jay" Alsop (police chief), and Joe D. Offutt (police judge).

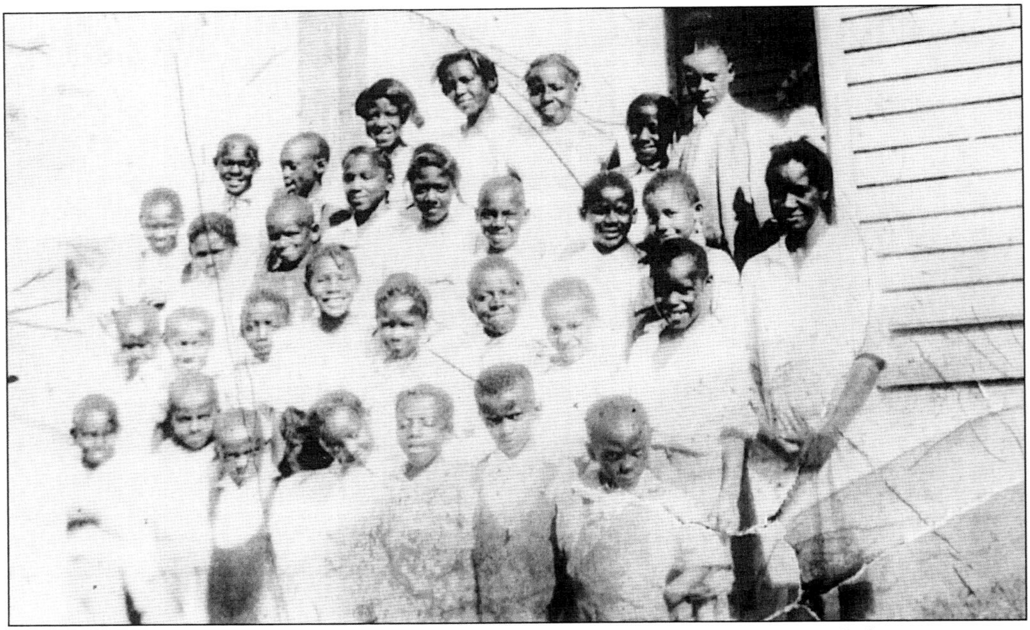

The children and teachers of New Zion School are gathered in front of their one-room schoolhouse in this 1931 photo. Pictured are Sarah Williams, Mattie Young, Roberta Clark, Oscar and Clarence Dishman, Leland and Zella Holman, Luther Figgs, Beron Sidney, Floyd Williams, Bessie Cayson, Martha Baltimore, Fannie Spotts, Richard Figgs, Walter Sidney, Artie Adams, Carl and Joseph Claybourne, and Margaret White.

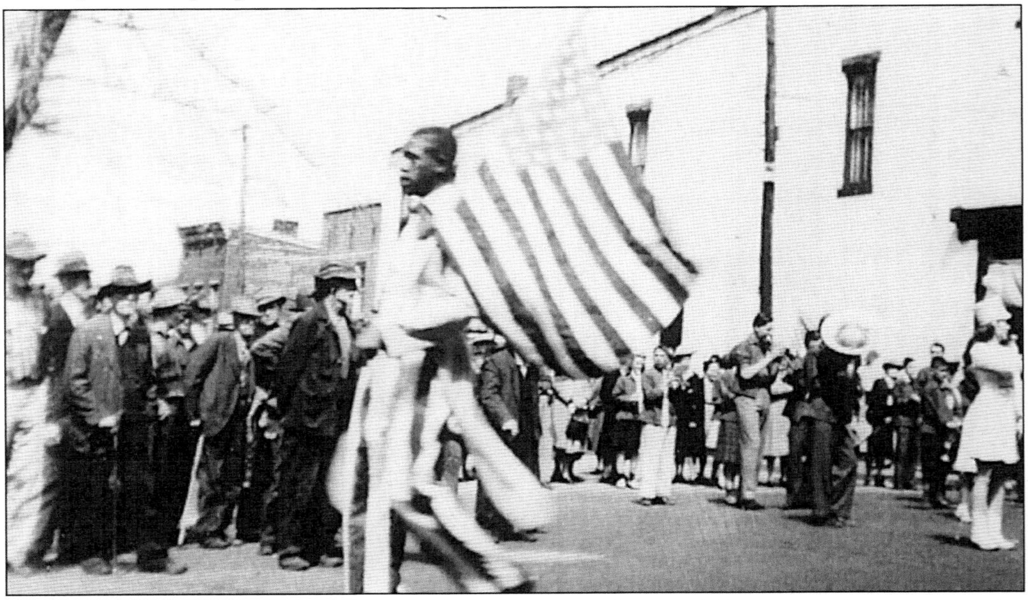

An estimated 2,500 persons participated in or witnessed one of Georgetown's largest parades ever on April 6, 1942. Among the participants in the community's first nationwide Army Day celebration was an African-American Uncle Sam. Maxine Bowling (now Mrs. Charles Friedly) photographed the parade. The *Georgetown Times* headlined its account of the parade, "All Organizations Well Represented."

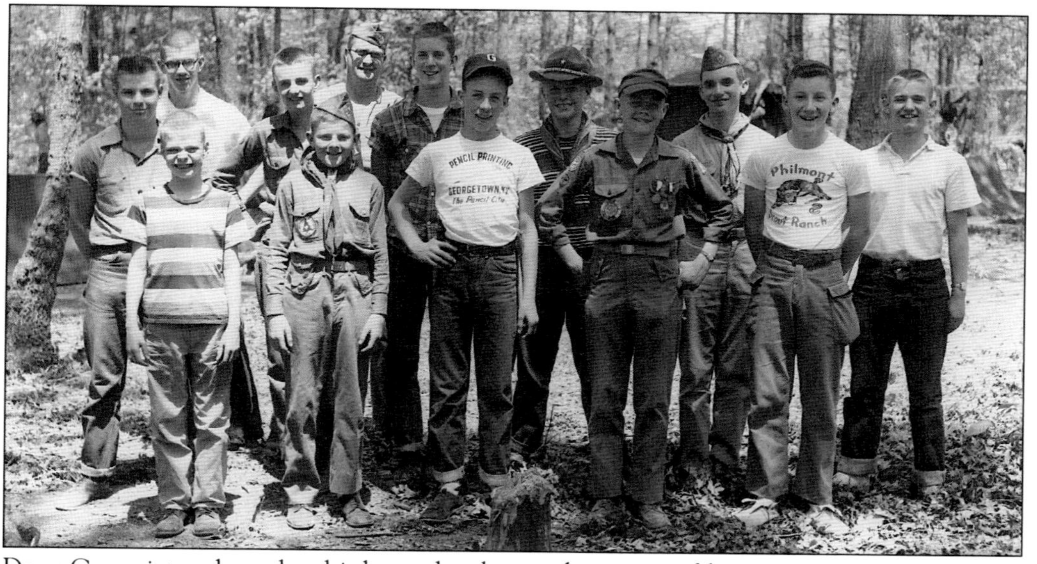

Doug Cox, pictured on the third row, has been a key spirit of boy scouting in Georgetown and the Daniel Boone District for more than five decades. Cox is shown with his 1955 Troop 177 taking a break from helping set up the council's Camp McKee. Pictured from left to right are as follows: (first row) Lynn Melzer, Bradford Gibson, Henry Walls, Jerry Robinson, and Don Wyatt; (second row) Ben Scroggin, Chan DeMoisey, Bobby Lewis, John Melzer, and Larry Prather; (third row) Jamie Ewing and Cox.

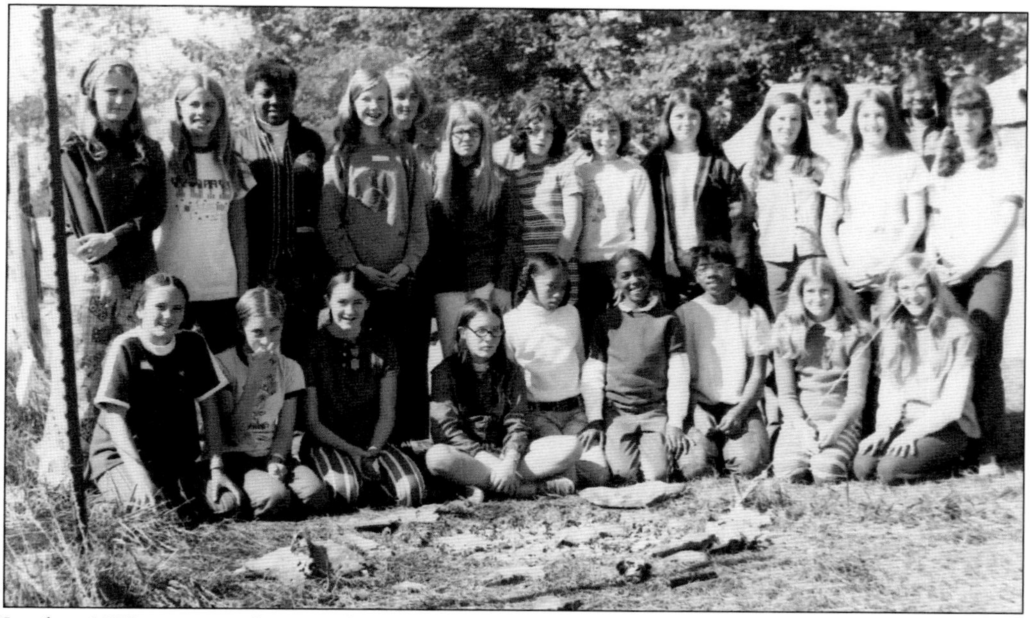

In this 1970s view, cadette and senior Girl Scouts are shown at camp. Pictured from left to right are as follows: (front row) Kathy Hill, Elizabeth Shirley, Vicki Mann, Marie Shirley, Denise Wilson, Rosalind McIntyre, Karen Taylor, Holly Brown, and Marchel Gilvin; (back row) Marilyn Johnson, Fran Bevins, Augusta Washington, Cheryl Gragg, Arlene Johnson, Sheri Gilvin, unidentified, Cindy Wohn, Pamela Vance, Bobbie Hill (leader), Brenda Walker, Teresa Wesley, and Debbie McFarland.

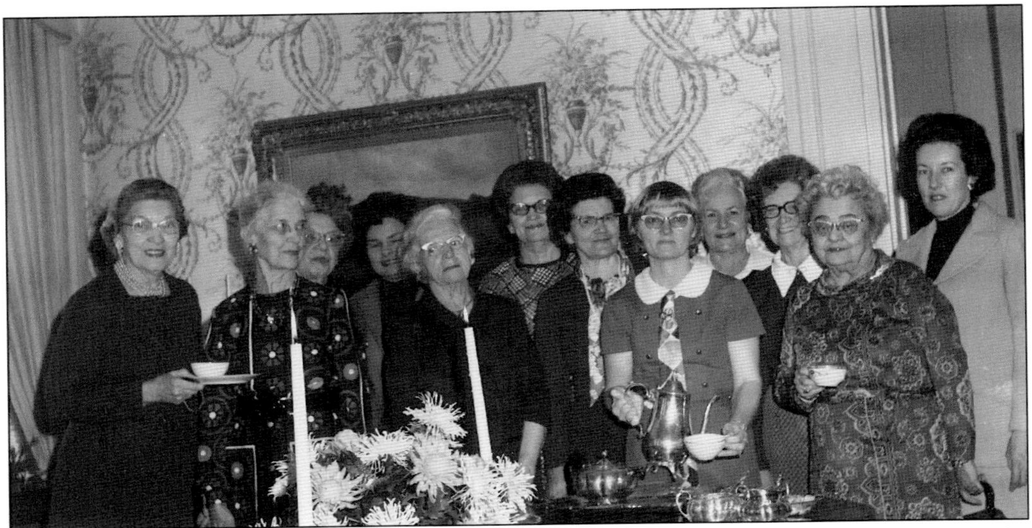

The Woman's Association of Georgetown College celebrated its 100th anniversary in 1998 by increasing its endowment fund for scholarships for women to $100,000. Leaders of the association posed for this photograph in 1973. Pictured from left to right are as follows: Eula Proctor, Mabel Johnson, Bertha Hall, Mary Overall, Mabel Lancaster, Carolyn Redding, Hetty Singer, Vonna Mallow, Jane Hope Oldham, Kate Snyder, Sara Hambrick, and Maribeth Hambrick.

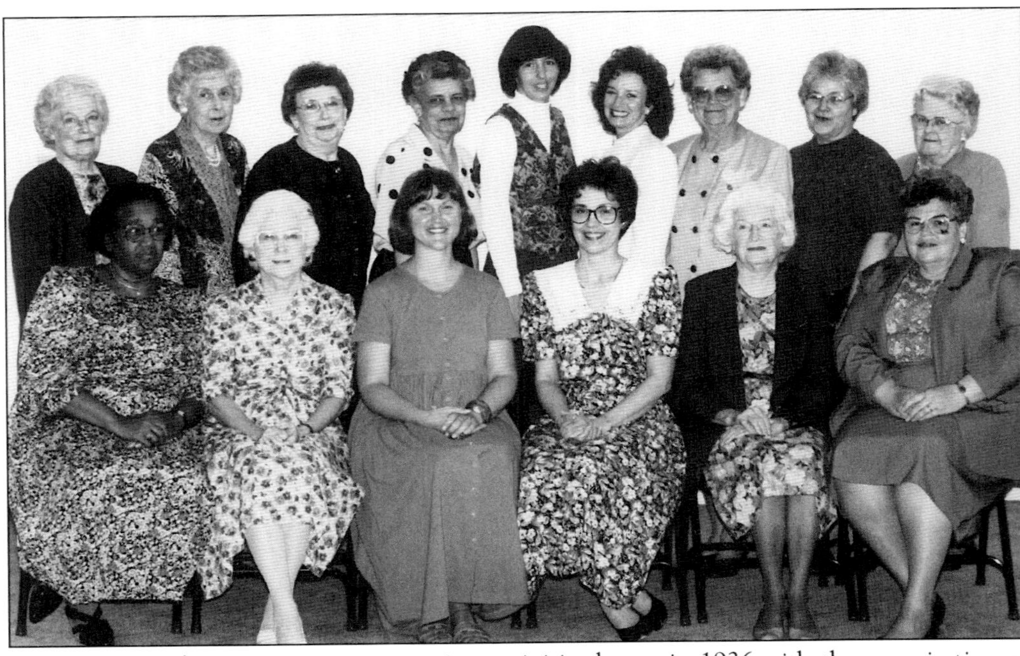

Scott County's home economics extension activities began in 1936 with the organization of a homemaker's club in the Stamping Ground area. Former presidents photographed in 1995 include, from left to right, the following: (front row) Sally Henderson, Geneva Carr, Jennifer Aldrick, Janice Parks, Genevieve Clark, and Thelma Duff; (back row) Mildred Clark, Lucille Hilander, Annie Barbara Friedly, Ida Figgs, Marjorie Baker, Jana Tylicki, Mildred Gregory, Billie Green, and Lucille Gibson.

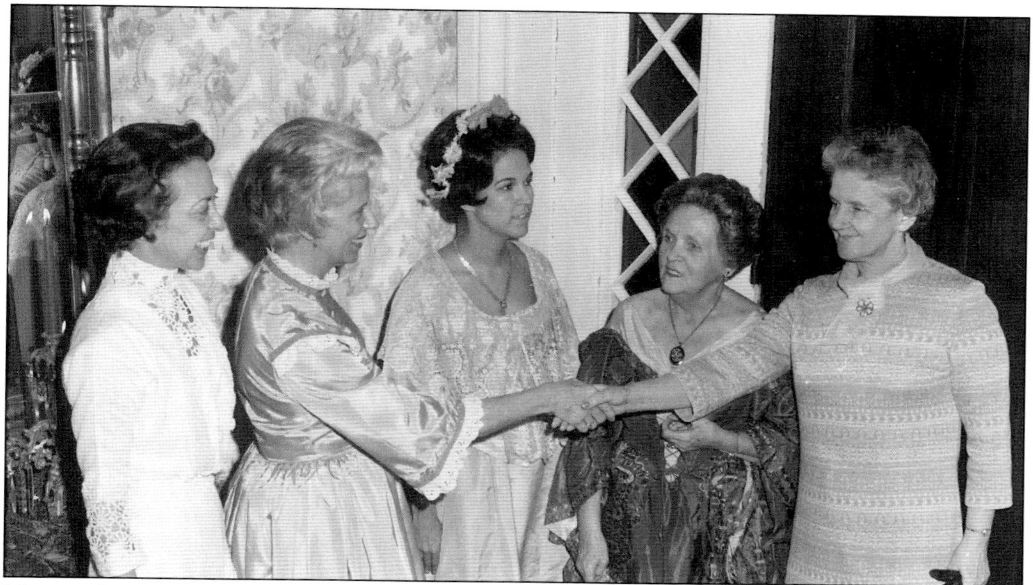

Historic house tours sponsored by the Scott County Woman's Club began in 1963. The tours helped increase appreciation of community history and raised funds for a number of causes. Proceeds from the first tour raised funds for a proposed community park at Georgetown's Big Spring. Pictured from left to right are as follows: Claudia Jett (president), and club members Evelyn Aulick, Kay Bell, and Lillian Jameson. Ms. Aulick is shown greeting a guest.

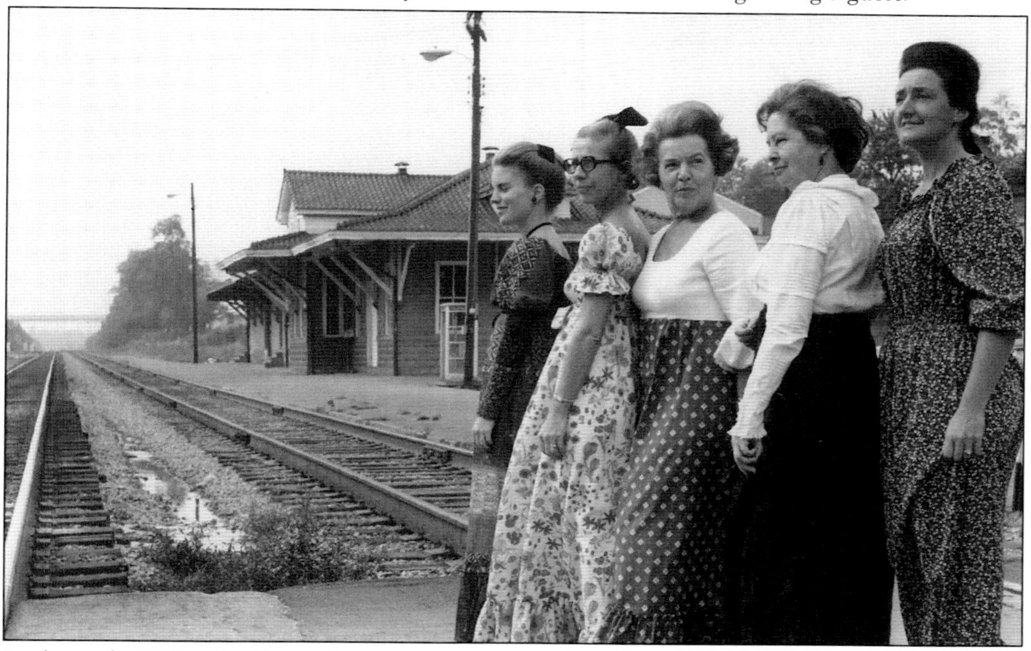

In the early 1970s, the Scott County community gathered at the historic Cincinnati Southern Depot on Maddox Street to raise funds for the hospital auxiliary's work at the John Graves Ford Memorial Hospital. The three hospital auxiliary-sponsored "Sentimental Journeys" raised $15,000 toward a new hospital wing. Pictured from left to right are as follows: Betty Wooten, Pat Watson, Nell Shropshire (chairperson), Edna McKnight, and Pat Mudd.

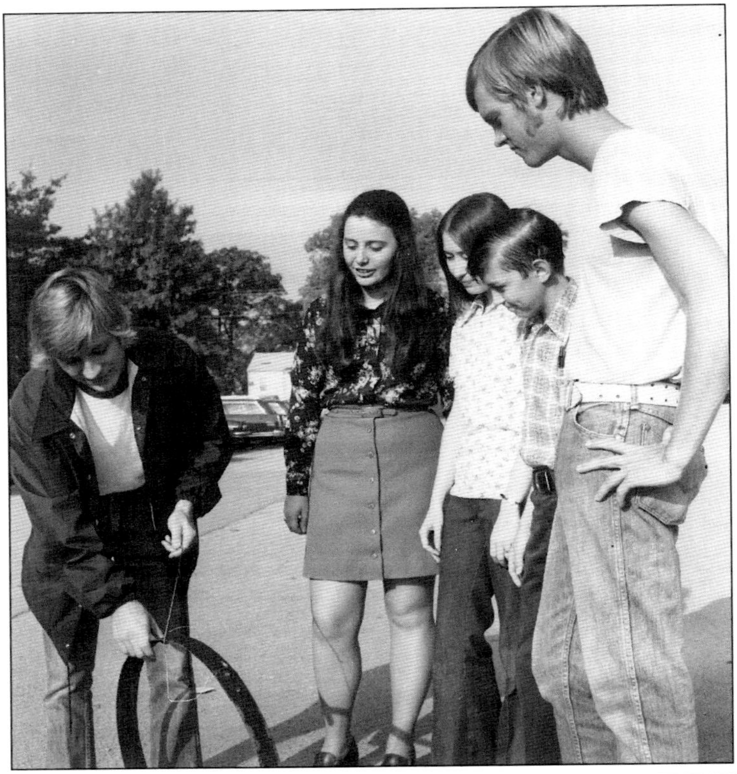

Scott County High School's young historians organized children's and youth activities during the 1974–1976 Kentucky settlement bicentennials. These members, demonstrating how to roll a hoop, are pictured from left to right as follows: Jeff Singer, Lynne McMaine, Janie Muddiman, Tim Stewart, and Parker Tucker. The younger historians sponsored several events during the three years of celebration, including an outdoor series of worship services and downtown pioneer-era competitive activities.

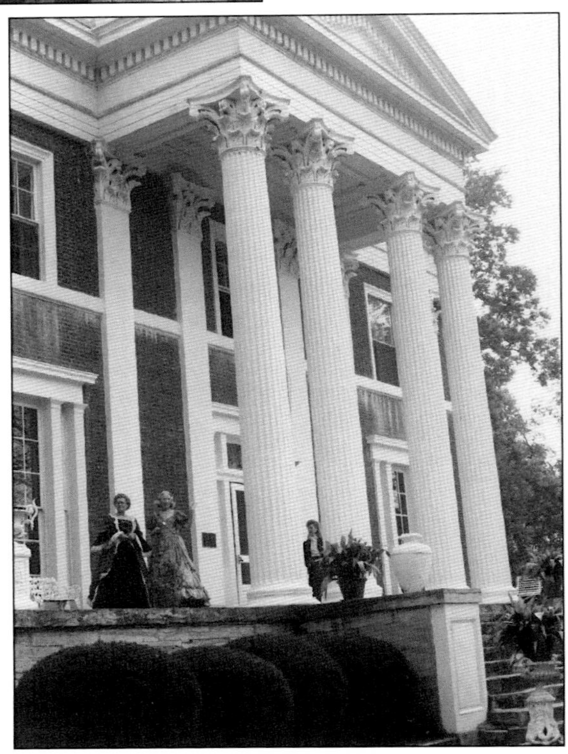

In 1979, Frances Susong Jenkins (second from left) met the challenge of developing her family's home, historic Ward Hall, into an historic house museum. She and her associate, Ruth Hutchins (right), guided visitors through the great mansion, Kentucky's largest and most ostentatious Greek Revival house for several years. Ward Hall was built in the 1850s for Junius Ward, local farmer, Mississippi planter, and grandson of Scott County's first permanent settlers, Robert and Jemima Johnson.

Nine
Having a Good Time

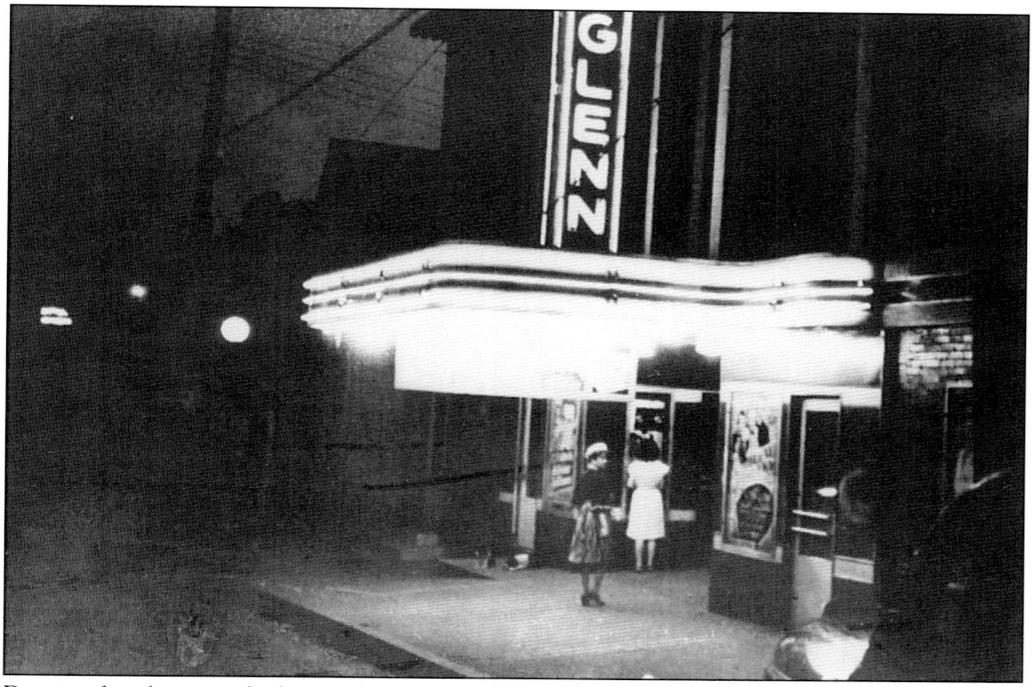

Despite the absence of a large urban center, Scott County residents have rarely been at a loss for entertainment. Generations created their own good times. Horseback riding, county fairs, or a splash in Elkhorn or Eagle Creek, or even a farm pond, provided respite from work that began for most people early in life. Church and local organizations also provided outlets for leisure activities. It was not until the late 20th century that an effective Parks and Recreation Department, jointly funded by city and county, began to create an impressive array of activities for young and old alike. Even before that, with help from the private sector, Suffoletta Park provided a swimming pool and ball fields for summer fun. Perhaps the most endearing symbols to long time residents were the Sweet Shop and the Glenn Theater. Above is a rare photograph of the Glenn Theater, undoubtedly taken on a summer Saturday night. That is nostalgia talking; the photograph evokes memories of many small towns in the 1940s and 1950s. The Glenn, always a little worn around the edges, was nevertheless a popular spot for movie goers in the 1940s, 1950s, and 1960s. On South Broadway, near the center of town, the Glenn provided access to new films until the theaters of Lexington became more accessible in the 1960s. In this picture, a young woman purchases a ticket while Clara Thomason looks at the marquee. The building was razed to make room for parking.

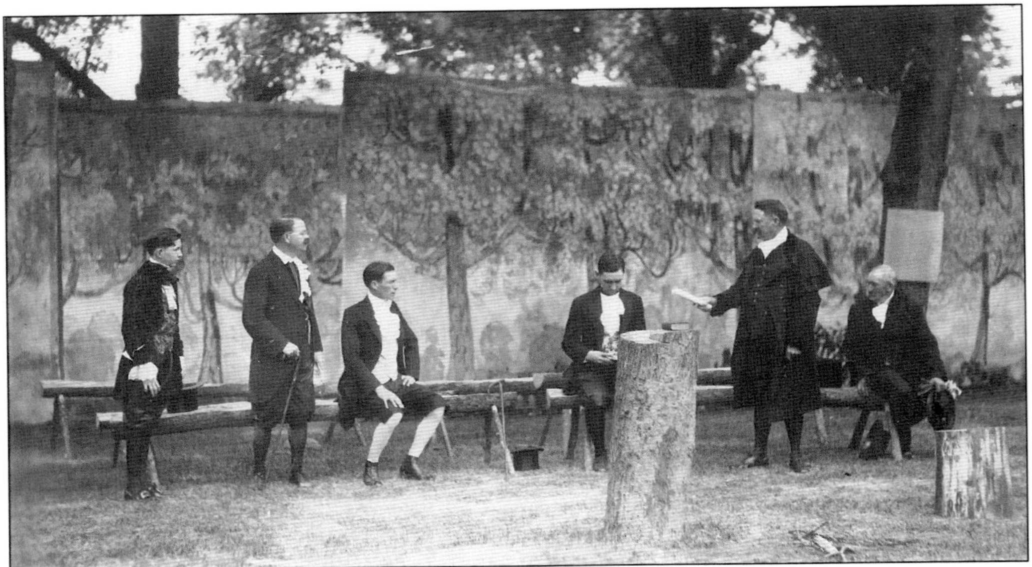

When formal entertainment was not provided, county residents created their own good times. In 1925, residents planned a historical extravaganza which celebrated local activities since the settlement era.

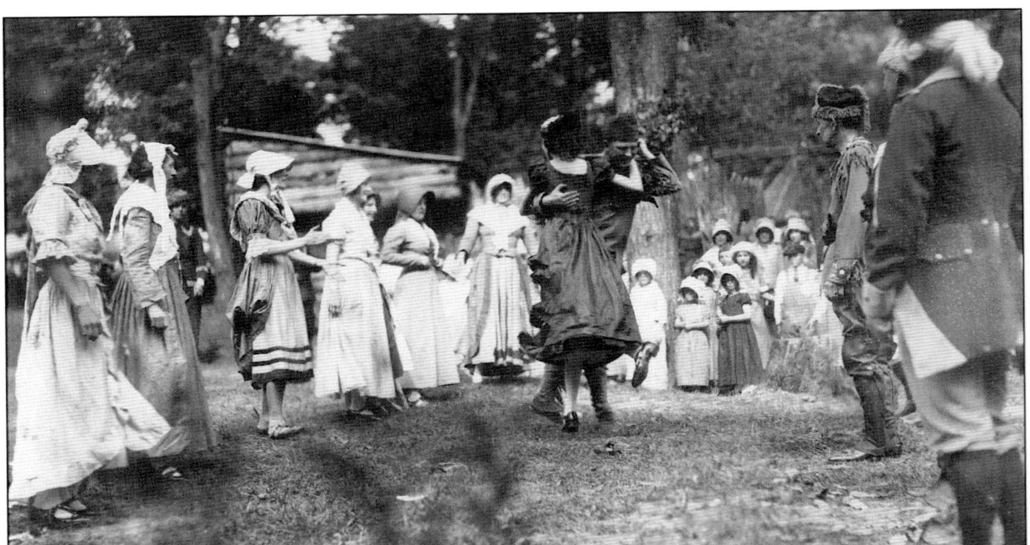

A series of programs said as much about the Scott County of 1925 as it did the past. Since 1925, local organizations have occasionally sponsored programs showcasing local talent.

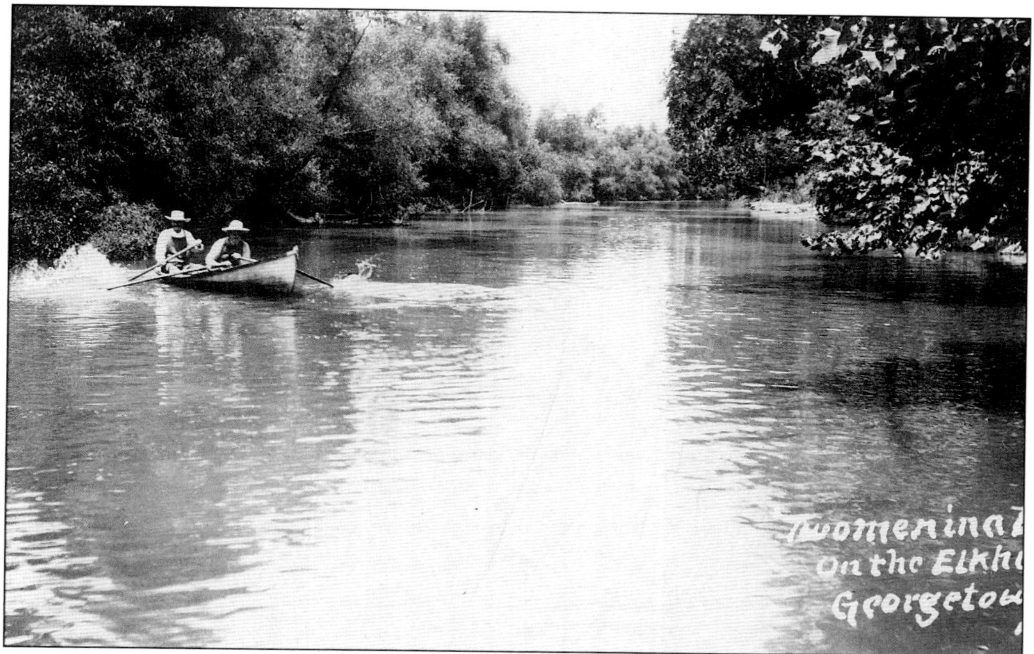

Elkhorn Creek has also provided many forms of entertainment throughout the county's history. In this view, two women canoe on a lazy summer day. The slow-running creek is ideal for canoeing in its deeper areas.

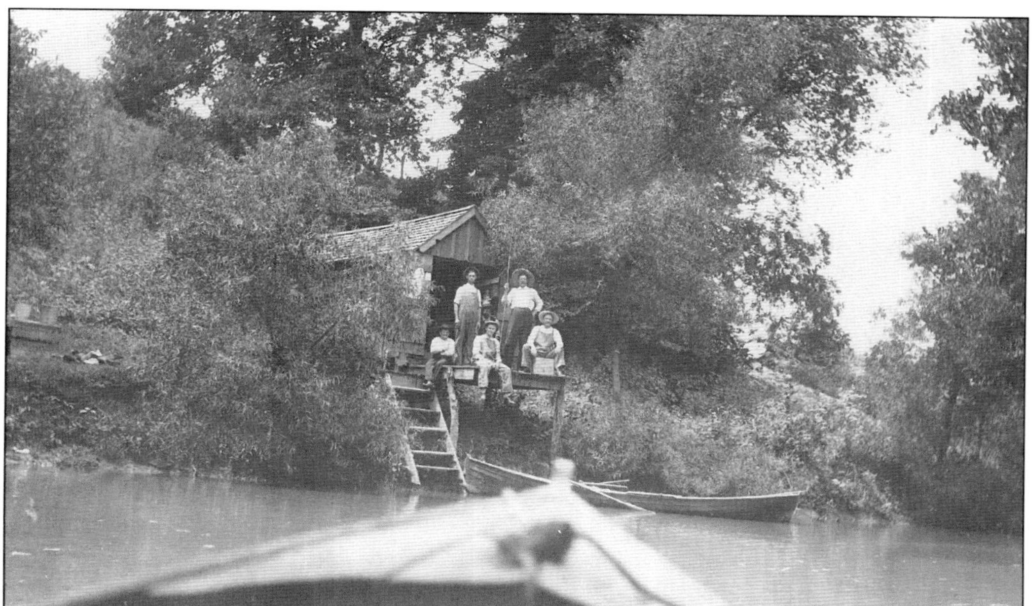

In this view of the creek, a group of people are seen on a fishing expedition. Elkhorn Creek was one of the best smallmouth bass streams in America, and a good angler can still have an afternoon of fun catching bass, bluegill, red-eye, and even a "newlight" or two.

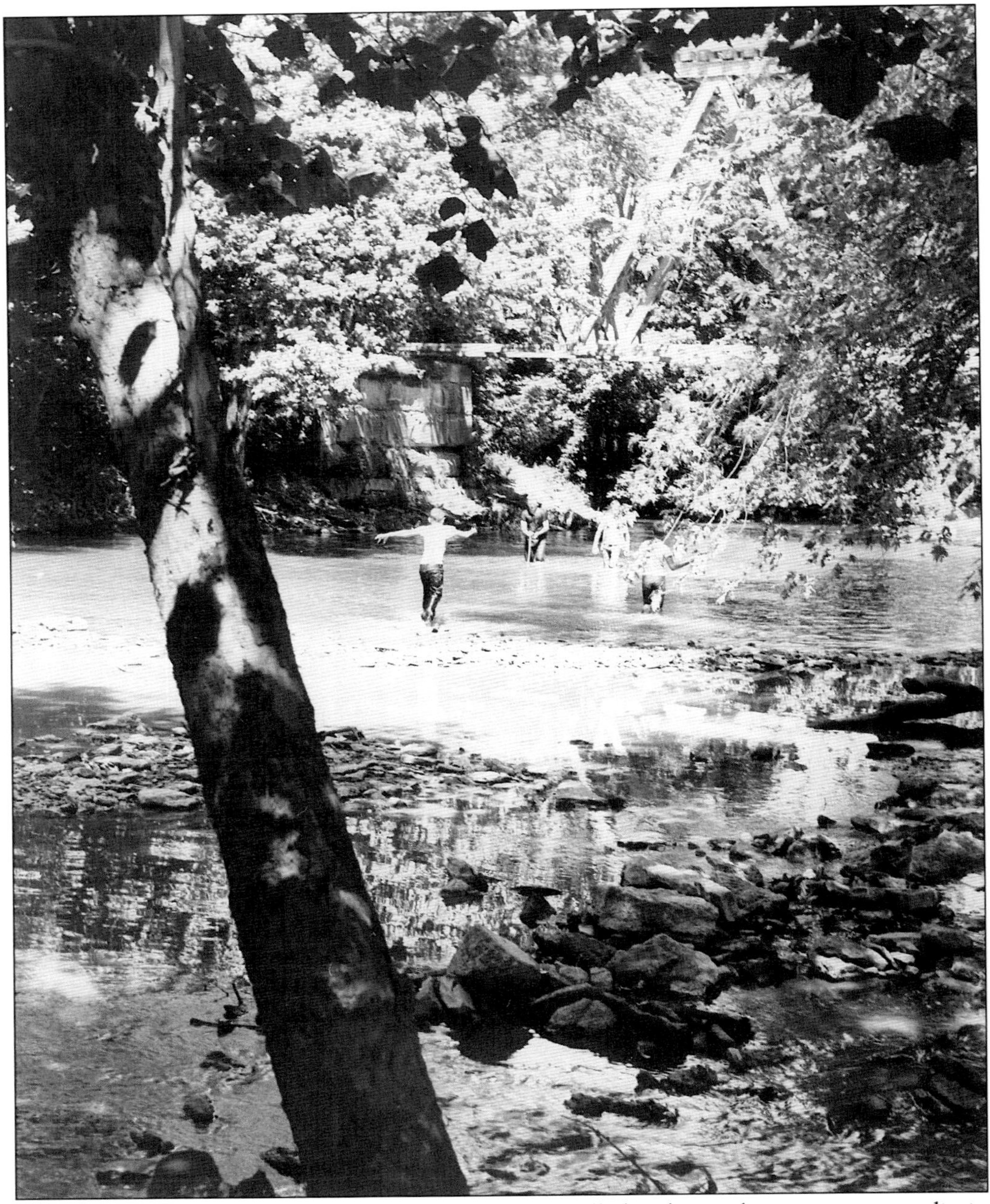

Enjoying perhaps the oldest summer pastime of them all, four boys take a spontaneous dip in the creek. Scott County provides excellent opportunities for such entertainment in Elkhorn and Eagle Creeks as well as other small streams. For generations, young people have seined minnows, created makeshift dams, and enjoyed the cooling effect of the water and the shade of trees lining the banks of the creek.

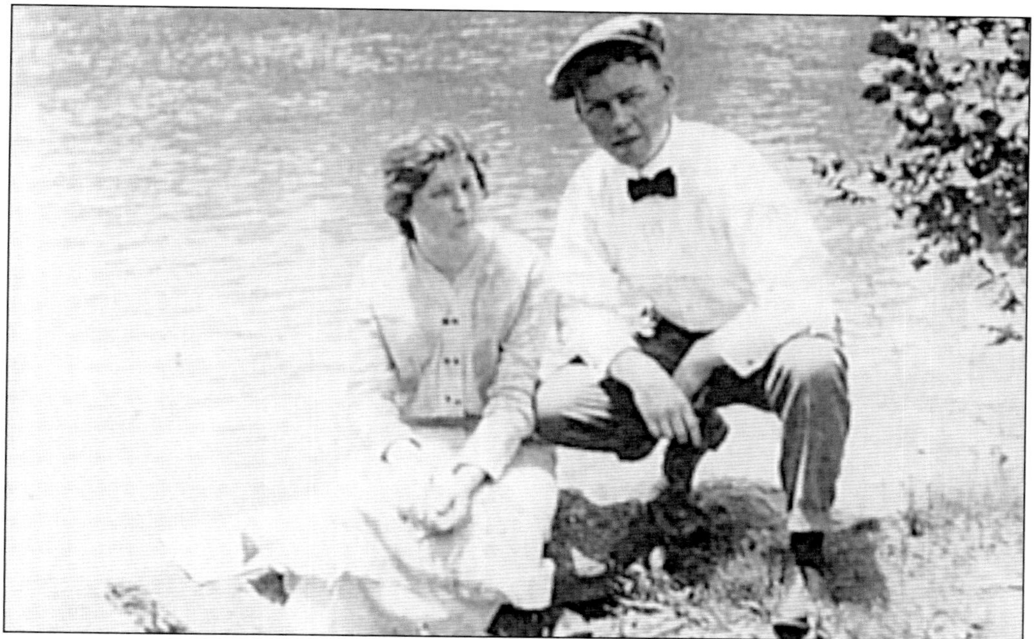

The creek also provides a wonderful place for romantic walks and picnic lunches. Two young people, photographed near the turn of the century, enjoy an afternoon of fun and relaxation. The bow tie suggests that there may have been some serious business about this picnic, but then again, perhaps people were just more formal in earlier days.

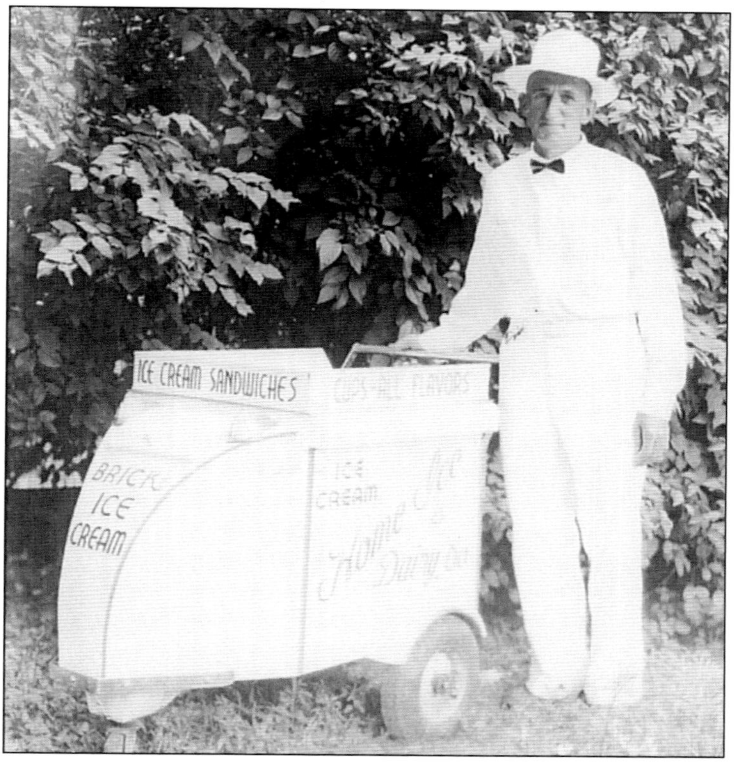

Arnold Eli Watson provided a bright spot in every Georgetown child's summer afternoon with his ice cream truck—no bells, whistles, or sirens needed. The pace of life was slower, and Mr. Watson's machine was propelled by him!

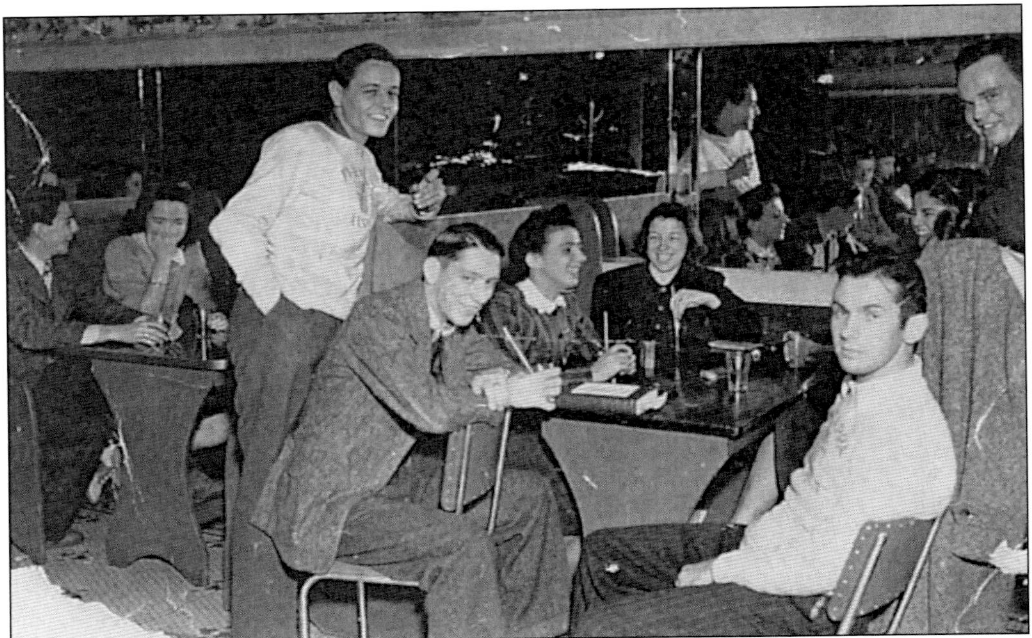

In the years after WW II, teenagers gathered at the Sweet Shop. In this picture, county residents Tom Porter, Gene Russell, Ruth Miracle, and Norris Wilson joined others for after-school sodas. They represent the hundreds of young people who frequented this teenage hangout on Main Street in Georgetown.

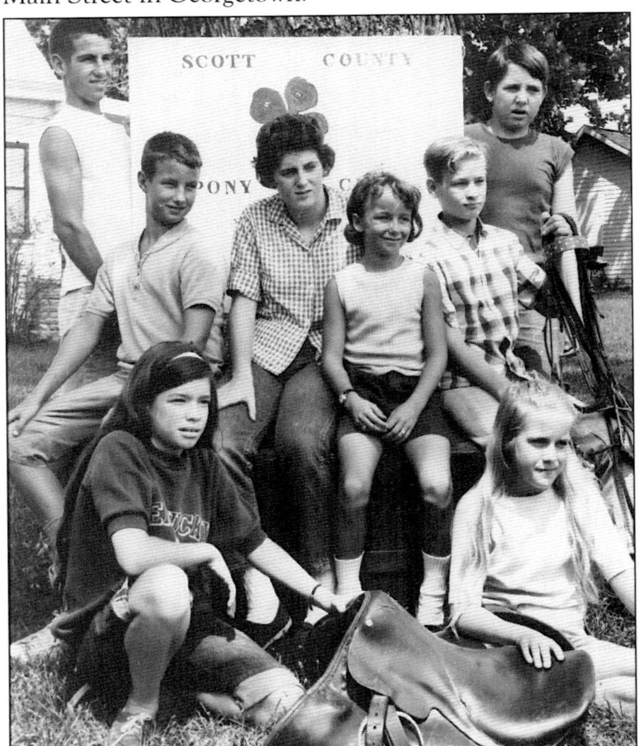

The Scott County Pony Club provided fun for some local youths. Whether in a formal way or just down on the farm, horseback riding has been a leisure activity since the county's beginnings.

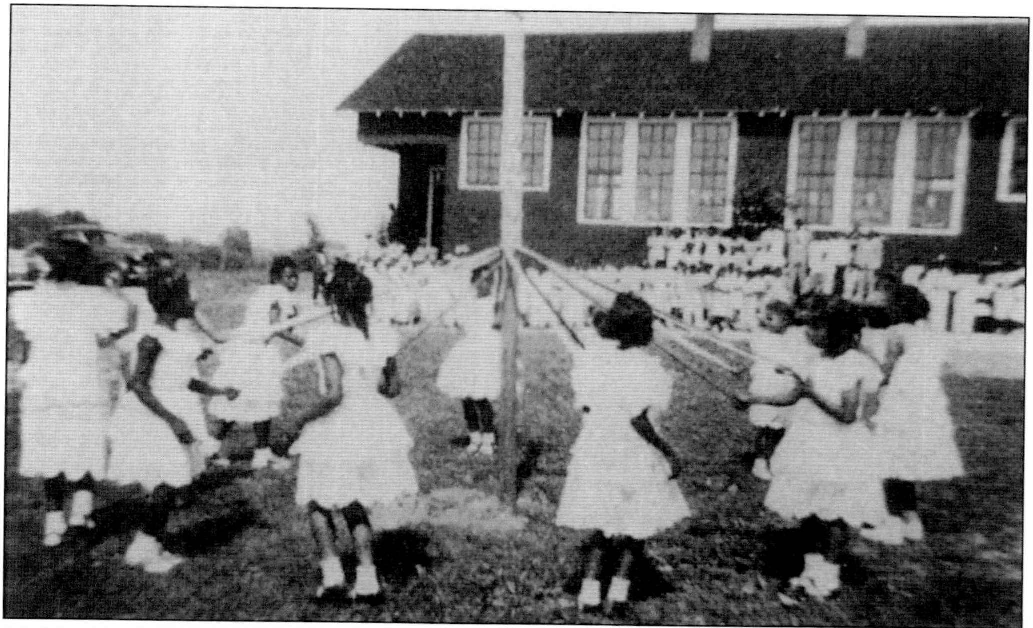

It's May Day! Young girls at New Zion enjoy circling the May Pole. May Day, almost a forgotten holiday in a modern world, was a time of celebration in earlier years.

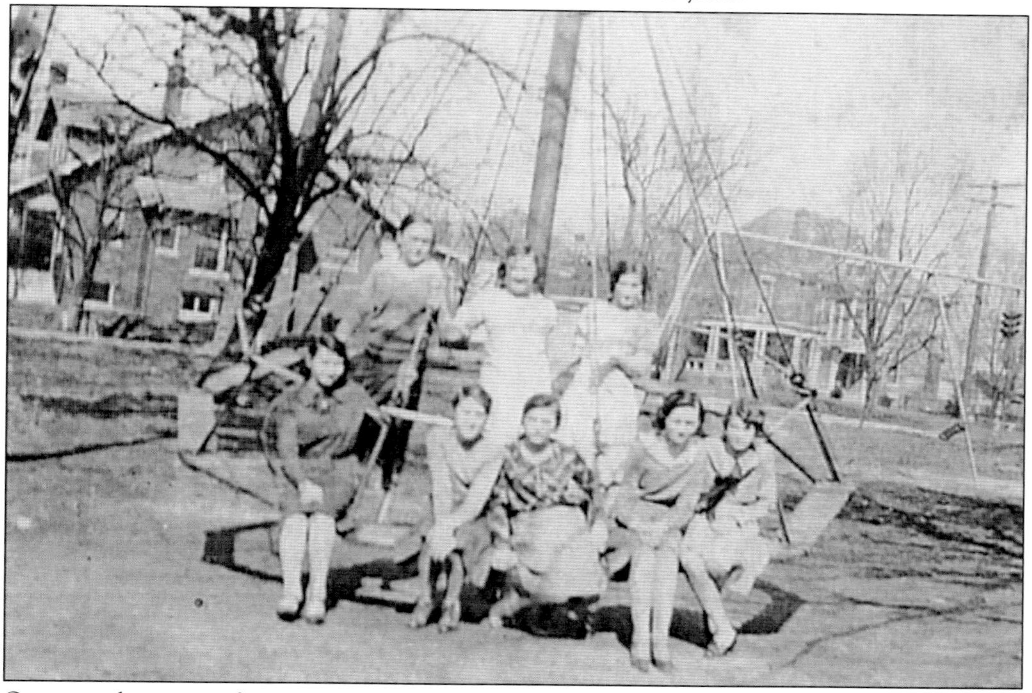

On an early spring afternoon in 1931, this group of ninth-grade girls pose on the merry-go-round at Garth School. The playground equipment may change, but school playgrounds across the county still draw young people on a warm summer day. Pictured from left to right are as follows: Mamie Spears, Dorothy Reed, Natalina Fava, Eileen Munson, Dorothy Traylor, Lois Steger, Mildred Morris, and Ruth Towles.

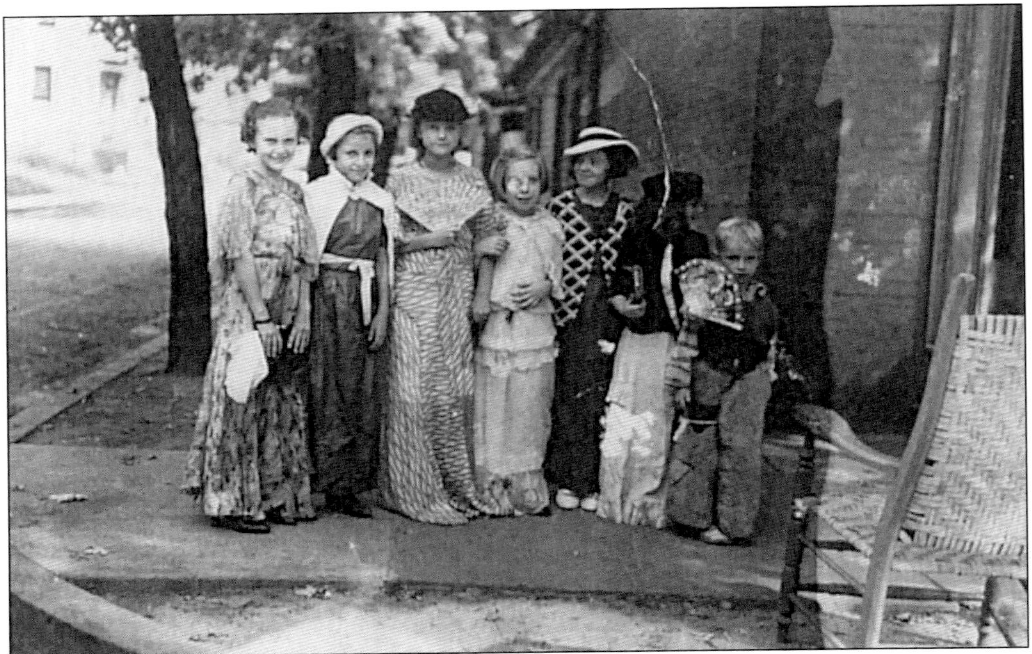

If all else fails, there is always an afternoon of make believe in mother's clothes. Betty Cassity, Louise Baston, Betsy Lee James, June Foree, Martha Jo Baston, Marian James, and Donnie Sharp create their own entertainment to fill a summer day.

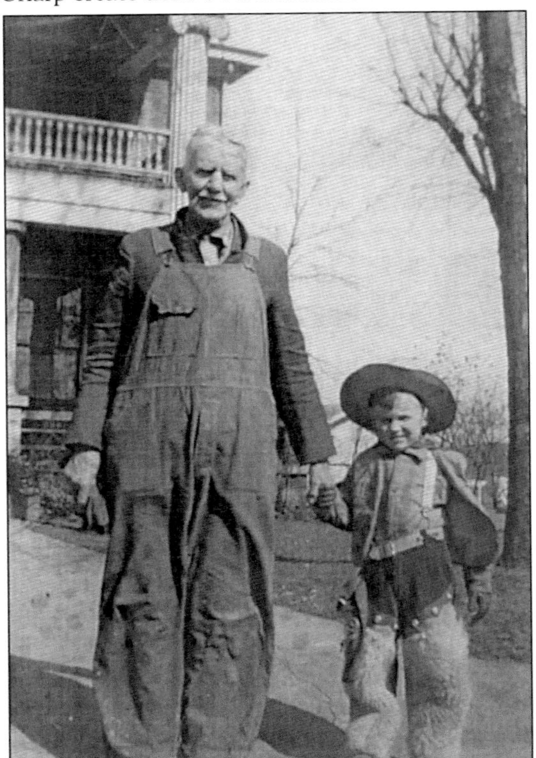

There were also days for playing "cowboys and Indians." All Bobby Smith needs is his horse and, perhaps, a leg up from W.T.Carrick.

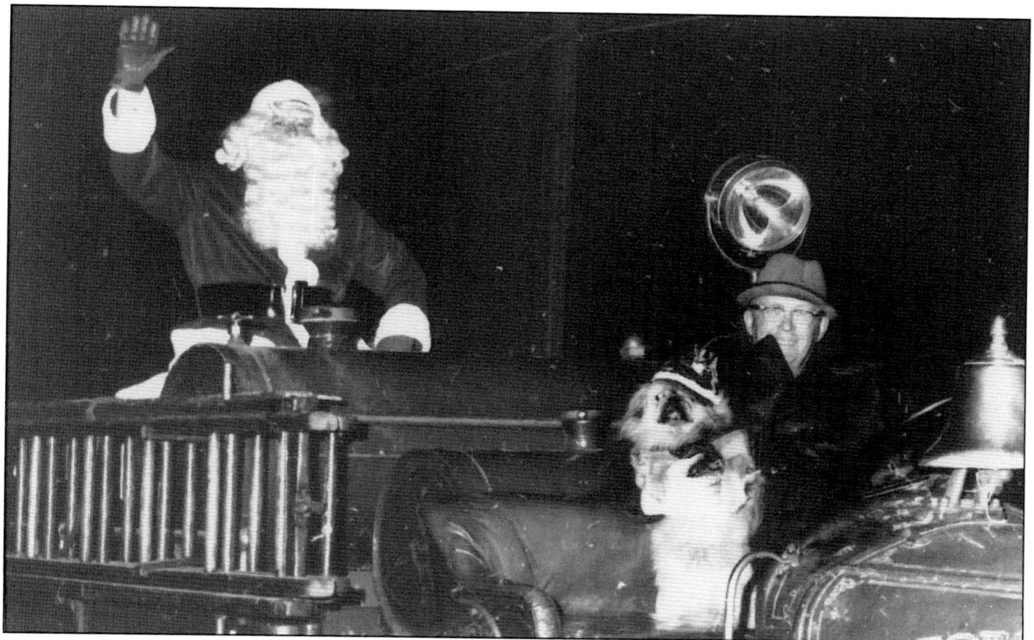

Christmas comes but once a year, and Santa Claus always rides the fire truck in the city Christmas parade. This appears to have been a white Christmas, but neither snow, rain, nor a cold, cold wind can keep a crowd away from the annual Christmas parade.

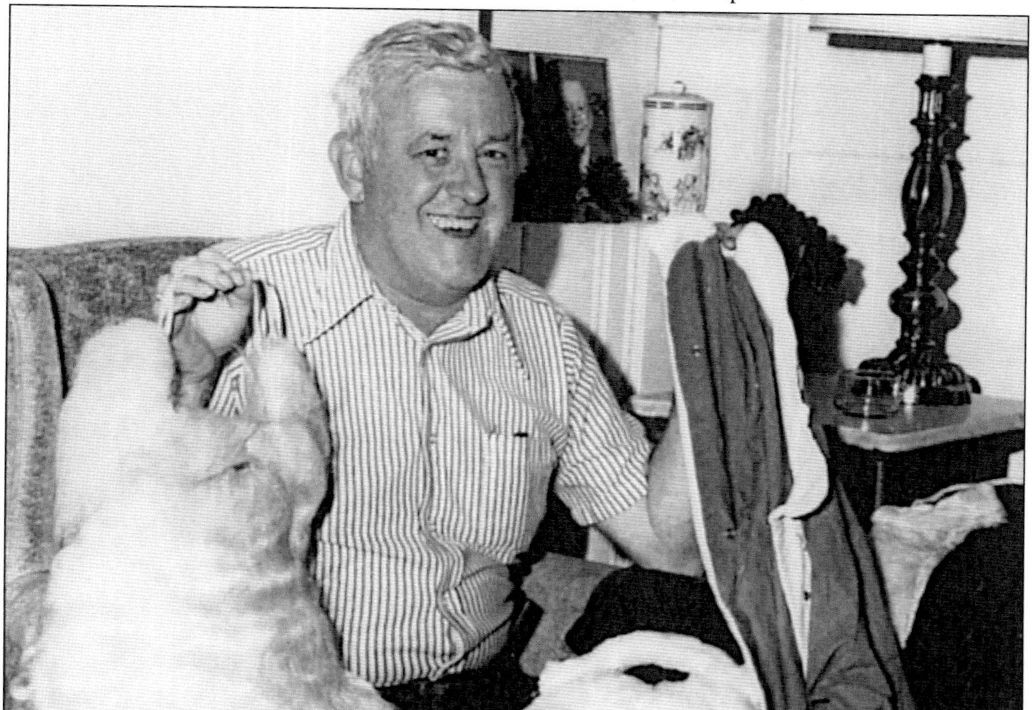

Pictured is jolly old St. Nick—or is it Santa's helper? Leland Perkins prepares to dress the part. Perkins played the role of Santa for Scott young people for many years.

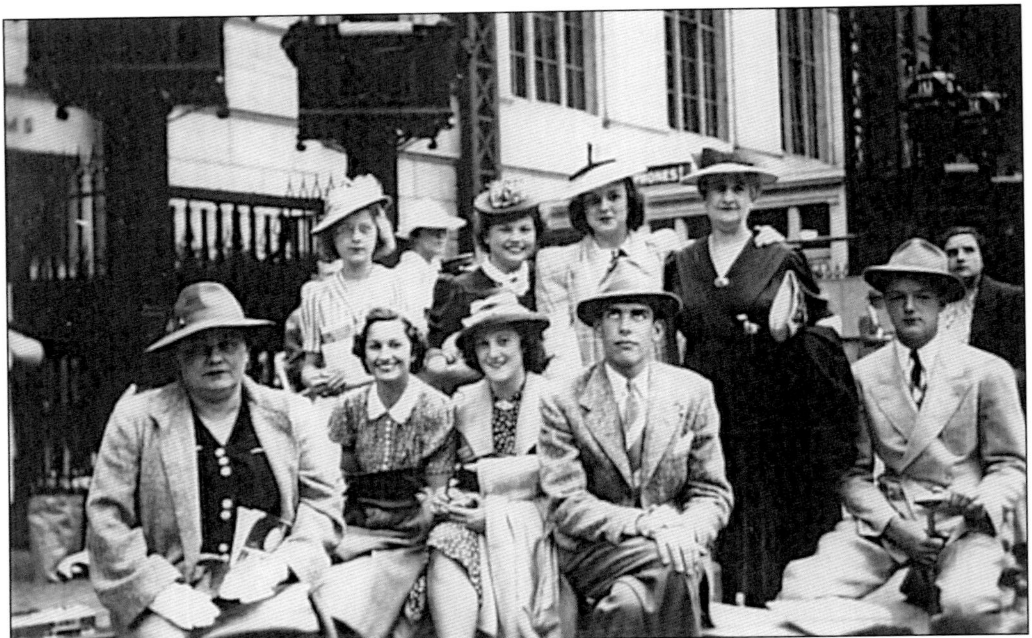

Some people found their entertainment in other places. This group attended the New York World's Fair, bringing home fond memories of a much bigger extravaganza than the home folks could provide.

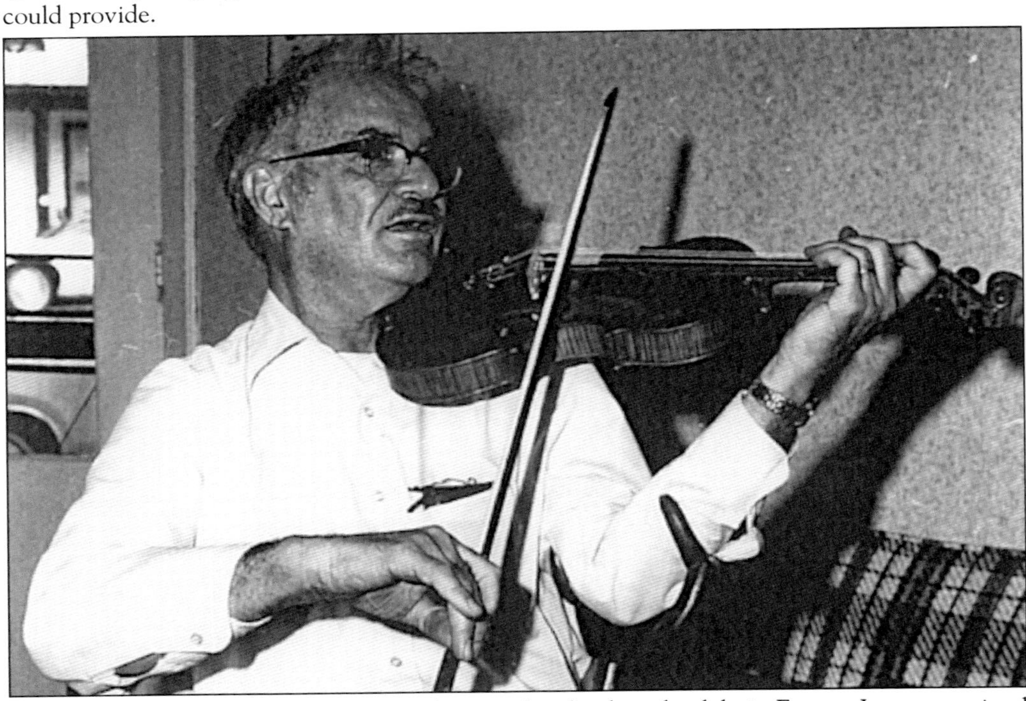

Good times are made by people. Even when confined to his wheelchair, Eugene Lee entertained himself and many others with his beautiful music. He made and played stringed instruments of many types. Wherever Lee went, there seemed to be music in the air, and although he is now gone, his picture recalls the melodies that put a song in Scott County hearts.

ACKNOWLEDGMENTS

The generosity of many persons yielded the hundreds of photographs that the authors pondered prior to their selection of the 210 presented between the covers of Georgetown and Scott County.

The *Georgetown News-Graphic* not only allowed the authors to borrow freely from the newspaper's archive of historic photographs, but also creatively provided space within its pages to let the people of Scott County know about our effort to put together a photographic history. Doug and Doris Jean Smith opened the photograph files of the old *Georgetown Graphic*, much of which was accumulated by Archie S. Frye, the publication's founding editor. Without the generosity of journalists, past and present, and the support provided by Terry Maurer and Ken Hisel of the Scott Shopper, the quality and diversity of the images presented in this volume would be considerably less.

Similarly, we took advantage of the store of photographs of the Georgetown and Scott County Museum, where we frequently met to work out the details of the project. Museum director John E. Toncray was helpful, and his gracious assistance as we developed the project is greatly appreciated.

Clara DeMoss of Stamping Ground prodigiously collected the best photographs from her community, which has suffered losses of landmarks as a result of at least two devastating fires and the 1974 tornado that swept away most of the rest of Stamping Ground. Assisting Clara was Elaine Reynolds. Owners of these photographs include DeMoss, Mary C. Prewitt, Betsy Adams Wigginton, Gene Wiley, Truitt Gaines, Henry Etta Johnson, Larry C. Johnson, Clemmie Hall, and Marie Clark Towles. Eddie Marshall and Mae Price were particularly helpful in providing photographs of historic Sadieville. The museum archives also had several photographs taken by the late W.A. Marshall, historian of northern Scott County.

John Farris generously shared historic railroad photographs and memorabilia through the years, and he allowed us to choose from the rarest of his collection. Over many decades, C.A. "Chic" Mifflin collected postcards and photographs from a variety of sources. Many of his photographs are included in the museum collection, and we deeply appreciate his generosity in sharing them. We are grateful to Gary Perry for allowing us to choose from his collection of railroad and local history photographs, many of which can be found in an exhibit in his place of business.

Others who shared collections include William McIntyre, Clay McKnight, Emily Askew Rawdon, Betsy Hall, Mary Susan Kring, David Stuart, Marian James Lynch, Sallie Tilford, Mattie Jo Lucas, Mary Lou Walker, Elizabeth Hartsfield, Horace Hambrick, Edith Clifton, Nancy Brown, Herndon Price, Jo Thiessen, the Georgetown Post Office, Virginia Paxton Gorham, Maxine Friedly, Betty Wooten, Betty Lou Graves, Mike Marshall, Katherine Tackett, Orie D. Sargent, Herndon Price, Rick Johnston, and Ann Bevins.

Individual photographs were provided by Frances Nash, Linda Power, Donna Atkins, Harold Prather, J. Rufus Dalton Jr., Betty Johnson, Phil Weisenberger, Hetty Singer, Mrs. W.T.

Withers, Warring Davis McFarland, Sarah Relford, Tom Payne, Helen Carroll Donaldson of Toyota Motor Manufacturing, Annie Barbara Friedly, and Connie Minch.

The several persons who provided assistance as we tried to identify individuals in group photographs include William McIntyre Jr., Augusta Washington Leslie, Sarah Relford, Carrick James, Edith Clifton, Patsy Swift, Clemmie Jameson Hall, Ruby Harris, Doug Cox, Maxine Friedly, John Toncray, David Stuart, Gary Perry, Charles Johnson, and Willa Gentry.

Limited space made it impossible to use all photographs that we would have liked. We thank the owners for letting us consider their photographs for the book and hope that someday they, too, may enter the annals of print.

Eugene Bradley graciously gave permission for the reproduction of the photographs of his father, the late Eugene Bradley, who was and continues to be nationally recognized for photographic art. It is a goal of the authors to compile a second volume in the Images of America series of the works of Bradley and, possibly, other great local photographers.

This publication is truly a community effort, and, as in many times in the past, the people of Georgetown and Scott County have proven that when there's a cause or a project, we really enjoy working together.